CW01560312

A STRANGER IN JERUSALEM

Geoffrey Ainsworth Williams

MINERVA PRESS

ATLANTA LONDON SYDNEY

ISBN 0 75410 747 7

First Published 1999 by
MINERVA PRESS
315–317 Regent Street
London W1R 7YB

Printed in Great Britain for Minerva Press

A STRANGER IN JERUSALEM

By the Same Author

Rachel Kay-Shuttleworth, 1885–1967: A Memoir

Viewed from the Water Tank: A History of the Diocese of Blackburn

Who Was John? A Study of the Johannine Literature in the New Testament

Locus Benedictus, The Story of Whalley Abbey

About the Author

Geoffrey Ainsworth Williams was born in Manchester and educated at the Manchester Grammar School, where he was a foundation scholar. He proceeded to be a scholar at University College, Durham, where he took his degree with honours in Theology. After a year of research, he was ordained to a curacy at Bury Parish Church in Lancashire. Ten years later he was appointed Vicar of Habergham in 1949 and remained there for fifteen and a half years, during the last four of which he was also Rural Dean of Burnley. He served for over twenty-five years as a Residentiary Canon of Blackburn Cathedral, which post he occupied first as Sacrist and then as Chancellor until he retired. During this period he was also Warden of Readers in the Diocese of Blackburn, Warden of Whalley Abbey, the Diocesan Conference and Retreat House, and Tutor for the WEA and the extramural department of Manchester University. He is still active as a teacher both of sixth formers in school and also of adults.

And one of them whose name
was Cleopas answering said unto him,
'Art thou only a stranger in Jerusalem
and hast not known the things that are
come to pass there in these days?'

Saint Luke
xxiv.18

Contents

Chapter I
Getting to Know the Plot

On a Sunday afternoon in the year 27, or 33, or maybe even 30, two people were walking quietly along the road from Jerusalem to Emmaus. As they walked they were deep in conversation, and the matters they were discussing were puzzling and sad. A third figure approached, joined them and questioned them about their talk which made them appear so serious. 'Art thou only a stranger in Jerusalem, and hast not known the things that have come to pass there in these days?' was the question put in answer to the uninvited interrogation. This question has been asked down the ages ever since. It is still being asked today and no doubt will persist, possibly to the end of time.

Whatever events did happen in those days, they constitute for all mankind, in many people's opinion, the most important and definitive weekend, as we should now call it, in the whole of history. Yet from the point of view of the historian, those four or five days are about the most well attested and documented period in recorded time. None of the great turning points in history, occasions such as the battles of Marathon, Salamis, Actium or Philippi, are nearly so well documented; of none of them has such attention been paid, and about none of them has there been anything like the same doubts, uncertainties and contradictions.

Of those events there are four fairly full and detailed accounts that provide the documentary evidence, which for something that happened nearly two thousand years ago is a fairly substantial testimony. Furthermore, there is a definite agreement that of those criminals executed in Jerusalem on a particular Friday one had been raised from the dead, restored to life and had been seen. This attestation came not only from a recording of the sight of the risen one, but also by means of the sense of touch in three of the four accounts. Added to these is an earlier reference to sightings from a letter actually preceding the writing of the fuller narratives, and in many other letters from Saint Paul and other correspondents there are repeated references to the occurrence, clearly defined as statements of fact. So indeed, it is true to say that from the documentary evidence, the resurrection of Jesus of Nazareth from the dead is the best-attested fact in history. When, however, we examine the four detailed accounts, there appear to be contradictions which are not easily reconcilable. It need not be stated that were four people who had attended a football match to write, after a lapse of time, an account of their recollections of the event, any reader of all four could be excused for wondering whether they had attended the same match. The spectators would be recording impressions, whereas the Evangelists are making statements about events. (Though at least none of the sports commentators would convey any doubts as to the fact that the match had been played on a certain day and at a particular football ground!)

It is inevitable that the followers of Jesus Christ would want to have as full and as accurate an account of His life on earth as was possible, and the search for the Jesus of history is certainly not confined to German theologians of the early twentieth century. To try to satisfy the popular demand of the last century, authors such as Dean Farrer tried writing a life of Christ in which all the events recorded in the gospels were conflated into one continuous record. These attempts have been sustained even into this century: one thinks of such writers as Patterson-Smythe and Anthony Dean. Readers of these books are nowadays struck by the lack of success attendant upon these biographical endeavours.

Perhaps the fiercest battle in the field of biblical scholarship was that waged some hundred and thirty years ago concerning the submission of the text of Holy Writ to the scrutinies of literary criticism, resulting in the subjection of the books of the Bible to those same structural analyses and historical investigations as were applied to other forms of literature. Eventually, it came to be generally recognised that the doctrine of inspiration of scripture did not necessarily preclude scholarly investigations, and a new form of biblical criticism was established. Scholars grew to accept as a general assumption that the Evangelists used stories and records which were basically oral traditions and adapted them to meet and appear relevant to the Church as it existed at the time when they were writing. The biblical exegete's job therefore was to try to strip away the accretions to the original accounts, which were in the form of adaptations to the needs of contemporary Christians, and then discover the event or saying as it first happened or was uttered. Thus was invented what came to be called form criticism. A further study involved in the attempts to trace the reasons for literary development, such as those differences which are found in the text of the Bible itself, and to discover why such adaptation has taken place. For instance, it was noticed that the Lord's Prayer in Saint Matthew's gospel is slightly longer than the form in which it is stated in Saint Mark, and that there should be some attempt made to discover the reasons for this. This scholarly activity came to be known as redaction criticism. Such activity's fascinations and the success with which they seemed to be rewarded led the scholars to realise that what we have in our present text of the New Testament is the result of a development process, in turn leading to the assumption that there must have been a considerable number of years intervening between the events recorded and their actual account in the text as we now have it. This made scholars ascribe a later date to the appearance of the gospels than was hitherto traditional, some going so far as to ascribe some of them to the later years of the first century, and even the latter part of the second. Thus it came to be generally accepted that, although the first gospel bore the name of Matthew, it could not have been written, in the form in which it now exists, by the Apostle of that name. This tendency became so widespread that it almost seemed that if a book in the Bible bore the name of a particular person, then the investigation would start with the assumption that that individual was the one person who could not possibly have written it. So generally accepted was, and is, this attitude, that when Bishop J.A.T. Robinson produced a book, *Redating the New Testament*, in 1976, in which he argued for nearly the whole of the New Testament to have been written before the fall of Jerusalem in AD 70, the silence with which the world of scholarship received it was positively deafening. It would seem that if Bishop Robinson were correct in his assumptions, and he certainly advanced most cogent and convincing arguments, then the whole of New Testament scholarship for the last hundred years and more had been working on the wrong lines.

All scholars seem to agree that the Evangelists were using source documents for the production of a book which at least gave a portrait of Jesus of Nazareth, if not an historical account of His life. Some indeed assert that Saint Mark's gospel was itself a primary source document, which was used as such by the authors of the first and third gospels. Saint Luke himself actually states that his sources were some 'which from the beginning were eyewitnesses of the word'. On the other hand, the fourth gospel would seem to rely upon a different tradition from Saint Mark, and therefore it came to be assumed that Saint Mark himself was dependent upon sources displaying a tradition separate from that which lay behind the fourth gospel. Eusebius, a church historian writing in the late third and early fourth centuries, says that Irenaeus, a bishop in Gaul in the second century, makes reference to one called Papias, whom he describes as a 'man of long ago', a contemporary of S. Polycarp. This Papias, who was probably born late in the first century, survived into the second. Eusebius tells us that, according to Irenaeus, Papias wrote five books which bore the title *Interpretations of our Lord's Declarations*, but these books have not survived. It would appear that Eusebius knew them, and had access to them. He writes that: 'Papias himself, in the Preface to his discourses, by no means asserts that he was a hearer and an eyewitness of the holy Apostles, but informs [us] that he received the doctrine of faith from their intimate friends.' He then proceeds to quote directly from Papias and says: 'I have never, like many, delighted to hear them that tell many things, but them that teach the truth... If I met with any who had been follower of the elders anywhere, I made it a point to enquire what were the declarations of the elders; what was said by Andrew, Peter or Philip; what by Thomas, James, John, Matthew, or any other of the disciples of our Lord; what was said by Aristion and the presbyter John, disciples of the Lord, for I do not think that I derived so much benefit from books, as from the living voice of them that are still surviving.' What this quotation provides is clear evidence that there was indeed an oral tradition as well as written documents on which Christians were relying for the reception of the Faith, even as early as that period in the history of Christianity when there were people alive who could, and did, converse with some of them who had actually been with Jesus when He was on earth.

Eusebius himself, in commenting upon this passage

from Papias, makes an interesting statement when he writes: 'It is also proper to observe that the name of John is twice mentioned, the former of which he mentions with Peter and James and Matthew, and the other Apostles, evidently meaning the Evangelists. But in a separate point of his discourse he ranks the other John with the rest, not included in the number of the Apostles, placing Aristion before him. He distinguishes him plainly by the name of presbyter.' Eusebius then makes the suggestion that there were in Asia two men bearing the same name of John, and advances in support of this that 'there are two tombs in Ephesus, and that they are both called John's, even to this day'. He further makes the suggestion that if the Apostle did not write both the gospel which bears his name and the Revelation of John, it was the presbyter John who could be advanced as the other author.

Eusebius also makes an interesting comment concerning the fact that, whilst the accounts given by the Evangelists in their gospels are accurate, they are not necessarily told in a correct chronological order. He states that their narratives were derived from word of mouth accounts, both of events in which Jesus was involved, and also in the reportage of what He said both in His discourses and, presumably not least, in the parables. He does recognise however that some of the stories which had gained currency and become part of the oral tradition, partook of the nature of legend rather than of fact. He says:

> The same historian [Papias] also gives other accounts which he says he adds as received by him from un-written tradition, likewise strange parables of our Lord and some other matters rather too fabulous... he has also inserted in his work other accounts given by the above mentioned Aristion respecting our Lord, as also the traditions of the presbyter John, to which

15

referring those that are desirous of learning them, we shall now subjoin to the extracts from him, already given, a tradition which he sets forth concerning Mark who wrote the gospel, in the following words, 'And John the presbyter, also said this, Mark, being the interpreter of Peter, whatsoever he recorded, he wrote with great accuracy, but not however, in the order in which it was said or done by our Lord, for he neither heard nor followed our Lord, but, as before said, he was in company with Peter, who gave him such instruction as was necessary, but not to give a history of our Lord's discourses.'

Eusebius iii.39

Since nearly the whole of Saint Mark's gospel is quoted either by the first or third gospels, and two-thirds of it by both, it is quite clear that behind these two gospels are documentary sources. In this way it can be clearly stated that those who wrote the first three gospels were all dependent upon certain information which came to them either orally or from written documents. Of the traditional authors of the gospels, Saint Matthew was one of our Lord's Apostles, one of the Twelve, and it would seem therefore that if this tradition is correct, he would have no need of sources of the kind mentioned, as his personal recollections would be sufficient for him to compose such a book. Because, however, we know that he did rely on sources, the author of the first gospel cannot have been Saint Matthew. Saint Luke certainly made no claim to be one of the people who had known and lived with Jesus when He was on earth, tradition identifying him with the 'beloved physician' of Saint Paul's epistle to the Colossians, and in all probability the companion of Saint Paul from the point in his missionary enterprise when he left Asia and crossed from Troas into Greece. As for Saint Mark, it would appear that he had at least some personal knowledge of Jesus in the flesh, since it would seem that his mother's house in Jerusalem became the headquarters of the Church after the Ascension; he was certainly attendant upon Saints Paul and Barnabas on their first missionary journey, subsequently travelling with Saint Barnabas, his uncle, to Cyprus. It has never been seriously claimed that he was one of the Eleven. If then the author of the gospel that bears his name was the John Mark of the New Testament, then he would need to rely upon sources of some sort if he were to be the writer of a gospel.

When we come to consider the fourth gospel, the traditional author is Saint John the Apostle, the son of Zebedee and the brother of James. From very early days doubts have been cast upon this tradition. Although the earliest references to the gospel that we have do ascribe the authorship to John, it seems that doubt arose as early as the end of the second century. There has subsequently persisted, however, the belief on the part of some that John the Apostle was the author; modern studies point, from a consideration of the internal evidence, to a growing realisation that the traditional Johannine authorship is capable of justification. If indeed this is so, the author of the fourth gospel would not have the same need to rely upon sources for his writing as with the other Evangelists. Nevertheless, he does appear to use episodic stories of Jesus' ministry in a similar way to that adopted by the other three. It is the very use of short passages in story form of actions or sayings of Jesus, pieces technically known as 'pericopes', that gives to the gospels the qualities making them unique in all literature. How then did they come to be?

There are always stories told about people who have fulfilled any kind of public office or ministry, and these stories are passed on in the establishing of an oral tradition.

One has only to remember the stories told of such political leaders as Winston Churchill to realise that some will undoubtedly be accurate recallings of ascertainable facts, others may well be a true reflection of the 'Churchillian character' but have suffered exaggeration in their retelling, whilst some are almost certainly apocryphal. The stories recorded in the gospels, however, and especially where we can see Matthew and Luke reproducing almost the exact wordings of Mark, are so close to the original that written sources would almost certainly be implied.

We must be careful though about the presumption that oral traditions established in the first century of the Christian era are similar to oral traditions which are in the process of being established today. We live in a world of almost universal literacy, even though the ability to read may not produce the ability to write or speak in what can be called literary language. Nevertheless, today there is little need to train the memory for the remembering of witnessed or recounted speeches: it is nearly always possible to have a document or book in which the forgotten fact may be recovered. If we have heard a speech or sermon which has impressed us, and we wish to be able to refer to it in the future, we ask the speaker or preacher to let us have his text or for the oration to be published. It is comparatively easy to look things up. But in those societies where literacy is by no means universal, where there is not the same accessibility to books or where the ability to read them is non-existent, it is necessary for the memory to be much better cultivated. Even in our own period it has been noticed that since learning by rote has largely been abolished from our educational system, the ability to recall is much less developed. In New Testament times quite ordinary people would have acquired the power to listen to quite long speeches, commit them to memory and then be able to reproduce them subsequently almost verbatim. Plato, for example, would be much more able to listen to Socrates's apology in court, store it in his memory and reproduce it almost word for word as delivered than had he been educated and living in our day. We must be careful not to read back into the world which existed before the invention of the printing press the mental attitudes and abilities which that great revolution in thinking brought about.

With regard to the oral tradition concerning the words and deeds of Jesus, there was an extra reason for care to be taken in the exact preservation of such records. On the first Maundy Thursday Jesus had supper with His disciples. After supper, He took the bread and when He had given thanks He brake it and gave it to them, saying, 'Do this in remembrance of Me.' Likewise with the cup He said almost the same words, with the proviso that when they did that which He had demonstrated, it should be done in remembrance of Him. Again, it must be recalled that the concept of memory in the ancient world was different from what it is to us today. When we think of ourselves as making an act of remembrance, the concept we have in mind is that of casting our minds back to a moment in the past. The saying 'God has given us memories that we might have roses in December' reflects this attitude. We are able by an act of remembrance to move in our minds back through time to a season when roses were in bloom. In the ancient world, however, the concept of remembering was such that the mind should have the ability to bring out of the past an event and make it actual, real and potent in the present. This is well illustrated by the story of Elijah in the First Book of Kings 17:18. Elijah had promised to the widow of Zarephath the birth of a son in reward for her kindness to him, and in due time the promised child had been born. When, however, the lad died and there was no breath left in him, the mother said unto Elijah: 'What have I to do with thee, O thou man of God? Art thou come unto me to call my sin to remembrance, and to slay my son?' By calling her sin to remembrance, he had caused her to bring out of the past whatever sin it was that she had committed, and it immediately became alive, present, dynamic and possessed of the power to do evil, and it slew her son. Such for the woman of Zarephath was the consequence of the act of remembering.

When therefore Jesus said, 'Do this in remembrance of Me,' that would suggest to the disciples that whenever they broke the bread and drank the cup in remembering Jesus, He would be brought alive in the present; He would be physically real in the eucharistic elements, and the passion, the risen Christ, would be fully available, alive and dynamic. For them there would be no possibility of argument or controversy about the nature of the real presence. In celebrating the Eucharist therefore, from the first days after the ascension, a necessary part of the rite, and condition of the fulfilment of the promise, would be to remember Jesus. It was not very long in the history of the Church before there were Christians who had not the ability to remember Jesus, because they had not known Him when He was in human form on earth. It would thus be necessary, within the rite itself, for there to be a public recognition of Jesus so that all could indeed remember. Someone who had known Him therefore would tell something that Jesus had said, or something that He had done, recalling an event concerning His life. The Holy Gospel, as an essential part of the eucharistic rite, would be much older than any gospel written by one or other of the Evangelists. As the number of congregations increased, there would be more celebrations of the Holy Communion than there were people available to give such an account, and so it would doubtless be desirable that some such narratives should be written down, so that they could be preserved and read in public. It must have been a process such as this which caused the appearance of documentary 'pericopes', and these would be available to the authors of the gospels. They would then not only have the authority of liturgical usage behind them, but also the guarantee of authenticity.

When the Evangelists came to write their gospels they were actually writing theological treatises for the instruction and edification of the Christians, and the liturgical pericopes would act as tools for the making of a book. This is not to assert that the historical accuracy of the stories is to be doubted, but rather that they would have been used to make points, and not to give a systematic chronology. Anyone who undertook to write a gospel would make a selection from material which was available, and the selection would be dictated by theological considerations and not biographical necessity. It is surely this fact which makes it impossible for anyone to treat the gospels as though they were biographies and which gives them their somewhat episodic structures. The editor-author of the last chapter of Saint John's gospel indeed assures his readers that 'there are also many other things that Jesus did, the which, if they should be written every one, I suppose that even the world itself should not contain the books that should be written'. There is the implication here that there were other accounts of what Jesus did, and presumably also of what He said, than those events contained within the gospel.

It is the underlying theological inspiration which causes the gospel writers to use their pericopes in such a way that they convey significance on a number of levels. On occasions this would necessitate the use of words so that meaning could be conveyed at a deeper level than the merely factual recording of the event, which may well have been how the language of the original source presented it. Investigations into the use of words in this way, and considerations of the reasons for this, together constitute the science of what has come to be known as form criticism.

A good example of what is meant by the above is to be found in Saint Mark's accounts of the incidents of the young man in the Garden of Gethsemane, the deposition of our Lord from the cross and the appearance of the messenger to the women at the tomb on Easter morning. The young man – and we shall defer for the present a consideration of who he might be – is described as having a linen sheet cast about his naked body. When the soldiers grabbed him he is said to have wriggled out of the sheet and run away with nothing on. At the obvious level the Evangelist is describing an event which actually happened and there is no need to doubt its veracity. He uses a word, however, for the young man – νεανισκος – which is not a common one and is not easily translated. The old English word 'stripling' best conveys its meaning, or perhaps the more modern 'teenager'. In the New Testament we find it used twice by Saint Mark in the passages under discussion; once by Saint Matthew in relation to the young man who had great possessions; four times by Saint Luke, one of them being in the gospel in reference to the young man, here described as the only son of his mother at Nain who had died; and three times in Acts, the first in a sermon of Saint Peter on the day of Pentecost, the second for the youth who fell asleep in one of Saint Paul's sermons and dropped from the window next to which he was sitting, breaking his neck, and lastly for Saint Paul's nephew in the account of his arrest at Jerusalem. In the Johannine literature the word only appears once, in the first epistle, when the author is appealing to the young men within the community as a whole.

The word used for the linen sheet is also even more unusual. The Greek word is σινδων, meaning a cloth of muslin or cambric. Herodotus uses it for describing the cloths wrapped about corpses in the process of mummification. Other examples see the word being used for the bandage placed upon a wound. From these considerations, therefore, it could also be used for describing a shroud. In any case it is a most unusual word, only appearing three times in the whole of the New Testament, twice in Saint Mark (of which this is one and the other to describe the sheet in which the Lord's body was wrapped at the deposition from the cross) and the third in Saint Luke, who in this case is following Saint Mark.

In giving this account the Evangelist tells that the young man had a sheet-cum-shroud wrapped around his naked body. We remember that the scene is set in a garden, and this very word in devotional literature to a (devout) Jew would call to mind the Garden of Eden. In the Genesis story the immediate result of Adam and Eve's sin was that their eyes were opened and they knew that they were naked, and they hid themselves, and they sewed fig leaves together and made aprons for themselves. In this story clothing is the covering of man's shame, the effect of his sin. For this reason to remove a man's clothing is, according to Hebrew concepts, to shame him, to expose the effects of his sinning and to make him ashamed in the presence of his peers. On the other hand, in the time of their innocence, before the sin had been committed, Adam and Eve were naked and were not ashamed. In Saint Mark's telling of the story of the young man, as well as writing exactly what happened, he does it in such a way that his readers will recognise that the boy's contact with Jesus had the effect of causing him to be exposed and his frailties revealed, while at the same time he is restored to the condition of his innocence when his sin has been remitted and therefore obliterated.

Saint Mark does not leave the matter there. When he is telling of the way in which the body of Jesus was removed from the cross, he says that it was wrapped in a σινδων. That which had covered the lad's shame, the sheet in which his naked body was wrapped, is now the shroud in which the Lord's body is wrapped. The incarnate Jesus, who was God, had thus allowed Himself to be clothed with the garments of our shame, the body of our sinfulness, such that He became tempted in all things as we are. It is, therefore, in His humanity that he is laid in the tomb.

Saint Mark continues his account of the Passion and resurrection of our Lord by telling of the visit of the women to the tomb on Easter morning. When they had arrived at the scene they found that the stone had already been rolled away from the door of the sepulchre, 'and entering into the sepulchre they saw a young man (νεανισκος) wearing a long white garment.' In all the other accounts it is an angel, or two angels, who convey to the women the news of the resurrection. There is no reason to doubt that Saint Mark considers this young man also to be an angelic apparition, yet he uses that infrequently used word, νεανισκος, to imply that, as the young man in the garden was made to represent all men, so humanity was indicated in the figure within the tomb. Textually, he is no longer wrapped in a σινδων, but wearing a στολην λευκην, literally a white robe. Not easy to translate, a στολη is a royal robe, the panoply of a king, and white is always representative of innocence and purity. Thus by the resurrection of Jesus from the dead man has been restored, Paradise regained; no longer is humanity clothed with the garment of shame but glorified with the royal robes of kingly magnificence. The human nature which God assumed in Christ, and which was buried with Him in the sepulchre, by the resurrection was thus also raised to the glory of the ascended Jesus. In this way Saint Mark gives a plain straightforward account of a series of historic events but, in doing so, he takes us to a more profound level of understanding and guides us into deep theological truths. It is this style of writing which has caused men throughout the ages to proclaim such books inspired, and this inspiration has caused them to be regarded as the word of God and canonical scripture.

This provides a useful illustration of the way in which the Evangelists used their sources in the compilation of the gospels. There is no need to doubt the historicity of the events they are recording, though we must recognise that they are the result of a selection process for theological purposes. Of the sources available, one Evangelist will choose some, another perhaps the same or differently. It is therefore not possible, using the gospels, to reproduce the life of Christ in the correct chronological order. It could be said that Saint Luke did make such an endeavour. At least he seems to have undertaken to do this when he says in his preface: 'Forasmuch as many have taken in hand to set forth in order a declaration of those things which are most surely believed among us, even as they delivered them unto us, which from the beginning were eyewitnesses and ministers of the word; it seemed good to me also, having had perfect understanding of all things from the first, to write unto thee in order, most excellent Theophilus.' Twice he uses the phrase 'in order', but this is not to say that it assumes chronological significance. Even if it does, Saint Luke the Gentile is totally reliant upon source documents, or what eyewitnesses had told him by word of mouth, and again he would have had to make a selection. However hard he may have tried to present the events of our Lord's life in correct succession, he would almost certainly have been bound to fail: the pericopes to which he would have had access and the verbal accounts which he may well have collected would almost certainly have defied any attempt to place them in a correct time sequence.

Nevertheless, all four Evangelists give a very full and detailed account of the events which occurred in Jerusalem between Maundy Thursday and Easter Day inclusive; it has even been said that the accounts of the birth, childhood and early ministry of Jesus in the gospels are but introductions to the Passion narratives. All certainly regard the events of those few days to be of paramount importance for the salvation of men and for the redemption of the world. If they considered these occurrences to be of such absolute worth it follows that their exactitude of reportage must receive careful attention. From the records the Evangelists have left us, it should be possible, while recognising that each made his own selection, for us to recreate something like a compilation of the events recorded in correct chronological order. Of course, there may well have been other events which occurred, but which were not recorded, or were not selected for inclusion in any of the gospels. Nevertheless, it behoves us, in attempting to recreate the events of those days in chronological order, not to omit any incident which any one of the Evangelists considered necessary to include. This has been attempted many times, but almost invariably apparent contradictions have compelled the narrator either to omit one or more of the incidents from his sequence, or else, in recognition of the apparent impossibility of reconciling all the contradictions, to take refuge in a declaration as to the fallibility of all human recollection, and even the deliberate alteration of facts on the part of some in obedience to the presentation of a theological point of view. It might be possible by careful readings of the text to discover resolutions to some of the apparent contradictions, but there are others which defy any such attempt.

The outstanding contradiction in the Passion narratives is the date of the crucifixion. All agree that it happened on a Friday, but was that Friday the day of Passover or not? The

Synoptists say quite categorically that the Last Supper was the Passover meal. Saint John says equally categorically that it was not. This is a contradiction which clearly is incapable of resolution: they cannot both be correct.

We have already seen that the Evangelists used historical events to convey theological truth. Both the Synoptists and the author of the fourth gospel are at pains to stress the sacrificial nature of the atoning work of Jesus. The Passion and the crucifixion indubitably took place at the time of Passover. There is no doubt at all that it was because Jesus, the disciples, the brethren and the women had gone to keep the feast that they all happened to be in Jerusalem at that time. It would, therefore, be salutary, before we begin to consider the relative merits of the divergent datings so as to ascertain the actual date, for us to consider what happened when a family went to Jerusalem to keep Passover.

It must first be remembered that the purpose of a sacrifice was not the appeasement of an angry God by the slaying of a victim, nor was it the taking of a victim's life as a substitute for one's own, because sin had rightly brought down upon the head of a sinner divine wrath and judgement. It is true that sin separates man from his God, because imperfection cannot be in complete union with perfection. If therefore the worshipper needs to be reconciled to a perfect God because he cannot make himself perfect or become perfect by an act of will, he will need to identify with a life which is perfect, other than his own, and offer that. Because that life is perfect it could be worthily offered to God and accepted by Him as a 'sweet smelling savour'. If the worshipper had identified himself with the victim's life and become united with it, then through that identification, God would also accept the worshipper. This would be possible in spite of the fact that the worshipper was a sinner, and by his sin had cut himself off from communion with God.

The book of Exodus gives an account of the institution of the Passover in the twelfth chapter:

> They shall take to them every man a lamb, according to the house of their fathers, a lamb for a house: and if the household be too little for a lamb, let him and his neighbour next to his house take it according to the number of the souls, every man according to his eating shall make your count for the lamb. Your lamb shall be without blemish, a male of the first year: ye shall take it out from the sheep or from the goats, and ye shall keep it up until the fourteenth day of the same month, and the whole assembly of the congregation of Israel shall kill it in the evening. And they shall take of the blood and strike it upon the two side posts and the upper doorpost of the houses, wherein they shall eat it... and the blood shall be for you for a token upon the houses where ye are; and when I see the blood, I will pass over you, and the plague shall not be upon you to destroy you, when I smite the land of Egypt. And this day shall be unto you for a memorial; and ye shall keep it a feast to the Lord throughout your generations; ye shall keep it a feast by an ordinance for ever.

There are certain points about this account worthy of special attention. Firstly, the lamb which is to be offered must be a male of the first year and must be without blemish, a perfect specimen of its kind. Secondly, the blood must be drawn out of the carcass and smeared on the doors and lintels of the houses. The blood must not itself be consumed with the lamb, because as we are told several times in the book of Leviticus, the blood is the life. This last point must receive special consideration. Ancient peoples noted that when an artery was opened in man or beast, the blood drained away, and as it was spilled so the life ebbed until, when the flow had ceased, the life had gone from the body. It was a reasonable deduction then that the blood was the life and the life was the blood. It will be remembered that after Cain had murdered his brother, it was the blood of Abel which pleaded for vengeance to the skies: 'And God said, what hast thou done? The voice of thy brother's blood crieth unto me from the ground' (Gen 4:10). In the Passover celebrations then, the life of the lamb was the blood and, if the lamb were perfect, here there would be a perfect life. In the land of Canaan, after the building of the temple and the establishment of the cultus, the blood of the lamb was sprinkled on the altar, the erection in the temple court which represented the presence of God with His people. A further point to be considered is a reference in the book of Deuteronomy in the sixteenth chapter where we read: 'And at the place where the Lord thy God shall choose to place His name in, there thou shalt sacrifice the Passover at even, at the going down of the sun.' At the festival then the killing of the Passover lambs could not begin until the sun had passed its zenith, that is after the sixth hour of the day.

We are now in a position to describe what would happen at Passover time in Jerusalem at the time of our Lord. On the fourteenth day of the month Nisan, the heads of the household would arrive at the temple either with their lamb or so as to purchase one from the temple market. It was probably the temple stallholders charging more than the market prices for the lambs they sold there, that so angered our Lord on the occasion of His overthrowing their tables. Not until midday had struck could the slaying of the lambs begin. It must be especially noted that the victim was not slain on the altar, nor did a priest perpetrate the act. It was the head of the household, acting on behalf of his family, who actually put the knife into an artery and caused the blood of the victim to be poured into a bowl. In the popular assumption the life of the lamb was then not so much in the dead carcass as in the steaming bowl. Because the worshipper was a sinner he dared not himself approach the altar, but needed a man specially appointed or ordained for this work, one of the priests; having found him, he would present the bowl to him so that he might take it to the altar and pour the blood upon it. First however, before he slew the lamb, the one making the sacrifice would have placed his hands on the head of the animal, thus making an expression of his intended identity with it. Before giving the bowl to the priest, he would have smeared the blood on his forehead. Thus part of the lamb's life would adhere to his person, and his identification with the lamb would have been established. The carcass would then be taken home and roasted for the Passover meal, a greatly valued family occasion when the household gathered around the family table. Thus the sacrificial action was completed by the eating of the flesh of the lamb whose life had been offered in sacrifice. There are then four parts to the action of the sacrificial ceremony: the identification of the worshipper with the victim; the slaying of the victim so as to make its life available, the blood smeared on the head of the worshipper and poured on the altar of God so that God and the worshipper are brought together as one in the offered life of the victim; the offering on the altar and the acceptance by God of the victim, and therefore of the worshipper who has become identified with it; and lastly, the consumption of the lamb in the sacrificial meal. For a Jew the day begins at sundown, so that the meal would be eaten on the fifteenth day of the month Nisan, the actual Feast Day, although the lamb would have been slain on the afternoon of the fourteenth. The Passover date was determined by the fact that it was the time of the first full moon after the vernal equinox.

All the Evangelists were anxious to establish the fact that it was only in the sacrifice of Jesus that the Passover had been fulfilled. The offering that was to be made had to be of a living creature, a perfect specimen of its kind, for only perfection would be acceptable by God. The animal victims, however, were only perfect in their physical properties; one could not say that they were sinless, because they were not moral beings. In the case of the men on whose behalf the lamb was being offered, the main cause of the separation from God which the sacrifice was intended to overcome had been caused by sin; humans are imperfect because they are sinners. So, for a sacrifice to be really effective in achieving the goal for which it was offered, the victim must be at least a moral being, and therefore at least human. Jesus was human and totally without sin, and was therefore an appropriate offering. Indeed He was the only perfect human being, for all others, to use scriptural language, shared in the sin of Adam. In this day and age that statement may well need a little further elucidation.

The myth of the Garden of Eden, as it stands in the book of Genesis, records that the human inhabitants were tempted to disobey God's prohibition to eat of the fruit of the tree which was in the midst of the garden, and suc-cumbed to temptation. The effect of that fall was the total fragmentation of the created order. If one tiny fragment of a piece of porcelain decides 'to go its own way', to live apart from the place in the artefact which the potter has made, the piece becomes broken, and every other particle of which the piece is composed shares in that imperfection. Since this accords with man's experience of himself and his consciousness of the imperfection of his being, there must have been a Fall; otherwise God would be guilty of creating a less than perfect world. That Fall then must have been cosmic in its effect, and every creature shares in the consequent fragmentation or imperfection. An atoning sacrifice, to be effective, could not be the offering of any of God's creatures, because what perfection it may have could only be physical. We are therefore confronted with a dilemma. If there were to be 'a perfect sacrifice, oblation and satisfaction for the sins of the whole world', the sacrificial life must not be that of a creature. But since it is the creation which needs to be redeemed, the perfect life offered must itself be a creature. This contradiction can only be resolved if the Creator Himself becomes a creature. This is why throughout the New Testament there runs the continuous theme that Jesus was in fact both Man and God, God made Man.

The identity of the people with the life of the Passover lamb was expressed by the householder placing his hands on the head of the animal and was realised in the Passover meal when the carcass of the lamb was eaten. In the sacrifice of Jesus His life was made available by His death upon the cross and His subsequent resurrection. Saint Mark emphasises one aspect, Saint John the other. It now becomes clear why Saint Mark, followed by the other Synoptists, tells of the institution of the Eucharist in his account of the Last Supper and why the fourth gospel does not, but gives a full statement of eucharistic theology in connection with the feeding of the five thousand.

There is a further indication of Saint Mark's sacrificial interpretation of the institution of the Eucharist. When Jesus said that the bread and wine were to be His body and His blood, He meant that those elements would become, when so used, the means by which His risen life would be made available. The life is expressed in and mediated to the material world by flesh and blood. Therefore, bread and wine used in this way are the means by which the risen life of Jesus is communicated and the identification is made complete. It is probably because of this connection that the Synoptists emphasise the point by making the supper the

Passover meal. It is also significant that when Jesus said 'do this', He used the Greek word ποιεω rather than the more usual πρασσω. The word ποιεω is sometimes used, particularly in the Septuagint, the Greek version of the Hebrew Scriptures, for 'make this sacrifice'. Other Greek writers also, in particular Herodotus, Xenophon and Thucydides, use the word in connection with the offering of sacrifices.

On the other hand Saint John is at pains to establish the fact that Jesus is the true Paschal Lamb. In the early part of his gospel he makes Saint John the Baptist declare, 'Behold, the Lamb of God.' He emphasises the atoning purposes of the sacrifice of our Lord on the cross, and it will be re-membered that for Saint John the crucifixion was the glorification of Jesus, when His hour was come. It is Saint John alone who gives us the word from the cross – τετελεσται – somewhat inadequately translated as 'It is finished.' But really it is a cry of triumph and victory, 'It is brought to an end,' or even more colloquially, 'I've done it.' Saint John is careful to equate the slaying of the Passover lambs with the death of Jesus on the cross. This receives greater emphasis from the outpouring of Jesus' blood when the soldier thrusts the spear into His side, knowing that He was already dead, which reflects the pouring of the victims' blood upon the altar in the temple, which would be going on at the same time. Saint John alone records this.

There is yet another reference to Saint John's insistence on the sacrificial aspect of the atoning work of Christ. After the last discourse, which occupies five chapters of this gospel and concludes with the High Priestly Prayer, he says: 'When Jesus had spoken these words he went forth with his disciples over the brook Kedron, where there was a garden.' The mention of the name of the brook Kedron may well of course have been just a geographical note in the narrative. Nevertheless, it would convey something more to a Jewish reader of Saint John's time. This section of the gospel is concerned with what happened at the time of the Passover on which Jesus was crucified. On the day before the feast, during the afternoon, when according to Saint John's chronology Jesus was dying on the cross, the blood of literally thousands of lambs was being poured over the altar in the temple court. The altar was built on a grating which covered a bowl-like excavation in the rock beneath. This had a sump which led into a pipe constructed through the rock so that the blood of the sacrifices could drain away and be disgorged into the brook Kedron. This little trickle of a stream, by three o'clock on Good Friday afternoon, would have become a river of blood. The naming of the brook then would put into the minds of the readers the blood of the Passover lambs and the fulfilment of what the ancient sacrifices foreshadowed – the outpouring of the life of Jesus – would further be emphasised.

It is now possible to see the reasons for the differences in the dating of the crucifixion. If, however, it were to be assumed that the Evangelists could take such liberties in the recording of an historic event to make a theological point, some may doubt *all* the historicity of the gospels. Yet it has come only comparatively recently to be considered that the historian's duty is primarily to record past events in chronological order. Before the eighteenth century historians regarded their prime function to be the recording of past events to reflect a personal attitude. After all, it does not really matter whether the Last Supper were the Passover meal or not; the vital point to establish is that Jesus is the Lamb of God, whose life has been available for men who can identify with it and become part of it. This is what the Evangelists were doing. The Synoptists and the fourth gospel were taking different aspects of the sacrificial procedures to make their points.

It is only natural, though, that we should want to know

which of these datings is correct. It may well be of more than passing interest to consider some of the facts pertaining to this matter to try to discover which of the Evangelists has got it right. It must be stressed, however, that if it were possible to discover that one of them was mistaken, this would not in any way impair the reliability of that author in the production of an authentic gospel. Gospels are not histories, although there is much that is historical within them. Neither are they biographies, although they tell us much about our Lord's life on earth. Primarily, they are theological treatises, and as such, although historical accuracy must not be allowed to be perverted by theological reasoning, neither must theological reasoning allow itself to be overpowered by considerations of historical accuracy.

According to which tradition we take as to whether the Passover meal was eaten on the Thursday or the Friday evening, we should be able to fix a date for the crucifixion. From all the gospel accounts the crucifixion happened on a Friday. If the Synoptists are correct, then the fifteenth Nisan would be the Friday, but if the fourth gospel is correct then it would be the Saturday. We know that the fifteenth fell on a Friday in AD 30, but a Saturday in both AD 27 and 33. According to the Synoptists then the crucifixion can be dated at AD 30, whereas according to Saint John it can either be AD 27 or 33. We are told by Saint Luke that at the time of His baptism, Jesus was about thirty years old. From a consideration of the feasts mentioned by Saint John in the public ministry of our Lord, we can calculate that the traditional period of three years is correct. This then would suggest that Jesus was born in 3 BC. We know for a certainty that whoever first calculated that the year A.U.C. (*ab urbe condita* – 'from the foundation of the City' – that is to say Rome) 753 was henceforth to be known as AD 1 had got it wrong. Herod the Great died in

4 BC and therefore, if Saint Luke is right, Saint Matthew is wrong, because he tells us that Jesus was born some time before the death of Herod, the most likely year being 6 BC. If we take that year and add the thirty years of Jesus' age, and then a further three years for the public ministry, we arrive at AD 27, which accords with the Johannine account.

There is a further complication when we consider the verse in Saint Luke's gospel (3:1) which tells us that John the Baptist's ministry began in the fifteenth year of the reign of Tiberius. If we reckon Tiberius' reign to have begun with the death of Augustus, this would give us AD 27 or 28. If we date the beginning of his rule from Augustus' taking him into partnership in the Imperium it would give us AD 26 or 27. If we allow for a three year ministry of Jesus this would bring us to AD 30 for the crucifixion, which would give credence to the Synoptists' dating. On the other hand, if Saint Luke himself is correct in making Jesus about thirty at the time of His baptism this gives a birth year of either 4, 3 or 2 BC. Such a date is not impossible, but in view of the known date for the death of Herod it is not very likely. From a careful weighing of all this information, then, it would seem that it is not possible to arrive at a firm date for the crucifixion or to make a decision about whether Saint Mark or Saint John is correct on the nature of the Last Supper. On balance the scales are tipped slightly in favour of Saint John, though this is still a matter of opinion. We must, therefore, look for other pieces of biblical evidence to see whether it is possible to find a greater degree of probability for one or the other.

If the Last Supper were the Passover meal as the Synoptists say it was, it is significant that there is no reference to the head of the household going to the temple to procure the sacrificial lamb for the eating. We ought therefore to examine the references to the preparation. It would seem that Jesus had made very careful preparations for this meal and that it would have had more significance for Him than a merely routine supper. He had arranged for it to be eaten in a house which had a large upper room and had also arranged for this room to be carefully prepared for the meal. This in itself might well argue that the meal was to have been the Passover. It would also seem that the house was not generally known to the disciples, for the two who were dispatched to make the necessary preparations did not know where it was. Again Jesus had made careful plans for a man, presumably a servant employed by the owner of the house, to be at the city gate at a certain time, making himself conspicuous by carrying a pitcher of water. It was usually the women who served as the water carriers. It could be that these two were also entrusted with the necessary liturgical duties in the temple. In that case it seems odd that the disciples were not named, and one would have presumed that this would have been done by Jesus Himself. It could be however that the proprietor of the house would fulfil that obligation and so the lamb would have been provided as part of the preparations. Saint Luke indeed does name the two disciples as Peter and John. If these were the two, it is strange that Saint Mark does not also name them. It must be remembered that Saint Luke was entirely dependent upon second hand information, and these names could have been subsequently provided. They are however somewhat significant because Saint Luke is at pains to name these two disciples in association with each other. In his second volume, the book of Acts, there are many accounts in the early chapters of Peter and John being together as the leaders of the Apostolic band. Again there is nothing conclusive to be found in this line of enquiry, but it does appear a little strange that no mention is made of the sacrificial lamb and it being ceremonially killed and offered. We are still therefore not able to come to a clear decision on the matter, but again, the scales do seem to be slightly

Printed by Expressions Offset Ltd, 01942 729256

№ 1977

CHRISTMAS FAIR DRAW

To be drawn on 5th December, 2004 at St Wilfrid's School, Golborne Road

1st Prize: £100.00

2nd Prize: Northern Feather's Bedding 3rd: Hamper

4: Bottle… Plus many more prizes.

St Wilfids V.A. RC Primary School

Promoter: St Wilfids School PTA Committee, Golborne Road, Ashton-in-Makerfield WN4 8SJ

TICKETS 20p

tipped in favour of the fourth gospel.

It is quite certain, however, that the Eucharist was instituted at this meal whether it were the Passover supper or not. So important was this for the Church, not only in the immediate post resurrection period, but throughout its history, that at first consideration, it seems strange that Saint John does not mention it, giving no account at all of the institution. He gives us instead the account of Jesus washing the disciples' feet as an introduction to the long discourse to follow. It could be, of course, that the author of the fourth gospel already knew the gospel of Saint Mark and that he did not consider it necessary to make a repetition of that which already had become well known. If that were the case it would mean that there must be a late date for the writing of the fourth gospel, which is by no means certain. We have already seen that there could well be reasons why the Synoptists say that the Last Supper was the Passover meal, and why Saint John did not give an account of the institution of the Eucharist then. The supper however does not need to be the Passover meal for Jesus to institute the Eucharist at it. This meal itself could not have been a Eucharist, because the crucifixion and the resurrection had not yet occurred. What happened at that meal must surely have been that Jesus gave a demonstration of how He wished His disciples to use bread and wine in the future, and promised them that when they did obey this instruction in conscious remembrance of Him, those physical elements would be the means by which His own risen and glorified life would be communicated to them. This is the only possible interpretation of the words of institution, for it is by our physical properties that our personalities are expressed in and mediated to the world in which we live, and without which we would not have the power to influence, direct and teach; in a word, to be effective agents.

Although Saint John does not give a direct account of the historic institution of the Eucharist, in the discourse attached to the account of the feeding of the five thousand there is abundant evidence that he gave great importance to the use of bread and wine as the body and blood of Christ for the salvation of the individual. Indeed there can be no other interpretation of His words than that entry into the Kingdom of Heaven depends upon the availability of the Eucharist (Saint John 6:48–58). He has no need to take his readers back into what has already been fully treated, by giving an account of the particulars at the supper the night before He was betrayed. The fact that Saint John does not record the incident in no way means that it did not happen. It simply was not in accordance with the selection the author made so as to stress that the glorification of Jesus had begun and that this glorification was His passion and death. That which the Synoptists are doing for their readers in their accounts of the Last Supper, Saint John does for his in the sixth chapter of his gospel. Indeed he spells out the significance of the Eucharist even more specifically than do the Synoptists and attaches it to his account of the feeding of the five thousand which has undoubted eucharistic overtones.

In telling of the events of Good Friday the Synoptists inform us that the chief priests were at the scene of the crucifixion and joined in the mocking. Saint Mark is quite definite on the point: 'Likewise also the chief priests mocking said amongst themselves with the scribes, "He saved others; himself he cannot save."' Saint Matthew and Saint Luke both follow Saint Mark in this passage except that Saint Matthew adds to the priests and the scribes the elders, and Saint Luke describes them with the inclusive term the rulers. If this day were the feast day of the Passover it is unlikely that the priests, or indeed a crowd, would have gathered to witness the events on Calvary. If, on the other hand, it were the day before Passover, then the priests would have been able to be there in the morning, but after the passing of noon, their presence would be required in the temple to cope with the rush of sacrificers bringing the blood of their lambs. To substantiate this the Synoptists say that Jesus was fixed to the cross at nine o'clock in the morning. At the time of our Lord's death, Saint Mark, having told us that the centurion said, 'Truly, this man was the Son of God,' says that there were also women looking on from afar. Saint Matthew refers to the centurion and 'they that were with him', presumably meaning the soldiers, and also states that many women were looking on from a distance. Saint Luke alone says that 'all the people that came together to that sight saw the things that were done, smote their breasts and returned'. Luke alone gives the impression that there was still a crowd at the end. The other two Synoptists give the impression that most of the people had departed, although they do not specifically say so. Saint Luke of course could not have been there and is an unreliable witness for details of this kind. Saint John makes no reference at all to a crowd, but only states that at the cross were the mother of Jesus, the Disciple whom He loved, Mary, the wife of Cleophas, and Mary Magdalene. He says nothing about the priests being there, except to say that they asked Pilate to alter the wording of the superscription. This in itself would imply that they had been present at the execution to see the title affixed.

Here there is another discrepancy between the Synoptists and the fourth gospel which is impossible to reconcile. The Synoptists say that Jesus was crucified at the third hour, but Saint John is quite definite that it was noon when He was nailed to the cross. In this particular, the Synoptists are more likely to be correct. Whichever date is correct it would not be likely that there were a crowd about to watch and mock if Jesus only hung on the cross during the three hours after noon. If the Markan dating is correct, then it would be the actual day of the festival, when most people would be in their homes or the houses where they were staying. If the Johannine dating is the right one, then the priests would be far too busy in the temple and most others would be making preparations for the Passover meal. It must also be remembered that for a Jew to see a naked corpse, he would be rendered ceremonially unclean; therefore, if it were at this late hour, he would be precluded from the ceremonial and ritual obligations of the feast, not having time to make the necessary acts of purification. We can however readily see why Saint John uses the time schedule that he does. It was against the law for the lambs to be slain and offered until the sun had passed the zenith, and Saint John is at pains to identify the crucifixion of Jesus with the slaying of the Passover lambs. He would therefore want to make this point by having Jesus nailed to the cross at the same time that the lambs were starting to be killed. If, however, the execution did not begin until noon, it would be a little difficult to explain the hurry with which Caiaphas conducted all the legal preliminaries. We know from the account of Peter's denial that Caiaphas was still conducting the trial when the cock crowed, presumably as dawn was about to break. If the sentence in Saint Luke's gospel that 'the Lord turned and looked on Peter' is an authentic tradition, then that trial must have ended immediately before dawn. That would give Caiaphas about three hours to go through all the other preliminaries to the execution. Pilate would have had to have been summoned, some time would be required for his own enquiry, possibly also the visits to Herod, the condemnations by the crowd, and the soldiers' barracking of Jesus while waiting for the preparations for Him to be joined to the other two criminals who were to be executed that day. This means that a lot would have had to have happened in those three hours, and some may think that this consideration is an argument for the Johannine time schedule. On the other hand, it would be impossible for the priests to be present at the scene of the crucifixion if the period on the cross did not begin until noon. Nevertheless, Caiaphas would indeed have had to move very quickly. We are given some indication of his impatience when, not readily finding two witnesses to tell the same tale, he lays aside the proper requirements of the law and appeals directly to the prisoner with his question 'Art thou the Christ?'

A further argument in favour of the Johannine tradition lies in the fact that Saint Mark, closely followed by Saint Matthew, states categorically that they were anxious that Jesus should be got out of the way if possible before the feast, even though it was only two days away. Saint Mark's words are:

> After two days was the feast of the Passover and of unleavened bread, and the chief priests and scribes sought how they might take Him by subtlety and put Him to death. But they said, not on the feast day, lest there be an uproar of the people.

Saint Matthew states it in different words:

> It came to pass when Jesus had finished all these sayings, he said unto His disciples, 'Ye know that after two days is the feast of the Passover, and the Son of Man is betrayed to be crucified.' Then assembled together the chief priests and the scribes, and the elders of the people unto the palace of the High Priest who was called Caiaphas, and consulted

> that they might take Jesus by subtlety, and kill Him.
> But they said not on the feast day lest there be an up-
> roar among the people.

Saint Luke however does not mention the feast day as an undesirable occasion for the execution, merely saying:

> Now the feast of unleavened bread drew nigh, which
> was called the Passover, and the chief priests and
> scribes sought how they might kill Him; for they
> feared the people.

Saint John gives a much fuller account of this meeting of the Council and informs us that the debate concerned the problem of what to do with Jesus. There was no doubt that He had performed many miracles, but if they did nothing, then He would draw away a large part of the people and trouble would ensue. The rights and rule that were still enjoyed by the Sanhedrin were conditional upon the peace being kept. Saint John says, 'If we let Him alone all men will believe in Him; and the Romans shall come and take away both our place and nation.' Caiaphas eventually clinched the argument by saying that it was necessary that one man should die for the people. Saint John makes much of this, writing:

> and this he spake, not of himself, but being High
> Priest that year, he prophesied that Jesus should die
> for that nation; and not for that nation only, but also
> that He should gather together in one the children of
> God that were scattered abroad.

He continues that from that day forth they took counsel that they might put Him to death. He makes no mention of the feast day or its inconvenience.

We can affirm then with some confidence that there was a determination that the whole business should have been completed before the actual feast, even though it was so near. In this it would seem that the Synoptists give testimony to the accuracy of the Johannine dating. A further piece of evidence is the necessity for the bodies to be removed from the crosses before nightfall. If the Johannine dating is correct, this is understandable, but if the Synoptists are right then it is inexplicable, for the actual crucifixion would have been carried out on the feast day itself.

Furthermore, there does seem to be some evidence from the Synoptists that the fifteenth of Nisan that year fell on the Saturday. Saint Mark says that:

> when even was come, because it was the preparation, that is the day before the Sabbath, Joseph of Arimathaea... went in boldly unto Pilate and craved the body of Jesus. And Pilate marvelled if He were already dead: and calling unto him the centurion he asked whether He had been any while dead, and when he knew it of the centurion he gave the body to Joseph.

It was the Roman custom when a man had been put to death by crucifixion to leave the body on the cross until it had rotted away or been eaten by birds of prey. But the Jews had a law which forbade this. In Deuteronomy 21:22 we read:

> If a man have committed a sin worthy of death, and he be put to death, and thou hang him on a tree, his body shall not remain all night upon the tree but thou shalt in any wise bury him that day.

In order then not to offend Jewish religious susceptibilities Pilate allowed the body to be removed from the cross and given to Joseph so that the Jewish law might be observed. It would have been necessary then for the burying to take place before the evening whatever the day. For it to be mentioned that it was the day of the preparation, there must be something especially significant about that particular Sabbath. It is Saint John who provides the explanation by telling us that that Sabbath was a high day, that is to say the day of the feast.

We can now understand the anxiety on the part of the priests that the whole business of the disposal of Jesus, who to them was a probable cause of troublemaking, if not actual rebellion, should be over and done with before the festival actually occurred. To them Jesus constituted a threat to public order, needing to be disposed of as quickly as possible, but to allow the execution of the death sentence to be carried out on the day of the festival would indeed be inviting an outbreak of violence because of the sacrilege which the desecration of the Passover would have caused. It was surely this consideration which caused the Council to be so determined to move quickly. In any case the city was so overcrowded at Passover time that there was always the danger of trouble and the risk of outbreaks of violence. Religious and nationalistic feelings would be running high, and it was the government's responsibility not to do anything which could inflame what was already a highly volatile situation.

From all these considerations it is not possible to produce a watertight case for proving which of the two contradictory dates is the correct one. Nevertheless, on balance it does seem more likely that Saint John's is the correct one by his placing of the fifteenth day of Nisan on the Saturday. If that is true, then the Last Supper was not the Passover meal, although it is indisputable that at that meal Jesus instituted the Eucharist. For the purpose of a working hypothesis then, the Johannine dating will be accepted as authentic. As far as the timing is concerned, however, we should accept that given by the Synoptists and accept that the execution took place at nine o'clock in the morning.

We have now seen that the pericopes were the oral traditions or even the written documents of those disciples who had known and been with Jesus when He was on this earth. The Evangelists selected from them what they needed to establish the theology which they were set on teaching. It is easier to make this statement than it is to define what the teaching specifically was. Each gospel has its own particular angle, but the pericopes are assembled and used at so many levels and with such profound significance (an example of which we noted in Saint Mark's treatment of the narrative of the young man in the garden) that these four books have kept scholars, evangelists and teachers busily occupied for nearly two thousand years, and there are no signs that the well of meaning will ever run dry. It is this fact which made readers, presumably from their first publication, realise that these books have a quality which cannot be adequately described, except to say that they are inspired scripture. Even before there was a canon of the New Testament, these books were known and valued throughout the world. There is evidence that Saint John's gospel, which we are led to believe was first written in Asia, was known and used in Egypt as early as the first quarter of the second century, and also that it was known, read and used in Gaul before the days of Irenaeus only a few years later. Indeed, the earliest manuscript of the New Testament that has so far come to light was, until recently, thought to be a small fragment of papyrus, now in the John Rylands Library in Manchester. It can be dated to the first half of the second century AD. That dating represents the moment when the fragment was discarded or dropped, and subsequently covered by sand. It would therefore be unlikely to have been at that time a brand new book, but more likely have been in someone's possession considerably before then.

In point of fact the papyrus fragment is written on both sides and, since the words written both come from the eighteenth chapter of Saint John's gospel, on one side from verses thirty-one to thirty-three, and on the other from verses thirty-seven to thirty-eight, it must have been, when complete, a page from a codex, rather than a piece of roll, which was the normal manner of producing books at that time. The fact that the piece seems to have been torn from the top of a page makes it possible to reconstruct the whole of the page; from the distance separating the words on either side in the actual book, the size of the page can also be ascertained. This artefact then must have been a very early book and the size would indicate that it was more what we should now call a pocket edition rather than a book for preservation in a library. These facts alone would give a clear indication that one of the gospels at least was so highly valued as to be available in a manageable form for frequent reading and also available for personal carriage. It must also have been produced no later than the early years of the second century. It is not likely to have been the autograph, but an actual reproduced book, which we believe first to have been written in Asia, than copied at least once, and produced for personal and presumably devotional use in Egypt not long after. This would indicate that an authority was already being given to this book not unlike that due to canonical scripture. Only a few years later we have proof that Saint Irenaeus, who lived in Gaul, also knew and used this and the other three gospels. Indeed there is full evidence that all four gospels were known and used generally by Christians and regarded as reliable sources from a very early period in the history of the Church. The Rylands papyrus at least bears testimony that Saint John's gospel, as we have it, was written not very long after the events described in it had occurred.

There are also three papyrus fragments in the possession of Magdalen College, Oxford, given by one of its alumni who had been stationed at Luxor in Upper Egypt and who had come into the possession of them while out there. They too have writing on both sides, and it has been recognised that they are part of a papyrus sheet coming from a copy of Saint Matthew's gospel. This would mean that here there is further proof that the first gospel, as well as the fourth, was known and used by Christians living in Egypt at an early date, and that the gospels were being produced in a codex or book form as well as on the more usual rolls.

Until recently these pieces were considered to have come from the late second century of the Christian era. Dr Carsten Thiede, an eminent German papyrologist, having examined them as recently as 1995, has reached the conclusion that they ought to be dated much earlier than that. The style of writing on the fragments is a distinctive script, common in the first century BC, but which had petered out by the middle of the first century AD. This would mean that the gospel according to Saint Matthew must have been written at a very early date, and only a comparatively short time after the crucifixion which it describes.

From all this comes the reasonable deduction that, given what now appears certain about the very early authorship of Saint Matthew and Saint John, the same would also apply to the other two gospels. These are very important discoveries, bound to have a devastating effect on much of the New Testament scholarship of the last hundred years. Rather than revealing a situation which existed in a fairly advanced period of Christian development, which had caused biblical critics to spend much effort in trying to trace back from what they hitherto believed to be a developed situation in order to find the authentic facts and words about Jesus in His life on earth, we now have a written record which comes from a much earlier time in the history of the Church. Indeed, this was a time when there would still have been many people who had personal recollections of what Jesus said and did. It gives the claim that is made in the preface to Saint Luke's gospel, that he had consulted with 'them who from the beginning were eyewitnesses and ministers of the word', an enhanced claim to authenticity. It also means that almost from the first days of the Christian Church there was felt a need for written records so as to facilitate the missionary outreach of the Church and to enhance the personal devotion of individual Christians. Indeed it could be said that this need resulted in the invention of the codex form of literary production.

The above, together with the regard of the Fathers for the writings of the Evangelists, gives to them an authority which not only developed eventually into the production of a canon of Holy Scripture, but also, even at this early stage, lent a reliability for being treated as source documents for them the events of our Lord's life. It is true, of course, that we have no complete manuscript of the New Testament from these early years, but the reverent attitude of the early Christian writers to these books would have resulted in a reluctance to allow any great changes to reproductions of further copies or to permit radical alterations to the wording of the texts. No doubt there would be copying errors, and theological considerations may well have caused certain adaptations and variations in the use of words, but the historical reliability of the incidents and quotations they give has no need seriously to be doubted.

On the uppermost and most clearly recognised level of understanding, we can appreciate that Saint Matthew, for example, wishes to demonstrate that in the birth, life, mission, passion and death of Jesus, the whole tale of God's dealing with His people the Jews, the chronicle of which is contained in the Old Testament scriptures, actually receives its fulfilment: all their prophecies and prognostications have been realised. There is much more meaning in Saint Matthew's gospel than that, but his consciousness of the relevance of the Old Testament prophecies is one of the outstanding features of his writing, and this would cause him whenever possible to draw attention to these facts. Saint Mark, on the other hand, is at pains to indicate that the ministry, passion and resurrection of Jesus is a new beginning. He makes this abundantly clear by the opening words of his gospel, which do not even constitute a sentence. 'The beginning of the gospel of Jesus Christ the Son of God' is a title, not a statement. It is also interesting that here Christ is used as a name rather than a description. This title receives most dramatic emphasis in the concluding words of the book. It can be assumed that the author really did intend the book to end at chapter sixteen verse eight with the words εφοβουντο γαρ,which can be translated as 'For they were afraid'. In English that is a complete sentence, but in the original Greek it is a grammatical impossibility. The Greek word γαρ can be translated as 'for' or 'because'. It is a conjunction which is also an enclitic, which means it is a word which can never begin or end a sentence. In practice this means that it is nearly always the second word in the sentence, although, when it is, the sentence must contain more than two words. 'εφοβουντο γαρ' then is the beginning of a sentence which is deliberately left unfinished. It is this that has made many people think that the end of Saint Mark's gospel has been lost, that the end of the scroll on which it would have been written, at some time very early in its history, must have dropped off and disappeared. Indeed the gospel according to Saint Mark, as it has usually been printed in our Bibles, contains attempts to provide a suitable conclusion. Since these appear in most of the earliest manuscripts that have survived, it must have occurred very early. Nevertheless, it would be difficult for the ending of a scroll to be lost, because that is the part which is attached to the wooden roller on which the parchment would be fixed, and would be the last to disappear. It seems certain then that Saint Mark concluded his gospel with the beginning of a sentence. In this dramatic way he fulfils his title and makes the whole of the gospel a beginning. All that he has written is a preliminary to the resurrection of Jesus from the dead. As the women went to the tomb they saw that the stone was rolled away and were frightened. A great power has been let loose in the world. It is a beginning.

Saint Luke actually writes a preface to his gospel in which he states that he is trying to put the events and the whole course of the book into some sort of order. It could mean that this order is the chronological one, but it does not specifically say what the order is in which the book is going to be written. He also states that he is dependent upon them that were from the beginning eyewitnesses and ministers of the word. He makes it clear that the purpose of the book is that the reader 'should know the certainty of those things wherein thou has been instructed'. It could be that the Theophilus mentioned was a particular person, or, because the word literally means 'Friend of God', Saint Luke could be using it as a general term, as some Victorian novelists sometimes insert into the narrative of their books the specific address 'dear reader'.

If the author of the fourth gospel were indeed the Apostle John, the son of Zebedee and the brother of James, he would not need to rely upon source documents or oral tradition, because he would have the events and discourses he sets down retained in his own memory. He depicts Jesus as the Word who was God – with God and in the beginning with God, that is fully God – who was the creator of all things and now has been made flesh and dwelt among us. He then is giving an account of a new creation, the first creation having been marred and despoiled by sin. The six miracles which he selects and which he clearly indicates as signs are chosen to illustrate, be signs of, the new acts of creation, following closely the six days of creation in Genesis.

With all the four Evangelists the details of the closing days of our Lord's earthly life, His crucifixion and resurrection, and the events that immediately precede them occupy more of each book than any other event which they relate. They all give the events between Maundy Thursday and Easter Day an importance that no other record receives. They all, with the exception of Saint Mark, who with consummate skill makes his account of the resurrection clearly a beginning, give a very full record of the events of Easter Day. The incidents they record, however, do not seem to be the same. Each makes his personal selection in accordance with his purpose in the telling of them. It is of interest, therefore, that the attempt should be made to recreate the events recorded and to see whether it is possible for all of them to be related to each other in such a way that a continuous story can be reproduced.

In the earlier decades of the twentieth century there was a great demand for the writing and production of Passion plays and Nativity plays so that the great moments of our salvation history could be presented dramatically. Many were produced, the value of which lay more in the attempt to present an evangelistic appeal than in the excellence of dramatic art. There was, however, a difficulty in that the convention of the time prevented the representation of our Lord on the stage. A much vaunted and extremely popular film of the immediate pre-talkie era was a great American epic production of a dramatisation of Lew Wallace's *Ben Hur*, which had as its subtitle *A Tale of the Christ*. Even in this the audience was not allowed to see any more of Jesus than His hand or His feet; it was considered blasphemous for a mere man to be seen in full representation of the Christ.

In 1940 Miss Dorothy Sayers was asked to write a series of plays about the life of our Lord for broadcasting by the BBC on the Sunday *Children's Hour* programme. Her acceptance was conditional upon the character of our Lord actually being introduced, using modern speech. Before the performance of the first episode, however, there was a press conference at which Miss Sayers herself read some extracts from the plays. A storm resulted: there were howls of derision in the press and the plays were lambasted. Some felt that the whole structure of sound religion in this country was being undermined. To treat the gospel story as any other historical drama was to reduce the gospel to a state which would cause the general public to lose respect for it and further the growing secularism of the age. The broadcasting of the second episode was delayed for two weeks to allow a special meeting of the Religious Advisory Committee of the BBC to meet and give the wisdom of continuing with the plays fuller consideration. At that meeting, at which were representatives of all the Christian Churches (an exercise in ecumenical cooperation which was only just beginning to be possible at that time) there was a wholehearted expression of approval and the plays went ahead. So popular and effective were they that they were repeated again during the Sundays of Lent for a number of years. This case thus released dramatists from the convention of not allowing Jesus to be portrayed on the stage. It *should* have resulted in a whole crop of Passion Plays with Jesus appearing as one of the characters on the stage. It had been after all very inhibiting to write a play without allowing the main character to appear. If the Last Supper were depicted, the scene had to be set in an adjoining room and the words of institution were heard, usually provided by the vicar's voice coming from the dressing room, or, if the play were produced in church as many of these productions were, from the vestry. There was also considerable episcopal uncertainty about the wisdom of allowing plays to be performed in church, and usually certain conditions were imposed, one of which was that only scriptural incidents should be depicted, and another that if the words of Jesus were to be heard by the audience, they had to be phrased in the words of the Authorised Version. Two factors thus prevented widespread production. In the first instance now that the same liberty was granted generally to what had previously only been tolerated in the ten yearly production of the Passion Play at Oberammergau, producers realised that there were also now available the old mystery cycles of plays, and these began to be revived. In the second case, after the Second World War, the demand for biblical plays waned.

It can still be an interesting exercise to see whether it is possible, using all the events that the gospels record of the period of the Passion and resurrection, to recreate as though for a play, the narrative of what was likely to have happened. Of course a certain amount of imagination will have to be used. Like any dramatist there will be times when we shall have to ask what would be the most likely course of action to be taken by this or that character in the given circumstances of the occasion, and then to see whether that action agrees with the canonical account. If this experiment were to be successful and it were possible so to tell the story using only the sources that we have in the canonical scriptures, to give a consistent account of the events of the period, then many arguments that are currently being advanced for disbelief in the actuality of the resurrection could be diminished or removed.

In order to do this it will be necessary to assemble the cast, those people who have to play a part in the drama. This will need an investigation into the relationships between the various groups of people involved, and our interest will be more centred upon groups such as the Twelve or the Brethren or the Women than upon the more prominent characters of the Passion story, the High Priest or the Governor. It will also be necessary to build the set, to consider the geography of Jerusalem and the various sites where the incidents to be recorded happened, the scenes in which the drama is played out. The story can then move through a number of Acts, according to the various times through which the drama moves. But in all this, let scripture be the guide.

Chapter II
Assembling the Cast

When sermons are preached on the personalities of the Passion, those who attend them expect to hear treatments of Caiaphas, Pilate, Herod, the centurion and possibly Saint Peter. If, however, we are to examine the evidence with which we are supplied by the New Testament and to try to understand what was happening, consideration must be given to our Lord's own immediate circle. We know that He had twelve chosen disciples, and we can learn quite a good deal about them and learn who they were if we approach the gospels with an unprejudiced mind. We know also that there was a circle of women who were attendant upon Jesus, were concerned for the welfare of Himself and the Twelve, and who travelled up from Galilee to Jerusalem on the occasion of the Passover about the time that Jesus was crucified.

Some of these women are mentioned by Saint Luke in his gospel before his narration of the Passion. In his account of our Lord's Galileean ministry, at the beginning of chapter eight he writes:

> And it came to pass afterwards that He went throughout every city and village, preaching and showing the glad tidings of the kingdom of God: and the Twelve were with Him. And certain women, which had been healed of evil spirits and infirmities, Mary called Magdalene out of whom went seven

devils, and Joanna the wife of Chuza, Herod's steward, and Susanna, and many others which ministered unto Him of their substance.

Of these ladies who are named two of them, Mary Magdalene and Joanna, are mentioned as being in Jerusalem at the time of the crucifixion. All four Evangelists say that Mary Magdalene went to the tomb on Easter morning, but Saint Luke is the only one to mention Joanna by name as one of the ladies who went to the sepulchre to complete the burial procedures. Susanna is not again mentioned by name apart from the passage already noted.

Neither Joanna nor Susanna are mentioned as being present at the scene of the crucifixion on Good Friday. All four Evangelists however do mention that some women were present. Saint Mark names Mary Magdalene, Mary the mother of James the Less and of Joses, and Salome. He also states that there were other women present, amongst whom were them that he named. Saint Matthew says that:

> many women were there beholding afar off, which followed Jesus from Galilee ministering unto Him: among whom were Mary Magdalene, and Mary the mother of James and Joses, and the mother of Zebedee's children.

Saint Luke, however, does not mention anyone by name but merely states that 'all His acquaintances and the women that followed Him from Galilee stood afar off beholding these things'. Saint John, on the other hand, writes, presumably quite soon after Jesus was nailed to the cross:

> Now there stood by the cross of Jesus, His mother and His mother's sister, Mary the wife of Cleophas, and Mary Magdalene. When Jesus therefore saw His

mother, and the disciple standing by whom He loved, he saith unto His mother Woman behold thy son! Then saith He to the disciple Behold thy mother!

It seems reasonable that the women attendant at the cross named by the Evangelists were the same three ladies. This is to omit Mary, the mother of Jesus, for she is only mentioned in the fourth gospel. All name Mary Magdalene, and use for her the same nomenclature. Then there is another lady called Mary, of whom both Saint Matthew and Saint Mark say was the mother of James the Less and of Joses; the Greek word which is translated 'the less' – μικρος – is capable of meaning either 'the younger' or 'the little'. Saint John refers to her as the wife of Cleophas. Since he also gives her name, Mary, it is unlikely that she should be anyone else other than the mother of James and Joses. The third woman to be named is described by Saint Mark as Salome, but Saint Matthew changes this to the mother of Zebedee's children, whereas Saint John tells us that she was sister to Jesus' mother. Zebedee's children were of course the Apostles James and John.

From these namings by three of the four Evangelists we can deduce a good deal about a group of people who are part of the Lord's inner circle and who are related to each other. In the first instance we can say that Saints James and John, the sons of Zebedee, had a mother whose name was Salome. It was Saint Mark who gives her name, and we have accepted that his was the first gospel of the Synoptists to be written. Saint Matthew does not give her name but tells us that she was the mother of Zebedee's children. This is understandable because the use of the single name might not convey much about her to the readers, whereas Saint Matthew's description tells in greater detail more about her. Saint John is at pains to keep names out of it, by describing her as 'His mother's sister'. It is significant that the fourth Evangelist never gives us the name of Jesus' mother, and he never mentions Zebedee or his children by name. This can be advanced as an argument for the assertion that the author of that gospel was John the Apostle, the son of Zebedee. If he were indeed the author, when he has to make reference to himself he uses the phrase 'that disciple whom Jesus loved'. A clue to the reason for this must also lie in the very close relationship between Zebedee's and Jesus' families; Saint John was unwilling to allow that fact in any way to detract from the force of the gospel by introducing personal allusions. This would mean that James and John, the sons of Zebedee, were Jesus' first cousins, whom Jesus would almost certainly have known all His life. John may well have been the little cousin for whom Jesus had to care when he was a baby. Certainly Jesus did not walk beside the Sea of Galilee and see two strangers whom he called to be His disciples in a moment of sudden inspiration.

The third woman to be named is another Mary. This one is the mother of James and Joses and the wife of Cleophas. Saint Luke, however, in giving an account of the events of Easter Day in chapter twenty-four beginning at verse thirteen, tells us that two of them went that same day to a village called Emmaus, which was about seven or eight miles from Jerusalem. A little later in the story he says that one of them, whose name was Cleopas, asked Jesus, who was then walking with them, how it could come about that, even though he were only a stranger in Jerusalem, he had not heard what had been happening there in recent days. It will be noticed that this man's name is spelt differently from that of the husband of the third Mary at the cross as given by Saint John. In spite of the difference in spelling, it is unlikely that they are different names or indicate different people. If they are one and the same it would

surely be reasonable to assume that Cleopas's companion
was his wife. It is significant that the two travellers are
described as 'two of them'. They therefore are not of the
Twelve, neither are they of the brethren. It is true that
Cleopas tells Jesus about certain women who were early at
the tomb and had had a vision of angels who told them that
Jesus was risen from the dead, and adds the words: 'But
Him they saw not', but that is not to say that the person
walking beside him was not a woman. We know that he had
a wife and that she was the mother of at least two boys.
Who else then would this fellow traveller be if it were not
his wife Mary?

Who was this Cleopas or Cleophas? The name is certainly not a Greek one. It would therefore be a man's name
in Aramaic or Hebrew. Aleph, the first letter of the Hebrew
alphabet, is a letter which cannot be transliterated into ours.
It is the epiglottal catch in the throat which precedes the
enunciation of a word beginning with a vowel, such as
'apple'. When this letter at the beginning of a word is
transliterated into English, it is often omitted and sometimes a letter 'a' is used. Transliteration into Greek could
give either a kappa, which is represented by the English 'c'
or by an alpha with a smooth breathing mark, which would
be in English as 'a'. The name obviously gives difficulty to
the Greek translators because Saint Luke spells it Cleopas,
whereas Saint John gives Clopas. It is therefore reasonable
that another way of putting this un-Greek word into Greek
would be to use Alphaeus or Alpheus. From Saint Mark's
gospel in chapter two verse fourteen we learn that Jesus
called to be His disciple one Levi, the son of Alphaius, who
was sitting at the receipt of custom. In describing the same
vocation, Saint Matthew names the disciple as Matthew,
whereas giving a list of the Twelve he says that one of them
was 'James, the son of Alphaius'. If this name Alphaius is an
attempted transliteration of the Hebrew, which is otherwise

transliterated as Cleopas or Cleophas, then it would appear that the Cleopas of the gospels had a son called James, and we have already seen that Mary, Cleopas' wife, was the mother of James. We are now beginning to put together Cleopas' family, but the question still remains as to whether there are any other clues as to who they might be.

Eusebius, the fourth century historian, an authority from whom quotation has already been made, quotes a man called Hegessipus, a Jew of the second century who had been converted to Christianity and who was probably a native of Palestine. In book two, chapter twenty-three Eusebius says, referring to the James often described as the first Bishop of Jerusalem:

> Hegessipus also, who flourished nearer the days of the Apostles, in the fifth book of his commentaries gives the most accurate account of him thus: 'But James, the brother of the Lord, who, as there were many of his name was surnamed Just by all from the days of our Lord until now, received the government of the Church with the Apostles.'

In a later chapter (book three chapter eleven), Eusebius goes on to say:

> After the martyrdom of James and the capture of Jerusalem, which immediately followed, the report is that those of the Apostles and disciples of our Lord yet surviving, came together from all parts with them that were related to our Lord according to the flesh. For the greater part of them were yet living. These consulted together to determine whom it was proper to announce worthy of being the successor of James. They all unanimously declared Simeon, the son of Cleophas, of whom mention is made in the sacred

volume, as worthy of the episcopal seat there. They say he was the first cousin of our Saviour, for Hegessipus asserts that Cleophas was the brother of Joseph.

This would mean that Cleophas and Mary must have had another son, Simeon, who was presumably younger than the James and Joses who are mentioned in the New Testament. Hegessipus lived within the living memory of them that had known and lived with Jesus. It would seem then that amongst the twelve disciples the one known as James the Less, or James the son of Alphaius, was the first cousin of Jesus on Joseph's side of the family, as were James and John on the distaff side.

There is a possibility that another of Jesus' family was one of the Twelve, but it is not very likely. The writer of the epistle that bears the name of Jude claims to have that name and to be the brother of James (verse one). Clearly that relationship would not have been mentioned unless the James to whom reference is made were a person of repute and was well known to the potential readers of the document. The letter is addressed to 'them that are sanctified by God the Father, and preserved in Jesus Christ and called'. A very wide readership is envisaged, and therefore brother James must have been well known generally. The most likely intended James is James the brother of the Lord; as far as we know, he was neither of those two Apostles who bore his name. This of itself does not preclude the writer of the epistle being that Jude who is described as 'not Iscariot'. Indeed Tertullian, a Christian writer who survived into the third century, does so describe the author of this letter.

Nevertheless, if the author of the epistle of Jude were one of the Apostles, he could hardly have written verse seventeen:

> But, beloved, remember ye the words which were
> spoken before of the Apostles of our Lord Jesus
> Christ, how that they told you there shall be mockers
> in the last time, who should walk after their own
> ungodly lusts.

It seems reasonable therefore to assume that the Jude who
wrote the epistle that bears his name was not one of the
twelve disciples. It is still an open question whether or not
he were a brother of the Lord. He was certainly the brother
of James, because he says so, and it may well be that the
James to whom he claims such a close relationship was
indeed that James who is usually called the brother of the
Lord and presided at the Synod of Jerusalem, having
probably been appointed to an apostleship and leadership of
the Church because of his kinship to Jesus. This, however,
is by no means certain beyond all reasonable doubt.

So far, the women who were attendant at the crucifixion
have revealed a great deal about the family connections of
Jesus and we have seen that it is likely that the three of the
twelve disciples were His first cousins. There is, however,
one other lady, whom all the Evangelists mention and to
whom they all give the same name, to whom we must now
give some attention. That is Mary Magdalene. After all, she
is a key figure throughout the events to which we are giving
consideration. She was standing by the cross on Good
Friday as all the Evangelists testify; she was present at the
entombment as both Saint Mark and Saint Matthew assert;
she was also at the tomb on Easter morning going with the
other women as the three Synoptists tell; she had a private
encounter with the risen Christ as Saint John narrates; and
she was one of the earliest messengers of the resurrection in
giving the news to the Apostles. If we were to attempt to
write the authentic Passion play, Mary Magdalene would
have to be one of the principal characters. It is thus natural

to ask whether we know anything from the text of the New Testament as to her previous history.

Saint Mark begins his account of the Passion with the story of the triumphal entry into Jerusalem and concludes with:

> And Jesus entered into Jerusalem, and into the Temple; and when He had looked round about upon all things, and now the eventide was come, He went out unto Bethany with the Twelve.

He continues his narrative by telling us that they left on the next day from Bethany, and on their way to Jerusalem Jesus became hungry and saw the fig tree which was without fruit, for it was not the appropriate season, and went on into the city. Saint Mark then gives us his account of the cleansing of the temple, after which they went out of the temple, and presumably the city as well. On the Mount of Olives, over which they were to pass returning to Bethany, Jesus delivered that discourse which has come to be known as the 'little apocalypse'.

The next event described is an incident in the house of Simon the leper (he must have been cured of the disease, but this is not stated, neither are we informed that Jesus was the Healer). Simon was certainly entertaining a group of people to dinner, and the implication is that it was quite a large one because Saint Mark talks about 'some of them'. While they were at table 'there came a woman, having an alabaster box of ointment of spikenard, very precious; and she brake the box, pouring it on His head'. After some of the guests had complained about the extravagant waste, Jesus reproved them saying that she had wrought a good work (Mark 14:3–9). Saint Matthew here follows Saint Mark very closely telling the same story, citing the incident in the house of Simon at Bethany, but giving the added information that the group which grumbled about the waste of the ointment were the disciples. It would seem then that they also had been included in the invitation to the dinner party.

Saint Luke adds to his account of the triumphal entry into Jerusalem the fact that when Jesus had reached the top of the Mount of Olives, whence He would be able to have that glorious and splendid view of the city laid out in wonderful panorama before Him, with the temple dominant, He wept over it, and foretold its future destruction. In this gospel the cleansing of the temple follows directly after the entry. Saint Luke goes on to tell of our Lord teaching in the temple and being questioned on many things by many people, including representatives of the government, who were trying to trip Him up verbally so that they could gain some reason both to arrest and to put Him quite out of the way, if necessary by putting Him to death. Saint Luke does not mention the sojourn at Bethany or the dinner party at Simon's house, but says that 'in the daytime He was teaching in the temple; and at night He went out and abode in the mount which is called the Mount of Olives' (21.37) Bethany was on the other side of the Mount of Olives to Jerusalem, so there is support here for the Markan and Matthean placing of the Lord's and the disciples' accommodation in Bethany.

Although the third gospel does not give an account of Simon's hospitality to Jesus and the disciples in Holy Week, he does give, in the midst of reporting our Lord's Galilean ministry (although no specific place is named) an account of a dinner party in a Pharisee's house. He says:

> One of the Pharisees desired him that he would eat with him. And he went into the Pharisee's house and sat down to meat. And behold a woman in the city, which was a sinner, when she knew that Jesus sat at

meat in the Pharisee's house, brought an alabaster box of ointment, and stood at his feet behind him weeping, and began to wash his feet with tears, and did wipe then with the hairs of her head, and kissed his feet and anointed them with the ointment (7.36)

The story continues that when the host saw what had happened he 'thought within himself' that if Jesus had been a prophet He would have known what sort of a woman it was whom He had allowed to touch Him. It was indeed clear what sort of a woman she was, for no Jewish lady would let her hair down in the presence of gentlemen. This action in itself would advertise the fact that she was a person of loose morals. Jesus detected what was going through the Pharisee's mind, and addressed him by name, 'Simon'. He then speaks about forgiveness, commends the action of the woman and assures her that her sins are forgiven.

The closeness of this story with the one told by Saint Mark and Saint Matthew would suggest that there must be a connection between them. Although it is implied that this particular Pharisee lived in Galilee, it is surely a significant fact that he shares a name with the resident in Bethany with whom Jesus dined. It must be remembered that Saint Luke gathered the information he required for the writing of his gospel from secondary sources. It would indeed have been easy to place the incident that actually happened in one place and at one period, in another village at a different time. It would certainly seem that Saint Luke was using Saint Mark because of the similarities of the details of the story, even to the fact that the box which contained the ointment was made of alabaster. There are however certain significant differences. Saint Luke says that the woman poured the ointment on Jesus' feet, whereas Saint Mark is quite clear that she poured it on his head. The question we are tempted to ask is, were there two distinct dinner parties at which our Lord was anointed by a woman who had an alabaster box of ointment, or are the Evangelists telling different accounts of the same incident? Any husband married for many years is often quite amazed at the differences, not only in time and place, but also in other details, which his wife recounts of occurrences in which they both shared and which are quite contrary to his recollection. It would be quite understandable if Saint Luke's informant similarly had certain defects in his or her memory.

Has Saint John anything to say which can throw further light upon this experience? First of all, let us concentrate a while on the place, Bethany. In chapter eleven of the fourth gospel he gives us the account of the raising of Lazarus. It begins with the coming to Jesus of the report that Lazarus is sick. The opening two verses give a great deal of information:

> Now a certain man was sick, named Lazarus, of Bethany, the town of Mary and her sister Martha. It was that Mary which anointed the Lord with ointment and wiped his feet with her hair, whose brother Lazarus was sick.

In the first instance the mention of the names of Martha and Mary point us to the story told by Saint Luke in chapter ten, verse thirty-eight and following. This is the well-known story of Mary sitting at the feet of Jesus listening to him. But before mentioning that fact there are the significant words 'He entered into a certain village, and a certain woman named Martha received him into her house'. We are not given the name of the village, but in the absence of any other it can be assumed that it would be Bethany. Secondly, Martha is certainly the senior of the two sisters, 'the lady of the house'. Thirdly, there is no mention of Lazarus, although in the telling of this particular incident there is no reason why there should be. Finally, the actual wording would imply that although it was Martha who received as the hostess, it was Mary who seemed to think that she had a proprietorial claim on Jesus' attention. If it could be assumed that Mary had made the acquaintance of Jesus before he had met her family, and she was the one who had invited Him to her home, then this wording would be more explicable. He accepted her invitation, Martha received Him as her guest, and Mary would feel that, because she was the one who had introduced Him to the family, she would be the one to entertain him while Martha got the supper ready. In any case, Jesus is shown to be at home with this family, and through His acquaintance with Mary He had become their friend.

Now let us return to Saint John. In introducing the story he reminds his readers of the identity of Mary as the woman who had 'anointed the Lord with ointment and wiped his feet with her hair'. From this it would seem that the incident had already happened and had occurred some time previously. It is also interesting to note that in the particulars of the part of the anatomy of Jesus which was anointed and dried, Saint John seems to be agreeing with Saint Luke. This could be used as an argument for the differing accounts being of two different occasions, although the circumstances are so similar that it seems hard to accept. If, however, the woman who did the first anointing of the feet at a later date repeated the exercise, but on this occasion poured the ointment on His head, then perhaps there could be a reconciliation of the differences. Without posing these notions of identity and repetition of the anointing, the difficulty will remain unresolved.

We are given the text of the message which Jesus received and are told that it was the sisters who sent it, and the wording is revealing: 'Lord, he whom thou lovest is sick.' The picture given is of a whole family of two sisters and a brother with whom Jesus is on very intimate and familiar terms. He is quite clearly well known as a guest in their home, and the custom had developed by which that house could be used as His pied-à-terre when He was visiting the capital.

After recounting the whole story of the raising of Lazarus, Saint John goes on to say (11.54) that 'Jesus therefore walked no more openly among the Jews; but went thence into a country near to the wilderness, into a city called Ephraim, and there continued with His disciples'. It would seem that His next move was to go back to Jerusalem for the final Passover, and, as usual, He stayed with the family at Bethany, having gone up, we are told, six days before the feast (12:1).

We have been given the information that after the raising of Lazarus, many of the citizens of Jerusalem, who had gone to express their sympathy with the sisters on the death of their brother, had been present when Jesus arrived and restored Lazarus to life. They returned to the city and naturally talked about such a wonderful event. It was indeed a most newsworthy story. Hearing of it, the Council was called to meet to discuss the situation, and a lively debate was finally brought to a conclusion by Caiaphas's remark that it might be necessary for one man to die for the people. Accordingly, they came to the decision that it was necessary for Jesus to be put to death. In chapter twelve, verse ten, there is an interesting reference to a corollary motion: 'But the chief priests consulted that they might put Lazarus also to death; because that by reason of him, many of the Jews went away, and believed on Jesus.' This must surely explain much which followed. Lazarus was a wanted man. It was essential therefore for his survival that he should keep what we would now call a 'low profile'. His sisters also would have to be careful, for they could be wanted for questioning. At least this would apply to Martha, and perhaps only to a less degree to Mary. If she had been away from home for a long period of time, she would not be so well known and therefore she would be less likely to be apprehended. This would make sense of much that was to follow.

We are told in the fourth gospel that six days before the Passover Jesus had installed Himself at Bethany:

> where Lazarus was who had been dead, whom he raised from the dead. There they made him a supper; and Martha served, but Lazarus was one of them that sat at the table with him. Then took Mary a pound of ointment of spikenard, very costly, and anointed the feet of Jesus, and wiped his feet with her hair: and the house was filled with the odour of the ointment.

From this it would seem that Saint John is telling us that the supper party was at the house of Mary and Martha where Jesus was staying. As usual Martha was doing the cooking and other preparations when Mary appeared with the ointment. It is perhaps significant here that there is no mention of the alabaster box, and once again we have the anointing of the feet and the drying of them with Mary's hair. There is no mention of Simon the leper, and it is certainly strongly implied that the meal was in the house of Lazarus. It is quite clear then that there is some confusion between the various accounts. For Saint John it is abundantly clear that the woman who anointed the Lord's feet and wiped them with her hair was Mary of Bethany, the sister of Martha and Lazarus. Even if he is referring to an earlier episode in chapter eleven, when he says 'It was that Mary which anointed the Lord with ointment'(11:2.), he is quite sure that the woman on both occasions was the same, and that it was Mary of Bethany. Where then was the Holy week dinner party, at Lazarus's house or at Simon's? One possible resolution of the difficulty would be to say that Saints Mark and Matthew had got the banquet at the house of a Pharisee whose name was Simon confused with the Holy Week dinner party in Bethany. In making his selection of pericopes to demonstrate the theological purpose of his gospel, Saint Mark could have chosen the account of the anointing and placed it at this juncture in his narrative to give greater emphasis to 'she hath done what she could; she is come aforehand to anoint my body for the burying'. In this case Saint Luke, although following Saint Mark in declaring that the container of the ointment was an alabaster box, differs so widely from him in omitting to say that the ointment was spikenard and by declaring that it was poured on Jesus' feet, and not His head, as Saint Mark affirms. It would seem that Saint Mark and Saint Luke in this particular are dependent upon different traditions. It would be possible for the accounts to be so similar in spite of the differences, given the historicity of the story. So far, so good. The fact remains, however, that three of the four Evangelists say quite clearly that there was an anointing at a dinner party in Holy Week, and the fourth, Saint Luke, does not deny it, although he does not mention it.

If, however, there were two anointings at different times, one in Galilee and the other in Bethany, whether at the house of Lazarus or Simon, the confusion could be understood and possibly explained. Saint John certainly gives more than a hint of this. In introducing the Bethany family he says that the Mary who was the sister of Lazarus was the Mary who anointed the Lord (11:1). Later in the gospel and after the retreat to Ephraim and subsequent return to Bethany, he gives the account of another anointing (12:3). In both, if indeed they do refer to two incidents, it is the feet that are anointed.

This still leaves the venue of the Bethany party unde-
cided. Wherever it was, it was a semi-public occasion,
because Saint John says:

> Much people of the Jews therefore knew that he was
> there: and they came, not for Jesus' sake only, but
> that they might see Lazarus also, whom he had raised
> from the dead (13:9).

This would seem to indicate that the meal would not have
been held at the house of Lazarus, but rather that of a well-
to-do neighbour, Simon, who was sufficiently well known
as to have the designation 'the leper'. Admittedly, there is
no proof of this, but it would at least seem likely. Perhaps
Simon, as well as being a neighbour, was also a close friend
of the brother and sisters, and when Jesus was staying with
them, invited them to dinner at his house, as well as
inviting others to meet Jesus. On this occasion however,
the guests were anxious to come not only so as to meet
Jesus, but also because they were desirous of seeing
Lazarus, about whose resurrection they had heard. It could
be that the sisters went also, not to recline at table, for we
are told that they did not, but to help with the preparations
and the service. This would explain Mary's entrance with
the ointment. If she had so anointed Jesus on a previous
occasion and in another place (which could have been their
first meeting, or near the beginning of their acquaintance)
she was doing so again to remind Him of this fact and all
that it implied for her.

There is another text which is here especially apposite.
When Saint Luke is speaking of the women who ministered
to Jesus of their substance, he mentions by name – along
with Joanna the wife of Chuza, Herod's steward, and
Susannah – Mary Magdalene, 'out of whom went seven
devils'. The condition of which she had been healed was

then what we should now call a psychological disorder, although the people of that time would have recognised it as demonical possession. The effects of such an ailment would largely be moral, and the behaviour of the woman who did the anointing, which Saint John insists was Mary of Bethany, in letting down her hair, as already noted, indicates she was a lady of easy virtue; because we are told that there were seven devils, it would appear that she was quite notorious. There may not be scriptural proof for the traditional belief that Mary Magdalene had been a prostitute, but there is certainly some justification for it. This receives further support from the narrative of the incident. The woman is described as 'a woman in the city which was a sinner', and the Pharisee is reported as having said to himself: 'this man, if he were a prophet, would have known who and what manner of woman this is: for she is a sinner.'

Saint Luke does not name the village or the town where the anointing occurred and where Simon the Pharisee lived, only that the woman who came in is a 'woman in the city' (ητις ην εν τη πολει). From the context of the story, however, it would seem to be in Galilee. Magdala, according to the Talmud, was about twenty minutes' walk away from Tiberias, the town on the western shore of the Sea of Galilee. Although there is nothing to prove that the place of the anointing or the city to which the woman belonged was indeed Magdala, there is equally nothing to disprove it.

It may be that we are now in a position to attempt a reconstruction of some of the events of Mary's life which will give coherence to the biblical accounts. When Jesus was preaching in Galilee, He came across a woman who was a notorious strumpet. As a result of this encounter the woman was made aware of her sin, which was great, and in genuine penitence and sorrow as a result of her meeting with Jesus, she was healed of that disorder which had led her into such wicked ways. Being by nature somewhat volatile, she could not restrain herself, but simply had to burst into the house where Jesus was dining to show her appreciation and gratitude by anointing Him. Because of the association between them, and her new way of life, it was important that she should go back home. Her home was in Bethany near to Jerusalem, and in gratitude and friendship she invited Jesus to meet her family. This would explain why Martha was the one to receive Him, and why Mary felt that it rested with her to do the entertaining while her sister did the cooking. Incidentally, it could be that when Jesus said 'Martha, Martha, thou art troubled about many things, but one thing is needed', given the context, he was telling Martha not to bother about preparing such an elaborate meal; one simple course was all that was needed. This then could be another case of the inspiration of scripture, where a simple historical narrative can have deep levels of communication and understanding. When, on a subsequent occasion (and, as it turned out, the last one) Jesus was staying with her family, she was moved to repeat the action which had brought them together in the first instance. This apparently spontaneous action would be an inspired one, and therefore of deep significance, as Jesus pointed out by His reference to the anointing for the burying. The details could have moved Mary so far as to acquire another alabaster box for the occasion. It would be a memorial of that which had brought her, Jesus and her family together.

One further question remains to be answered. Why is she always referred to as Mary of Magdala, and not as Mary of Bethany? Many reasons could be advanced for this. It could be that that was the name by which she had come to have been known in the days of her notoriety, and it stuck. It could also be, because she had been away for such a long time, and Magdala had been the place where she had spent most of her adult years. It even might be that the early Christians, her own associates and companions, referred to her in this way, because by so doing they would draw attention away from Bethany. The vigilance of the authorities, who were bent on arresting Lazarus, would make it advisable for himself and his sisters to be as inconspicuous as possible. Whatever the reason, Saint John is quite adamant that it was Mary Magdalene, who was the sister of Martha and Lazarus, who anointed Jesus. Twice he makes the point. In introducing the family of Bethany he writes in parenthesis that it was that Mary who anointed the Lord with ointment, and in describing the anointing in Holy Week he writes: 'they made him a supper, and Martha served, but Lazarus was one of them that was at table with him. Then Mary took a pound of ointment of spikenard...' From this evidence then it would seem to be certain that Mary of Magdala was also Mary of Bethany, one and the same.

We have now discussed in some detail the group of women who were attendant upon our Lord. The next group of people who feature in the gospel narrative of the Passion is the Twelve, the group of disciples who were to become Apostles. We have already ascertained that three of them were first cousins to Jesus: James and his brother John, and James the Less, or young James as he would probably be called today. The next two we must consider are Andrew and his brother Peter. We know from the fourth gospel that John the Baptist was baptising at Bethabara beyond Jordan (John 1:28). In narrating the story, Saint John writes: 'The next day John seeth Jesus coming unto him, and saith, Behold the Lamb of God, which taketh away the sin of the world.' After recounting that John had seen the Spirit descending from heaven like a dove and that it alighted upon Jesus, the Evangelist went on to say, putting the words into the mouth of the Baptist:

> He that sent me to baptise with water, the same said unto me, 'Upon whom thou shalt see the Spirit descending and remaining upon him, the same is he which baptiseth with the Holy Ghost.' And I saw and bear record that this is the Son of God.

The day after, we are told, John was standing with two of his disciples and, as Jesus again passed by, he said to the two, 'Behold the Lamb of God', and the two, hearing this, left John and followed Jesus. Seeing this, Jesus asked them what they wanted. They asked where He was living and He invited them to follow. They went with Him and stayed there for the rest of the day, as it was by then about four in the afternoon. Jesus must then have been staying temporarily in the neighbourhood of the River Jordan. We remember of course that John the Baptist was also Jesus' cousin and Saint Luke tells us without any hesitation that Elizabeth was Mary's cousin (Luke 1:36), although the Greek word used could be translated as aunt. It means literally that they were near of kin. This would make Jesus and John first cousins or first cousins once removed. One of these two disciples was, we are told, Andrew, Simon Peter's brother, but the other is not given a name. Saint John, almost in parenthesis, tells us that Andrew 'findeth his brother Simon'; this would imply that Simon was not with him at Bethabara, although he could not have been far away. It must thus be gathered that Andrew had become a disciple of John. There is, however, no record of John being attended to by a specific group of accredited disciples. Could it be then that Andrew and his unnamed companion had gone out to the place where John was baptising and had been so much moved by the spiritual experience they had received there that they had stayed, as also presumably others would have done, to learn more about the way of life into which they had entered? There can be no doubt that Saint John's preaching had reached far abroad and that crowds had gone out to hear him. Saint Mark says (1:5): 'And there went out unto him all the land of Judaea, and they of Jerusalem and were all baptised of him in the River Jordan.' Saint Matthew extends the area from which the people came by saying: 'Then went out to him Jerusalem and all Judaea, and all the region round about Jordan.' Saint Luke implies that Saint John himself was somewhat peripatetic: 'He came into all the country about Jordan, preaching the baptism of repentance for the remission of sins.' Saint Luke goes on to indicate that the crowds were large and that they included, as well as ordinary folk, tax collectors and soldiers. Saint Matthew also says specifically that many of the Pharisees and Saducees also came (Matthew 3:7). Saint John states that amongst the multitude that came to hear his preaching there was a special deputation from the Pharisees (1:24). Saint John the Baptist was conducting a very popular mission and, although it is nowhere specifically stated that people came to hear from as far away as Galilee, it is quite certain that they did come from a very wide area, and this may well have included some from the North.

Having told us about Andrew, his anonymous friend and Andrew's brother Peter, who had been brought to Jesus and given him the soubriquet Cephas or Peter, Saint John the Evangelist then announces that:

> the day following Jesus would go forth into Galilee, and findeth Philip and saith unto him, 'Follow me.' Now Philip was of Bethsaida, the city of Andrew and Peter. Philip findeth Nathaniel…

Bethsaida, incidentally, is on the shore of the Sea of Galilee to the north-west, not far from where the Jordan enters the Lake. Nathaniel certainly seems to have been already known to and friendly with Philip, while Philip, Peter and Andrew would probably have known each other from their early years. Although we are told that Bethsaida is their city, at least Andrew and Peter were not living there at this time. Could it be possible that the unnamed disciple of John's who attached himself to Jesus with Andrew was Philip? It would seem to be more than likely. So now there are four disciples who together with Jesus were about to leave the region of Jordan and go to Galilee. We tend to think of the region of Jordan as being the country around Jericho but, of course, the river itself flows through the Sea of Galilee, entering in the north and flowing out southwards from the southern end. After the account of the acceptance of Nathaniel, Saint John says that on the third day there was a marriage in Cana of Galilee, and also that the mother of Jesus was there, and that both Jesus and his disciples were invited to the marriage.

It will be remembered that it was at this wedding that Jesus turned the water into wine, and the account ends with the words: 'This beginning of signs did Jesus in Cana of Galilee, and manifested forth his glory, and his disciples believed on him.' From this it would seem that, by the time of the marriage, the whole band of the twelve disciples had been gathered. In that case it would also seem that Saint John has got his time sequence somewhat awry. Here again we remind ourselves that gospels are not histories or biographies, and that their authors have made a selection of incidents, events, conversations and sermons and arranged them in such a way that the theological implications can be brought out and emphasised. One can criticise the arrangement, but this does not necessarily imply the authors' invention or cast doubts upon the historical accuracy of the events described.

When we turn to Saint Mark, we find a very different account of the calling of the first disciples. He tells us first that after our Lord was baptised by John, He was driven by the Spirit into the wilderness and that He was there for forty days. Forty days, like forty years, was a convenient way of saying that a period of some considerable time had elapsed. Forty years stands for a generation, although one does not need a sociologist to tell us that this is a mere approximation and must never on any account be taken literally. The other two Synoptists also say that after the baptism there was a period of temptation in the wilderness, and they give the temptations in specific details which Saint Mark does not do. Saint Mark on the other hand proceeds immediately to write: 'Now after John was put into prison, Jesus came into Galilee, preaching the gospel of the Kingdom of God.' Whence did He come into Galilee? The Evangelist does not say. It could be assumed that He had come from Nazareth, but that is in the district known as Galilee. There also seems to be some evidence that, by the time of our Lord's public ministry, Jesus, if not all His family, had moved to Capernaum, which was on the shore of the Sea of Galilee (Matthew 4:13). The most sensible interpretation may well be that as this verse follows the statement that Jesus was in the wilderness, it means no more than that some time afterwards He was in Galilee, and that the words 'Jesus came into Galilee' are no more than a hinge to lead into the next pericope.

Saint Mark continues by saying that as Jesus walked by the Sea of Galilee, He saw Simon and Andrew his brother casting a net into the sea, for they were fishers.

> And Jesus said unto them, 'Come ye after me and I will make you fishers of men.' And straightway they forsook their nets and followed him. And when he had gone a little further thence he saw James, the son

of Zebedee, and John, his brother, who were also in the ship, mending their nets. And straightway he called them; and they left their father Zebedee with the hired servants, and went after him. (Mark 1:14–20)

Here we are given a picture, not so much of a group of simple fishermen operating individually, but rather of a fairly large commercial enterprise. There are at least two boats belonging to the firm of Zebedee and Sons, and the sons could be spared to leave their father because there were hired servants to keep the business going while they were away. We learn a little more about this concern from Saint Luke. In telling the story of the miraculous draught of fishes (Luke 5:4–11) he mentions two boats and says that one of them was Simon's. Later in the story, after the enormous catch has been landed, he says that 'He was amazed and all that were with him, at the draught of the fishes which they had taken; and so also were James and John, sons of Zebedee, who were partners with Simon'. It would appear then that Simon was some sort of a foreman in the business.

Many fish were needed in Jerusalem, especially when the population of the city from time to time was greatly swollen by the arrival of pilgrims from all over the world at times of festival. Saint Luke in the second chapter of Acts gives us some idea of the extent of the area from which the pilgrims came. The Jews were not a seafaring people, and therefore the nearest and most plentiful fishing grounds were in the Sea of Galilee. The Dead Sea, the other large stretch of water in the country, was so saline that no fish could possible live in it. The fishes when caught would have to be pickled, and we know that there were saline deposits which made this possible at the southern end of the lake. Then, of course, there was the distribution, which would involve a base in the capital itself. We know that John had some sort of house in the city, because he was known to the High Priest and seems to have been so well known that he was on more than nodding terms with the domestic staff at the palace (John 18:15). From all this we gain the impression that Zebedee and Sons was an important industrial concern which had bases both at Capernaum and in Jerusalem. This would involve the employment of a considerable number of men. Because of such statements as the mention that one of the boats was Simon's, and the ease with which he and his brother, as well as 'the boss's sons', could get away, it would seem that the two brothers from Bethsaida had come to Capernaum to join the firm and now occupied positions of foremen in the business.

It also means that Jesus' family would be well known to those in the firm, because Zebedee's wife was Jesus' aunt, and James and John his cousins. This must mean that Zebedee's family had close connections with John the Baptist, and when the news of the prophet's mission reached Galilee, it could well have been that someone was sent to see what was going on. After all, we do know that when Jesus Himself was engaged in His missionary campaign His mother and brothers went with Him, presumably to try to persuade Him to come home. (Mark 3:31). This reflects a close-knit family which was a caring unit, and as we pursue our course through the narrative of the last days of our Lord's life on earth, this impression will be substantiated. This therefore is a possible explanation for the presence of Andrew at Bethabara, even though there is no biblical reference to people going to hear John, and to be baptised by him, from Galilee.

If this were the case, and Andrew were with John at the time when Jesus'was seen approaching, John's words about Jesus being the Lamb of God would be of special interest. Andrew would certainly know who Jesus was and it would be the most natural thing in the world for him to follow and ask Jesus where he was staying. As we know he went along with Him and spent the night there. As soon as he was reunited with his brother he would of course have told him all about it, and Peter would have wanted to see Jesus for himself. They had gone to see what John was up to, and then Jesus, the boss's nephew, turns up to be baptised; surely some sort of an explanation was necessary. It was probably at this point that the brothers decided that they would attach themselves to Jesus as His disciples when the time was ripe. At this point, as we know from Saint Matthew and Saint Luke, Jesus himself had much sorting out to do in His own mind and went into retreat in the wilderness. When He returned to Galilee and went to find the brothers at their work, He told them that the time had come. They would have been expecting this and therefore were ready to go at once. No doubt they would already have given some warning to Zebedee. If Jesus had, as it would be natural to assume, been in close touch with His cousins, they too would have had some prior warning and were doubtless waiting for the call.

Of course, much of this is speculation. It does, however, explain certain features of the story as the Evangelists tell it, and resolve the contradictions, as they appear to be, regarding the place of the calling of Andrew and Peter. It also offers a reason for the immediate response on the part of the four disciples to Jesus' summons and the apparent ready acceptance of the situation by Zebedee. None of these four would have been strangers to Jesus, and He would have made His selection prior to the start of the public ministry. They would in a sense have been waiting for the call.

After the five of them had attended synagogue worship the following Sabbath, according to Saint Mark, Jesus adjourned to the house of the brothers Andrew and Peter in

Capernaum, taking James and John with Him, because no doubt they would have needed to have had a meeting. In the synagogue there had occurred a very public miracle of healing in the case of the man with the unclean spirit. Many questions were being asked by the people and the news was flying about (Mark 1:27 28). This reference to the house being the home of both the brothers is significant of a closely knit family relationship. The brothers are together. One of them at least has a wife, and her mother is living with them. Saint Paul refers to Peter's wife in his first epistle to the Corinthians (9:5) when he says: 'Have we no right to lead about a wife that is a believer, even as the rest of the Apostles and the brethren of the Lord, and Cephas?' She must therefore have been living at the time when her mother was ill, and Jesus cured her fever. It is interesting to note that as soon as the old lady was better she was up and about, and ministering to them! One wonders about the existence of children, but there is no mention of them anywhere in the New Testament.

The three Synoptists agree that one of the disciples was a tax collector, and therefore a man who was socially unacceptable in Jewish circles. Saint Mark and Saint Luke tell us that his name was Levi, and Saint Matthew that he was Matthew. So far we have been able to glean certain facts about the background of seven of the Twelve. James, John and young James were first cousins to our Lord; Philip was a native of the same city as Andrew and Peter; and Nathaniel, who elsewhere is called Bartholomew, which literally means 'son of Tolomeus' (and therefore the full designation may have been Nathaniel, son of Tolomeus), seems to have been at least an acquaintance, if not a close friend, of Philip. Of the other five, there are the two Judes. One of them we know is a man of Kerioth, for that in Hebrew would be Iscariot, who was the traitor, and Kerioth was a place in southern Judaea. There is a remote possibility that the other is one of the Lord's brothers, but, as we have already seen, that is not very likely. There is nothing else to tell us anything about him, as is the case with Simon the Zealot, whose surname at least assures us that he was politically motivated and that he was strongly opposed to the Romans as the occupying power.

That leaves Thomas. It is to Saint John that we owe most of our information about him. It was Thomas who, when he saw that Jesus was determined to go into Judaea because his friend Lazarus had died, is reported to have said to his fellow disciples: 'Let us also go that we may die with him' (11:16). During the last discourse in the upper room, it was Thomas who asked the question 'Lord, we know not whither thou goest; and how can we know the way?' (14:5) Thomas was also the doubter. For some reason or other he was not with the other disciples on Easter Day, and when he was told of the Lord's appearances he said: 'Except I shall see in his hand the print of the nails, and put my finger into the print of the nails, and thrust my hand into his side, I will not believe' (20:25). Finally, it is to Thomas that Saint John gives what we could call the curtain line of the gospel: 'My Lord and my God' (20:28). He is described as Thomas called Didymus (11:16 and 21:2) which means a twin. We are told nothing at all about the other one of the pair.

It may be that a little more light can be thrown upon the personalities of the Twelve by a consideration of the appendix to Saint John's gospel which we know as chapter twenty-one. Most scholars agree that this chapter comes from another hand than that which wrote the rest of the book. In the opening verses we are given an account of the disciples back in Galilee after their Easter experiences. It would seem that they are trying to return to normality:

> There were gathered together Simon Peter, Thomas called Didymus, and Nathaniel of Cana in Galilee, and the sons of Zebedee and two other of his disciples. Simon Peter saith unto them, 'I go a-fishing.' They say unto him, 'We also go with thee.' They went forth and entered into a ship immediately, and that night they caught nothing. (John, 21:2–3)

Of the disciples named in this passage, we know that Peter and the sons of Zebedee were fishermen and engaged in conducting quite a large commercial concern. It would be reasonable to assume that the other members of the party were also fishermen, or else they would not have embarked upon such an expedition. We have already noticed that it would appear that Nathaniel was known to Philip, who brought him to Jesus. We know also that Philip was of Bethsaida, the city of Andrew and Peter. Here we are told that Nathaniel came from Cana of Galilee. It is true that Cana and Bethsaida are not very far apart from each other, but the question as to how these two men became acquainted does present itself. It would appear then that Nathaniel was also a fisherman, but there is no suggestion that Philip was. It is true that there is no suggestion either that he was not. He was, however, not of the party which went out on this night excursion. Does this mean that Nathaniel also had been employed in the same firm as Peter, Andrew, James and John? On the other hand, we also know that Jesus did have friends living in Cana, who were close enough to Him to invite Him and the disciples to the wedding where the water was turned into wine. Saint John also states (4:46–54) that after the conversation with the woman in Samaria, through which Jesus was passing on His way from Jerusalem to Galilee:

> when he was come into Galilee, the Galileeans re-

ceived him, having seen all the things that he did at Jerusalem at the feast: for they also went unto the feast. So Jesus came again into Cana of Galilee.

He continues by recording the healing of the nobleman's son and notes that it is the second sign that Jesus gave in the same village. Jesus then would certainly have been a well known figure in Cana, and yet from the account of his being introduced to Jesus by Philip, Nathaniel does not expect Jesus to know who he was, for he says to Jesus 'Whence knowest thou me?' Jesus, however, *does* appear to know who Nathaniel was, because when he sees who it was that Philip was bringing to Him he declares: 'Behold, an Israelite indeed in whom is no guile.' Nathaniel then asks Jesus how it comes about that He knows him, and Jesus does not say that he recognised him from Cana, but makes the remark that 'Before that Philip called thee, when thou wast under the fig tree I saw thee'. This calls forth the exclamation 'Thou art the Son of God; Thou art the King of Israel'. (What had Nathaniel been doing under that fig tree?) The most that can be said is that it was unlikely that Nathaniel had been employed by Zebedee, that he was a friend of Philip's and that his native village was Cana. Although it would seem that both he and Thomas had experience of fishing, it cannot be said with any degree of certainty that they were professional fishers. What can be said, then, is that the company of men that Jesus gathered about Him as His disciples were not strangers about whom He knew nothing, selected by random inspiration, but that they were a group composed of relations and friends, some of whom He had possibly known all their lives.

There was a fourth group of people surrounding our Lord other than the women, the others and the Twelve, and that group was the brethren. In the fourth chapter of his gospel Saint Matthew tells us that Jesus 'leaving

Nazareth came and dwelt in Capernaum which is upon the sea coast' (4:13). All three Synoptists tell of a return to His home town during the public ministry – Mark (6:1–6); Matthew (13:53–58); Luke (4:16–30) – and Saint Luke gives the text of an account of the substance of His sermon in the synagogue, telling that the effect it had upon the congregation was so devastating that they attempted an assassination. The account of the other two, however, is rather less dramatic. Neither Saint Matthew nor Saint Mark give the text or the substance of the sermon, but both say that he preached in the synagogue and tell of its effect upon the people. According to Saint Mark:

> They were astonished, saying, 'Whence hath this man these things?' and 'What is the wisdom that is given unto this man and such mighty works wrought by his hands? Is not this the carpenter, the son of Mary, and brother of James and Joses and Judas and Simon? And are not his sisters here with us?' And they were offended in him.

Saint Matthew says the same things but with slightly different wording:

> Whence hath this man this wisdom and these mighty works? Is not this the carpenter's son? Is not his mother called Mary, and his brothers James and Joseph and Simon and Judas? And are not his sisters all here with us? Whence then hath this man all these things? And they were offended in him.

There is little significance attached to the difference in the listing of the names of the brothers. Both accounts number them as four: Joses and Joseph are obviously the same; the order of naming Simon and Judas is different, but to find any relative significance in this is pointless.

There is significance, however, in the different references to Jesus Himself. Saint Mark says that He was the carpenter, Saint Matthew that He was the carpenter's son. In a sense both of them are correct, because Joseph was indeed known as the carpenter, and there is no reason to doubt that Jesus learned His foster father's trade. The Greek word τεκτων is used for any worker in wood, but its significance in the world of our Lord's day is considerably wider than our use of the word carpenter. It is the word from which we derive our English word technician, and that means a man specially adept at working with his hands in a variety of ways. In Nazareth Joseph would have been the carpenter or the technician. He would therefore have occupied a position of honour and respect within the community. He would not only be the man who produced furniture, tools and wooden structures, but would also fulfil the role of what today would be the architect, the builder and the structural engineer. He was certainly not an artisan who would be considered to hold an inferior position within society, but an important person in the life of the town, more of an honoured tradesman than a humble worker.

From Saint Mark's wording it would seem that Joseph had died and that Jesus, the eldest son, was continuing to run the business after His father's demise. Saint Matthew's phraseology implies either that Joseph was still alive or that Jesus had not followed in His father's footsteps. We know that Jesus did not begin His public ministry until 'he began to be about thirty years old', and He must have been doing something until then. Of course, in the ancient world men did not come of age until they were thirty, and it was only when they attained that age that they acquired what franchise there was. The reason for the description of Him as the carpenter's son may also have been induced by a reluctance to tie our Lord to any particular trade. On the other hand, since there is no mention of Joseph when Jesus had reached adult years, despite several references to His mother and His brethren, it would seem that Joseph had died and Jesus was maintaining the family structure as the heir.

Reading the gospels without any devotional or theological overtones, these passages quite clearly state that Jesus was the son of Mary, and that the other children in the family were four boys and at least two girls (although Saint Matthew's reference to all of them would seem to indicate that there were rather more). The boys in each case are mentioned by name, and the girls are reported as being 'with us'. This would seem to imply that the boys had moved away and that the girls were still living in Nazareth, no doubt because they had married Nazarenes. We are told that Jesus had gone from Nazareth to live in Capernaum, and since the boys are mentioned as going with their mother to see Jesus, it could be that the whole family had gone to live there. If Mary had been left as a widow with a large family, it would be understandable if she went to live nearer to her sister, whom we have seen to be the wife of Zebedee.

There has been a tradition from very early times that Mary was not only a virgin at the time of her conception of Jesus, but that she remains ever virgin. It seemed to many that one whom God had chosen to be the mother of His incarnate son, to be indeed the Mother of God, could not then live a normal married life and have other children. As the years have unfolded this opinion has been enhanced by the teaching of a large part of Christendom and has developed into the doctrine not only of the perpetual virginity of our Lady, but also to the doctrine of the Immaculate Conception, which teaches that she herself, to fulfil the part that God required of her, would be herself without sin in the womb of her own mother. Later still this led to the promulgation of the doctrine of the Corporeal Assumption, by which it is believed that she was corporeally taken into Heaven to share the glory of her resurrected Son. It must be stated categorically that there is no scriptural evidence whatsoever for these doctrines. If however they are to be accepted, the existence of these children presents a difficulty. Attempts have been made to resolve this by saying that they were the children of Joseph by a previous wife, but there is no suggestion at all that when he became betrothed to Mary he was a widower. If he had been it would be strange indeed for the fact not to have been noted. Another suggestion that has been made is that they were not the brothers and sisters of Jesus but His cousins. It has been remarked that we know that two of the children of Mary Cleopas have the same names, James and Joses, as two of the brethren mentioned in the gospels. There is also the account already reported from Hegessipus, that there was a third son of Cleopas who became the Bishop of Jerusalem in succession to James. His name Simon or Simeon is also the name of one of these brethren. This would make them children of Cleopas who was believed to be Joseph's brother. If this were so, it is surely incredible that the Evangelists should have used the words for brother and sister, and not the word for cousin or kinsman.

On the other hand, in more modern times there have been others who have felt that the whole conception of the Virgin Birth is a creation of theological speculation and devotional reverence, rather than the reproduction of an historical fact. Such people point out that the word παρθενος means only a 'girl' or 'maiden' and is not necessarily capable of conveying the idea that a person so described is *virgo intacta*. Although there is no scriptural authority for the perpetual virginity of Mary, there is abundant evidence for parthenogenesis, whereby that which was conceived in her womb was God the Son and not the generation of an earthly father. The two Evangelists who write a birth narrative state quite categorically that this was so. Saint Matthew says that the angel who visited Joseph in a dream told him that the baby in Mary's womb had been conceived by the Holy Ghost (1:20). Saint Luke makes Mary say: 'How shall this be, seeing I know not a man?' There can be no doubt here that the Evangelists believed that neither Joseph, nor any other man, was the father of Jesus, but that He was miraculously conceived by God. They know that this is necessary if the truth that Jesus was both God and Man is to be maintained, and that such a belief is needful if Jesus is to be the Saviour of the world. If He were the result of a natural union between a man and a woman then He would be a man. Perhaps He could be an unusually good man, perhaps the best man who ever lived, but still a man, and nothing more. If the Godhead were to be manifested in Him to the extent that He could be called divine, then He would have been 'adopted' into the Godhead. Adoptionism was a heresy which was very soon promulgated and firmly condemned by the Church. It was then recognised that if Jesus were not essentially divine, then He could not be without the taint of sin, which is the result of the failure of God's creatures to live lives entirely for Him and with no other consideration. If He were not fully human, then He could not be the Saviour of human beings: 'By man came death, by man came also the resurrection of the dead.' Although the people who deny the Virgin Birth may not recognise it or acknowledge it, they are adoptionists. Such a doctrine could never be a development of a justifiable tradition.

There is every evidence then that Joseph was not the natural father of Jesus, although Jesus would doubtless know him as His father and call Him by that name. Indeed, in telling the story of Jesus as a boy in the temple, Saint Luke reports that when His parents (*sic*) found Him Mary said, 'Thy father and I have saught thee sorrowing' (Luke 2:48). By reading the scriptures without any theological convictions or prejudices, there seems to be no reason why, after the birth of Jesus, Mary and Joseph did not come together as man and wife and that their union should not have been blessed with the gift of children. Saint Matthew makes this quite clear when he says: 'And Joseph, rising from sleep, did as the angel had commanded him, and took his wife; and knew her not until she had brought forth her son!' (Matthew 1:25) If he knew her not until she had brought forth her son, presumably he did know her when she had done so. To deny this would be to make grammatical nonsense of the sentence as it stands. Indeed some early manuscripts of the New Testament have added the word 'firstborn' before 'son' in Saint Matthew's gospel, and the use of the same word in Saint Luke (2:7) appears to belong to the original text. If Jesus then is described as 'firstborn', the implication must be that others were to follow. Otherwise the word would be 'only-begotten' or simply 'only'. An unprejudiced reading of the gospels, then, leaves us no alternative but to believe that in the home at Nazareth Jesus was the eldest of a large family of children, both boys and girls. Later in the gospels the Evangelists tell of the care and concern that Mary and the brothers have for Jesus, and there is evidence that his eldest brother became a leader and pillar of the Church in Jerusalem and that at least one other took a prominent part in the life of the Church and the promulgation of Christianity. From these short references we can glean a picture of a united and loving family, caring for each other and sympathetic to each other.

These then are the four groups of people with whom we shall be concerned: the women, the disciples, the others and the brethren. There were, of course, others involved in the events of these momentous days, but in the main these groups constituted our Lord's intimate circle. There was, for instance, the young man in the garden who has already been discussed. Traditionally, this was the author of the gospel in which the account is found, the young John Mark. We know that the early Church in Jerusalem had its headquarters at the house of Mary, the mother of John, whose surname was Mark (Acts 12:12). If this lady's house was large enough to hold a meeting of the Church in it, then we already have a house with a large upper room. What could be more likely then for the early Christians in Jerusalem to have met in that place where the Lord had chosen to eat His Last Supper with the Apostles, especially as we know that there was a large room within? It can then be said with a reasonable degree of certainty that this house had become the place where the followers of Jesus gathered together. Saint Peter, delivered from prison and left to himself in the streets of the city, knew where his friends would be and where he could find them.

In this way we can learn that there was in Jerusalem another family who were intimately connected with Jesus. We recognise that to the Evangelists, writing after the events, the key figure was a young man called John, whose surname was Mark. Mark is, of course, the Latin name 'Marcus', and this may well indicate some personal characteristic of the young man. Could it be that he was generally accepted as a companion both by his fellow Jews and also by the associates of the occupying power? Whatever the reason, he and his mother lived in rather a large house in Jerusalem. As there is nowhere any mention of his father, it seems reasonable to assume that Mary, his mother, was a widow. She was obviously known to Jesus, for He arranged for the Last Supper to be eaten at her house. Its exact locality, however, was not known to all the disciples, and certainly not to the two whom Jesus despatched to make the necessary preparations. Otherwise He would not have had to go to the trouble of making the somewhat elaborate arrangements for one of the male servants of the house to be at the gate of the city carrying a pitcher of water. It is Saint Luke who gives names to these men and says that they were Peter and John. We do remember that the author of Saint Luke's gospel relies upon secondary sources for his information, and certainly in the early days after the resurrection we hear of Saints Peter and John being frequently together, acting as spokesmen for the whole band, and even journeying together into Samaria to receive formally into the Church those Christians whom Philip the deacon had converted. It is perhaps excusable then for Saint Luke to assume that these two would be the ones whom Jesus had sent to make the preparations for the supper. If they had been, it seems a little odd that the other Evangelists did not also name them. In any case if John, as seems most likely, lived for part of the time at least in Jerusalem (he was well known to the High Priest and also to the portress at his palace) he would certainly know where the house was, and there would be no need for the man bearing a pitcher of water.

As well as knowing of John Mark and his mother Mary, we also know the name of one of her maids; for it was Rhoda who heard and recognised Peter's voice when he was trying to gain admission. By this time anyway, Peter must have become very well known to the household. Saint Paul, in writing to the Colossians from Rome, gives the greetings of Mark, the son of the sister of Barnabas. Saint Barnabas appears to have been particularly attached to his nephew, given his quarrel with Saint Paul about him. When he and Paul were on their first missionary journey and when they had come to Perga in Pamphylia, John Mark, whom they had taken with them as their junior assistant (which is a better translation of the Greek word than 'minister'), had departed and returned to Jerusalem. We do not know the cause of his departure, but when it was suggested that he should again accompany them, Saint Paul objected:

> And some days after Paul said unto Barnabas, 'Let us go again and visit our brethren in every city where we have preached the word of the Lord, and see how they do.' And Barnabas determined to take with them John, whose surname was Mark. But Paul thought it not good to take him with them, who departed from them from Pamphylia, and went not with them to the work. And the contention was so sharp between them, that they departed asunder one from the other: and so Barnabas took Mark and sailed into Cyprus; and Paul chose Silas and departed, being recommended by the brethren unto the grace of God. (Acts 15:36–40)

It is enough to learn that Saint Paul and Saint Mark were eventually reconciled, and that Mark was with Paul when he was in Rome. This family of which Mark, Mary and Barnabas are members were somewhat involved, then, if only peripherally, with the events of that Passover which we are discussing.

The other characters of the Passion narratives, Pilate, Herod, Caiaphas, the soldiers and the centurion are external to the family and intimate circle of which Jesus was the central figure. As we trace the unfolding of the story, like the writers of Passion Plays tried to do, these men will occupy an 'offstage' position. So it can now be said that we have assembled the cast. To recapitulate, there is Jesus, and it was largely the convention that He should not be represented on the stage that caused so many of the Passion Plays that were written to fail from a dramatic point of view. There are the women, and of them we know the names of the husbands of three of them, Zebedee, Cleopas and Chuza. We also know a little more of the family connections of a few, for it would seem that Mary Magdalene is the sister of Martha and Lazarus of Bethany; that Salome is the mother of James and John; and that Mary Cleopas is the mother of James the Less. Then there are the disciples, and we have managed to abstract quite a lot of information about them. Next come the brethren, and we have been compelled to come to the conclusion that they were the younger brothers and sisters of Jesus, children who were born to Joseph and Mary after they had come together and assumed normal married relations. Lastly, there was another Jerusalemite family, that of yet another Mary, whose son was the only one who had an onstage part in the drama.

Chapter III
Building the Set

The events that the gospels record as happening between Palm Sunday and Easter Day all occurred within the city of Jerusalem and its immediate environs. To attempt to reproduce these events in a chronological sequence, and to try to understand how the movements of the various characters fit in with each other, we really need to know something of the geography of the places where they happened. Here we are immediately confronted with a difficulty. Although the old city of Jerusalem still stands on the same geographical site of the city of the period of the second temple, nothing of the city that existed in our Lord's day remains. When the Roman army which had besieged the city for over sixth months finally made a breach in the walls, captured the whole of Jerusalem and brought the Jewish War to its conclusion, Titus, the Emperor Vespasian's son, who was then the general commanding, ordered everything to be destroyed. The gospel prophecy that not one stone should stand upon another was literally fulfilled. The walls, the temple, every building in the city that was standing were totally destroyed. Only one small part of the fortifications, now known as the Citadel, was allowed to remain, so that a guard could be installed there to see that the order for no Jew even to stand upon the site, could be maintained. What had been the great city of Jerusalem and the magnificent temple of Herod which was one of the architectural wonders of the ancient world, had been levelled with the ground. Everything had been flattened and the whole site had been declared a 'no go' area. Never before had there been such a devastation. That was in the autumn of the year AD 70.

Jerusalem had been built upon two spurs of the Judaean Plateau running southwards. The eminence on the western spur was Mount Zion, and that on the other eastern one, was Mount Moriah, the apex of which was considered to be the traditional site of the attempted sacrifice of his son Isaac by Abraham. Dividing these spurs were three valleys, which met roughly at the deep depression of the Pool of Siloam. The westernmost was the valley of Hinnom, the central one the Tyropaean valley and the one in the east was the valley of the brook Kedron. It was around the rock of Moriah that the temple had been built.

In 63 BC Pompey the Great had entered the city with his army because a civil war had been disturbing the peace and causing considerable devastation. When the government of the country passed into the hands of Herod, he set about a major work of reconstruction, so in our Lord's day much of Jerusalem was new, including the temple. Herod was an indefatigable builder and was determined to make his temple the biggest and most splendid building of his time. In order to achieve this he first had to build up around the Rock of Moriah an artificial mound to create a large platform on which the temple and its attendant courts and porticoes could be erected. To maintain this he had to build a retaining wall on the west side of the Tyropaean valley, which in some places was a hundred feet deep. Access across the valley into the temple area was by bridges. The remains of one of these bridges has recently been uncovered and named 'Robinson's Arch' after the man who discovered it. Herod began the building of the temple in 20 BC and we know from the New Testament (John 2:20) that it took forty-six years to build; it would not have been completed when Jesus was presented in it and was held by Simeon, nor when as a boy He was discovered amidst the doctors both hearing them and asking them questions. Mount Zion or the Upper City had by this time become a residential area, and on it were the dwellings of many of the prominent people in Jerusalemite society and the wealthier citizens. This was the city that Titus ordered to be destroyed in AD 70, after which it had become a waste land, deserted save for the garrison in the Citadel.

So it remained for sixty-five years until the reign of the Emperor Hadrian, when in AD 135 a new city was erected on the site, a typical Roman colonial town given the name of Aelia Capitolina. Because of the significance of the place for all members of the Jewish race, no Jew was permitted to enter it on pain of death. Before the city was built, however, the inconvenience of having the Tyropaean Valley running through the middle of it was removed by its being filled in. This brought the level of the town nearly up to that of the temple mound, thereby making it suitable for building development. At the point where the valley broadened, so as to make this operation impracticable, the developers cut the infilling off, leaving exposed the southernmost end of Herod's retaining wall, and the southern end of the Tyropaean Valley. This is why, to this day, there is a broad low level square, one side of which is dominated by this wall and known as 'The Western Wall', or perhaps more recognisably in the Gentile world as 'The Wailing Wall'. Because this is all that is left of Herod's work, although it is strictly speaking not part of the actual temple building, it is a very holy place of prayer for the Jewish people.

Part of the existing Via Dolorosa, the traditional route taken by our Lord on His last fateful journey from the Roman Praetorium to His crucifixion on Golgotha, and along which countless pilgrims down the ages have walked thinking that they are retracing the steps that Jesus trod, is actually on top of this infilling of the Tyropaean valley, and therefore could not have been the authentic path. Two of the stations are affected by this, but not the Church of the Holy Sepulchre. It is this Roman city of Hadrian's reign that is now being excavated, and much has been revealed. A great deal of the Cardo, the main street which ran through the centre of the city, has largely been uncovered. Indeed Jerusalem could be described as an archaeologists' playground, and there have been exploratory digs ever since the days of the Emperor Constantine.

At the Battle of the Milvian Bridge outside the city of Rome in the year AD 311, Constantine was victorious and as a result found himself the sole ruler of the Roman Empire. He had been brought up as a sun worshipper, as indeed most of the emperors had throughout the third century. He was a religious man and anxious that there should be a favoured religion which could be established throughout the Empire, which could act as a kind of spiritual cement to bind together the many countries and peoples that it included. Sun worship and Christianity seemed to be the two main contestants, and no doubt, at least in some measure due to the influence of his mother, who herself had become an intensely devout Christian, Constantine decided in favour of Christianity. In AD 313 he promulgated what history has come to know as the Edict of Milan, which made Christianity a *religio licita*, that is to say a permitted religion, and removed all the statutory penalties for the profession of the name of Christ, which for many years had been a capital offence. This conversion initiated a determined search for the holy places, and none was more determined than the Emperor's mother, Saint Helena. It was she who revealed to the Emperor that there was such a shrine beneath a heathen temple which dated from the time of Hadrian. When his workmen dug beneath that temple there was discovered a cave tomb, which was accepted as the tomb in which the Lord's body had been deposited on Good Friday. The temple above was destroyed and a Christian church was built over the tomb which was incorporated within it. One argument in favour of the authentication of the sepulchre was that it was a custom of the Romans when they occupied or conquered a country to build over local shrines or holy places, a temple dedicated to a god or goddess of the Roman pantheon. It was hoped that this would prevent its use by the local population as a centre of dissidence, nationalistic enthusiasm and possible rebellion. The fact that when Aelia Capitolina had been founded a temple was built in this place is an indication that it was on a site which had in the past received veneration. The argument against this being the site of the sepulchre was that no graves were ever allowed within the walls of a Roman city, and the Church of the Holy Sepulchre is well within the city wall. It was this fact, among others, which persuaded General Gordon that he had discovered the authentic tomb outside the wall.

The walls which exist today only date from the sixteenth century and were erected on the orders of Suleiman the Magnificent, the ruler of the Ottoman Empire. He had wished to restore the original walls, but unfortunately his workmen made a grave miscalculation and omitted to include within the city the hill of Zion. It is said that the poor men paid for this mistake with their lives. Its long history has made Jerusalem a heap of deposits from previous eras. After the Byzantine period, in which the city was Christian, it had fallen to Muslim occupation, then was conquered by Crusaders in 1099, whilst the coming of Godfrey de Bouillon established the Kingdom of Jerusalem which lasted until 1187, when the city fell to the Muslim leader, Saladin. Each occupation naturally left its mark. The destruction in AD 70, however, was the most complete. Of course, even Titus could not remove all traces of the previous occupations. There are still features like the tunnel of Hezekiah by which the water supply for the city, which was provided by the Gihon spring outside the wall, could be channelled through the rock and into the reservoir, which we now know as the Pool of Siloam. There is also the cave of Zedekiah, so named because King Zedekiah was thought to have sought refuge by hiding in it from the Babylonians, in which attempt he was not successful. This is not a natural geological formation but a man-made quarry, and there is no reason to refuse to accept the tradition that it is from this subterranean source beneath the city, that Solomon acquired the stone with which to build the first temple.

Even more interesting are the archaeological explorations recently conducted outside the crusader church of Saint Anne which have revealed what could only be the remains of the structure built over the Pool of Bethesda. In Saint John's gospel (5:2) we read that 'In Jerusalem, by the sheep market a pool which is called in the Hebrew tongue Bethesda, having five porches'. The structure which has been here revealed does indeed have five porches. It is discoveries such as this which are persuading more and more people to attach to the New Testament accounts more credibility than most modern critics have allowed. Such revelations have moved scholars like John Wenham, a member of Latimer House in Oxford and who has lived in Jerusalem, to accept all the gospel narratives as being reliable accounts of what actually happened.

It is Wenham who, in his fascinating book, *The Easter Enigma*, reports that since the Second World War excavations conducted by Kathleen Kenyon seem to have shown decisively that the wall at the time of our Lord did in point of fact have an indentation which would bring the Church of the Holy Sepulchre outside. This indentation would be easily explained because of the uneven and somewhat rocky terrain in this area, which would provide a suitable site for the execution of criminals and also for the creation of a garden. Now that this fact has been established, there is no reason to prefer the site of General Gordon's Garden Tomb as being the authentic one. Indeed there are many similar tombs about Jerusalem dating from this period, any one of which would answer to the biblical accounts. The fact that the General saw in the rock formation at this point a vague resemblance to a skull and judged from this that this must indeed be the real Golgotha shows that the assertion belongs to the realm of archaeological speculation rather than to that of historical fact. The rock at this point in any case is a soft limestone, and it is most unlikely that it would present identical features in the first century and earlier to those that prevailed in the nineteenth when General Gordon made the discovery. It seems that Queen Victoria, having received a letter from Gordon telling her of his discovery, and in her reply thanking him for his opinion adding 'For ourselves, we are content to trust the discoveries of our cousin Helena', was justified by later scholarship.

For those who are able to visit Jerusalem, there is a fascinating model of the city as it would have been in the time of our Lord in the grounds of the Holylands Hotel, a short distance away. It is built in the scale of one to fifty, and as far as possible, the same building materials have been used as would have been in the actual buildings of the time. The archaeological and topical data were supplied by the late Professor M. Avi-Yona of the Hebrew University, who also supervised the building of the model. Since his death care has been taken to make any alterations which later archaeological explorations have revealed. It shows quite clearly that north of the spur of land which is the hill of Zion, the wall, which has been proceeding in a northerly direction, swings slightly to the east, and then continues in a northwesterly direction, thus making a kind of enclave. This enclave would provide a suitable arena for public events like the crucifixion: it was outside the city, close to the wall and would have provided a convenient backdrop.

Of course, the natural features of the area have remained the same. The Mount of Olives still stands where it did, as does Mount Scopus, and they present much the same shape as they would have done twenty centuries ago. The buildings upon them have changed, but the terrain has not. The valleys of Hinnom and Kedron are still there, although the ravine of the Tyropaean has disappeared under the labour of Hadrian's employees. As the modern pilgrim makes his way over these hills and across these valleys, he is indeed experiencing the same geographical conditions as did the twelve Apostles and our Lord Himself. We are therefore now in a position to be able to build in our mind's eye the setting in which the drama of the Passion would have been enacted.

There is no difficulty in siting the temple. The mound on which it was built is still there, and the Dome of the Rock makes it the most conspicuous landmark of the city, as the temple would have been in the first half of the first century. The rise of Mount Zion is now made even more conspicuous by the erection of the Church of the Dormition with its tower, and we know that it was in this area that the High Priest had his palace. From the biblical narrative it would also appear that the house where John lived would indeed be in this area, because we are told not only that he was known to the High Priest, but that he was so familiar as a neighbour that he was also well known to the portress on duty at the time of Jesus' arrest, when he and Peter gained admission (John 18:15–16).

It might seem that to place John's house in this part of the city, near to Caiaphas's palace, in what we know to have been a residential area of the well-to-do, is to be more than a little unrealistic. After all, traditionally the disciples were supposed to be simple fishermen and, if Zebedee and his family had a domicile in Jerusalem, it would surely have been in a more working class district, presumably somewhere near to the fish market. John Wenham does indeed tell us that there is a little coffee shop near the site of the old Fish Gate (which was through the north wall of the city) which claims to be on the site of John's house, but this is totally unsupported and therefore not really worthy of any credence. The tradition that all the disciples were poor men, is one which was born of devotional thinking, one could almost say wishful thinking, and receives little or no support from scripture.

There is, however, one verse in Saint John's gospel which could be interpreted that the Holy Family belonged to the poorer strata of contemporary society. That is to be found in chapter seven at verses fourteen and fifteen which read: 'Now about the midst of the feast Jesus went up into the Temple, and taught. And the Jews marvelled saying, "How knoweth this man letters having never learnt?"' In point of fact this passage would not have implied to the first readers of the gospel that the Jews were claiming that Jesus was not literate. The reference is to His being allowed to teach in the temple without having received a formal education in a Rabbinic school. It could be paralleled in modern parlance by some folk making reference to a university teacher, and saying, 'How is he allowed to teach when he hasn't got a degree?' In any case literacy at that time was not necessarily an indication of social status, although it is unlikely that many people who occupied positions of authority in industry or commerce would not be able to read and write. In any case, however, there is adequate scriptural evidence that Jesus was not only literate, but that there can be made a strong case for asserting that He was also multi-lingual. Saint Luke, in his account of the visit of our Lord to Nazareth, says that:

> And He came to Nazareth, where He had been brought up; and He entered, as His custom was, into the synagogue on the Sabbath day, and stood up to read, and there was delivered unto Him the book of the prophet Isaiah. And He opened the book and found the place where it was written 'The Spirit of the Lord is upon me...' (Luke, 4:16)

As a first century Jew, brought up in Galilee, Jesus would undoubtedly be speaking Aramaic in His own home and with His own people. He would also be able to speak Greek, which was the *lingua franca* of the Roman Empire. It does not need to be emphasised that the New Testament was written in Greek, and Jesus had no language difficulty in conversing with the Syro-phoenician woman, who, as Saint Mark says: 'was a Greek, a Syro-phoenician by race, and she besaught Him that He would cast forth the devil out of her daughter. And He said unto her...' (Mark 7:26). In Saint John 12:20 we read of Greeks who were anxious to converse with Jesus. To be able to read the scriptures in the synagogue, He would also be familiar with the Hebrew in which they were both written and read. We also read of a dialogue with Pilate, which would almost certainly have been conducted in Latin, Pilate's native tongue and certainly the language in which Roman court proceedings would have been conducted. It is significant that Pilate ordered that the placard and superscription attached to the cross of Jesus was to be written in Hebrew, Latin and Greek (John 19:19). It should be added that to be quadralingual in the first century was not an extraordinary achievement. It must be assured though that Jesus was certainly not illiterate.

There is strong biblical evidence that Zebedee was in

quite a successful line of business. He seems to have possessed a fleet of fishing boats and to have employed a considerable number of men. We know that even after James and John, Andrew and Peter had left him, there were still hired servants, who presumably provided a sufficiently large work force to carry on the business. The proprietor of such a concern would be in his own society a man of considerable power and influence, and there is no reason at all as to why his town house should not be cheek by jowl with the residences of the others who would have been his social equals, business associates and, in many cases, personal friends.

It might be said that John's house in Jerusalem would be the one in which Jesus would stay when He was in the capital, as Zebedee and Salome were His uncle and aunt. In that case it can be considered a little extraordinary that arrangements had to be made for a room in another house to be made available for Jesus and His disciples to have the Last Supper in it. It is surely true that such arrangements were made, and that the house in which the supper was to be held was not known to all the disciples, because elaborate arrangements had had to be made for them to find out where it was. This in itself, however, does not pose a convincing argument that John's house would be inadequate. It would seem that staying within the house for the festival were, as well as Salome (the fact that Zebedee is not mentioned causes one to speculate whether he was already dead or had not come up to Jerusalem for this festival but stayed in Galilee to supervise the Capernaum branch of the business), the Mother of Jesus, who was Salome's sister, as well as the other Mary and her husband Cleopas. It also seems likely that Jesus' brothers were also in the neighbourhood, because Jesus, meeting the women on the day of His resurrection, according to Saint Matthew's account, said to them: 'Go, tell my brethren that they go into

Galilee, and there shall they see Me.' It would seem unlikely though that they too were staying in John's house, even though they were first cousins, because there is no mention of them being present at any of the reported resurrection appearances. On the other hand, He would not have instructed the women to tell them to go to Galilee, and that He would see them back at home, unless they had been somewhere near at hand, either in Jerusalem or in the surrounding country.

Whatever the accommodation in John's house, it would appear that Jesus was especially anxious to hold this Last Supper somewhere else. He had clearly gone to great pains to make the arrangements. If indeed it was the house of Mary the mother of John whose surname was Mark, which was the one with the large upper room, as would seem to be likely, Jesus must have gone there sometime beforehand and made known His requirements, because we read that He told the disciples whom He sent to make the final preparations that they would find the room already furnished and ready (Mark 14:15). It is also clear that the house would be unknown to the two who were to go, and that they might not be recognised by the people in the house, because care was taken that the correct formula of words was to be used: 'The Master saith, where is the guest chamber where I shall eat the Passover with my disciples?' It is therefore abundantly obvious that Jesus was anxious to have this meal, not at Bethany, where there would be Lazarus and his sisters, and not at John's house, where there would be a number of relations, but somewhere where He would be undisturbed, alone and apart, only the Twelve being with Him. Had He not singled them out for a special commission in the carrying on of His work? Knowing that this would probably be the last opportunity before His death for a quiet talk, He had made arrangements for them to be on their own, where they would not be disturbed.

Such a supposition would receive support from Saint Luke, who reports that when they arrived at the place, Jesus said: 'I have desired to eat this Passover with you before I suffer.' It was also important that there should be the institution of the Eucharist and that the men be shown what to do with bread and wine in order to perpetuate the real presence of Christ. The last discourse reported by Saint John must embody the substance of what Jesus said there. The High Priestly Prayer could only have been said at that time. It is almost impossible to imagine a Christian evangelist, however close to Jesus Himself, and however deeply appreciative he may have been of the theological significance of Jesus' death and resurrection, inventing the High Priestly Prayer contained in the seventeenth chapter. And with equal certainty it can be said that there is no other time than at the Last Supper that it could have been said. Another example of what is meant here lies in the Lord's statement about peace. 'Peace I leave with you, my peace I give unto you; not as the world giveth give I unto you' (John 14:27). Then He breaks off and, leaving them with the unanswered question as to how His peace would be given, continues: 'Let not your heart be troubled, neither let it be afraid.' The answer comes when, in all probability in the same room and with the same company, on the evening of Easter Day, Jesus, appearing to them where they were gathered together, the doors being shut, said 'Peace be unto you' twice. The first would be His usual greeting, but the second would give the answer to the unanswered question on Maundy Thursday. We can be sure that Jesus arranged to take this meal alone with His disciples.

Joanna is also one of the characters who has a part to play in this ultimate drama, and we know that she was the wife of Chuza, Herod's steward, because Saint Luke has told us so (8:3). We also know that Herod's court was in Jerusalem, and again Saint Luke is our authority (23:7): 'As soon as he [Pilate] knew that He belonged unto Herod's jurisdiction, he sent him to Herod who also himself was at Jerusalem at that time.' Presumably Chuza, as one of the courtiers, would be living in the palace where Herod held court and his wife would be with him. There were two palaces in which Herod could have stayed, that built by Herod the Great and the Royal Palace of the Hasmonaeans. Although they were fairly close to each other there is no indication as to which the Herodian Court would occupy. The Hasmonaean Palace was contiguous to the temple but on the other side of the Tyropaean valley, the approach to the temple area being across one of the bridges.

The Castle of Antonia was also contiguous to the temple, having been built at the north-east corner at a height which enabled the Roman garrison to overlook the temple courts. It can be assumed that the governor would have stayed here when he visited Jerusalem. Normally he would reside at Caesarea on the coast. It is in this castle that the soldiers would have been quartered, and therefore where Jesus would be mocked and whence He would be taken on the road to Calvary.

It is now possible to build a picture of the city in our Lord's day and to have some idea of the location of the various houses and buildings which are involved in the unfolding of the Passion narratives. Attention must now be turned to the sites and places outside the city walls.

The first of these must inevitably be the Garden of Gethsemane. In point of fact it is not so much a garden as a grove of olive trees. The production of olives was one of the major industries of ancient times in Mediterranean countries. Olives were not only edible, but were one of the major sources of oil, necessary for cooking, heating and lighting, as well as used as an unction for anointing the body, a necessary precaution in lands where the sun's rays are intense. This olive orchard then would almost certainly have been enclosed, and no doubt admission would have been obtained by the use of a key. Because Jesus and His disciples 'ofttimes resorted thither', it would seem that its custodian had entrusted a key to our Lord so that He could have access to a retreat away from the rush and turmoil of the city. The site which nowadays claims to be the Garden of Gethsemane is about the only one of the holy places which has not got a duplicate. There are two sites which claim to be the scene of the stoning of Stephen, and there are two places which claim to be the site of the Holy Sepulchre. There can be no argument about this one. Saint John is quite explicit when he tells us that it was situated just across the brook Kedron:

> When Jesus had spoken these words, he went forth with his disciples over the brook Kedron, where was a garden into which he entered, and his disciples. And Judas also which betrayed him knew the place, for he ofttimes resorted thither with his disciples. (18:1–2)

Nothing could be clearer to delineate the geographical position of the garden.

If the Last Supper had been held on the hill of Zion, the little party would leave the city by a gate at the southern section of the wall, where there would then have been a path, as there is now, running outside and underneath the wall and passing beneath the temple mound. It then descends sharply to the brook and immediately across to nestle at the foot of the Mount of Olives, where is located Gethsemane. When one visits it, the place is indeed memorable. On the one side is the Mount of Olives, with a steep incline leading to the summit, more of a domed plateau than a rocky peak, and on the other, towering above the olive trees, is the steep rise towards the high wall of the temple, which from the garden gives an impression of great height overhanging the garden.

This crossing of the brook Kedron is at a junction of four paths. Jesus and the disciples, on Maundy Thursday evening, would have come down from the path running under the temple area, at which point would have been a road turning left to lead back into the city (the direct approach to the temple), and a third going straight on to join the main road from Jericho, which gave access to the city from the north. The road on the right would have then, as it still does today, taken the traveller up the very steep incline to the summit of the Mount of Olives. Somewhere near the top another road would have branched off to the left to join the Jericho road some distance further to the east than the path leading to it from Gethsemane. A traveller coming from Jericho whose destination would have been Bethany would naturally have taken this road as a short cut to avoid the summit of the Mount of Olives. It would have been a short step from this junction to the summit, from which the incomparable view of the city could have been obtained. Going from the city to Bethany one would not have taken this turning, however, but carried straight on over the hill to the little village standing on the other side.

Jewish travellers from Galilee to the capital would not normally follow the most direct route across the plain of Esdraelon, because that would have taken them through the land of Samaria and, as we know, the Jews had no dealings with the Samaritans (John, 4:9). Saint John, however, tells us that on at least one occasion Jesus did follow this quicker route. In chapter four, verses one to four we read:

When therefore the Lord knew how the Pharisees had heard that Jesus had made and baptised more disciples than John – (though Jesus himself baptised not, but his disciples) – he left Judaea and departed again into Galilee, and he must needs go through Samaria.

To avoid this passing through hostile territory, devout Galileans on their way to Jerusalem to observe one or other of the Jewish festivals would have taken an alternative route, crossing the Jordan after it had left the Sea of Galilee, proceeding down the east bank and recrossing the river by the fords at Jericho. They would then have walked up the twisting road, with its many recesses in the mountainous terrain providing opportune ambush places for robbers and assassins. For this reason they would usually travel in convoy, and *that* is how it could come about that Joseph and Mary could go a day's journey without noticing that the boy Jesus was not in the party. A long stiff climb would eventually have brought them to Jerusalem, passing along the lower ground between Mount Scopus on the right and the Mount of Olives on the left. It would appear that they considered the hazards of robbers to be less frightening than the unpleasantness of having to deal with Samaritans.

Bethany lay on the other side of the Mount of Olives to Jerusalem, and the main road from one to the other would have passed around the Mount of Olives to the south. There was however a rough track over Olivet which would have cut a considerable distance, although it would have involved the necessity of climbing over the hill. It is by no means certain that the present village of Bethany is on exactly the same site as the one which is mentioned in the gospels. We are told that a Sabbath Day's Journey, that is the distance one was permitted to walk on a Sabbath day without infringing the Sabbath law, was somewhere around three-quarters of a mile. It is reckoned that a Sabbath Day's Journey from Jerusalem would take a walker to the summit of the Mount of Olives, and it would seem that Bethany was just about as far again on the other side.

Saint Mark, in this instance followed by Saint Luke, speaks of another village in the neighbourhood, Bethphage. He begins his account of the triumphal entry into Jerusalem with the words:

> And when they came nigh unto Jerusalem, unto Bethphage and Bethany, at the Mount of Olives, he sent two of his disciples, and saith unto them, 'Go your way into the village over against you.' (Mark 11:1)

If we cannot be certain that the present village bearing the name of Bethany is the same place as the biblical village, the site of Bethphage must be even more uncertain, for it seems to have disappeared without trace. We can however gain one or two suggestions. From the verse quoted above we learn that it was near to Bethany and that it was on the Mount of Olives. Bethphage is mentioned first, before Bethany, and this could imply that Jesus would pass through that village before the other. We know that He was approaching Jerusalem by the Jericho route. In chapter ten verse thirty-two Saint Mark says: 'And they were in the way going up to Jerusalem,' and in verse forty-six: 'And they came to Jericho, and as he went out of Jericho with his disciples and a great number of people, blind Bartimaeus, the son of Timaeus, sat by the wayside begging.'

After the Evangelist narrates the entry into the city he says: 'Jesus entered into Jerusalem into the temple: and when he had looked round about upon all things, and now the eventide was come, he went out unto Bethany with the Twelve.' Bethany then was to be the village where he was going to stay that night. Coming up the road from Jericho, we learn from the narrative that He did not follow it into the city, but came to the Mount of Olives; He would have taken the pathway to Bethany. Before he reached that village, however, the road over the summit of the mount would have turned off to the right, descended to the brook, crossed it and climbed into the city. The nearest gate to that path at that time would have led directly into the temple. It is implied in the gospel that this was the route they took. Therefore it would seem that Bethphage must have been somewhere on the path from the Jericho road to Bethany, either at or before one comes to the turning to the right. This would seem to be a reasonable deduction.

We have now considered the area in which the events of the Passion were to be enacted. Scenes will be enacted inside the city; in John's house; in the house of Mary the mother of John whose surname was Mark; in the palace of Caiaphas; in the Castle of Antonia; and just outside the wall, in the enclave caused by an indentation on the west side, that rocky arena in which our Lord was crucified. Nearby was the garden in which Joseph of Arimathaea kept the new tomb in which he permitted the body to rest. We have been able to reconstruct a reasonable account of the geography of these places, which should enable us to follow the paths of the various characters as the greatest, most important drama of all time and all history unfolds itself in our reconstruction.

In the country *outside* the city walls, we have been able with some degree of reasonable certainty to plot the sites of the various pathways and roads, many of which still exist today, the sites of the villages and the Garden of Gethsemane. Put together, we are now in a position to study the entire narratives of the New Testament and to reconstruct the one true story of what we have been told happened. The two basic assumptions of the exercise are that each of the Evangelists has made a selection of the episodes and events of the full story, and that the selection so made was determined by the author's need to bring out a particular point or truth which he wished to emphasise. The second assumption is that the events recorded and the stories told are not pieces of fiction, or pulpit illustrations invented to make the desired points, but are indeed recordings of what actually happened. That said, it must be recognised that the points to be brought out, the truths to be emphasised and the theology to be presented are so vast that, as the author of the appendix to the fourth gospel writes:

> And there are also many other things that Jesus did, the which, if they should be written every one, I suppose that even the world itself could not contain the books that should be written. Amen.

Chapter IV
Act One: Maundy Thursday

It is agreed by all four Evangelists that some days before the Passover, Jesus made His triumphal entry into Jerusalem. All four also agree that quite elaborate preparations had been made for this event. A donkey had been procured and was produced at an appointed place and a scheduled time. Saint Matthew places the meeting between Jesus and the donkey when, on His journey up to Jerusalem, having crossed the Jordan at Jericho and there having healed two blind men, He came to a place known as Bethphage, on the Mount of Olives. Pausing there, he sent two disciples into the 'village that is over against you' (Matthew 11:1) to fetch the ass which they would find waiting, and gave them the password which would authenticate them as having been sent by Jesus. He then continued His journey into the capital by riding on the animal. By this gesture He would surely be making a public claim to Messianic status, after the prophecy of Zechariah (9:9): 'Behold, thy king cometh unto thee: he is just, and having salvation; lowly, and riding upon an ass, and a colt the foal of an ass.' Then, as Jesus and His party proceeded, people came out of the city and gave to the Lord a pilgrim's, if not a royal, welcome. It must be this poetic duplication of the ass and the foal which causes the first gospel to tell that there was a foal waiting along with the ass, whereas Saint Mark, who in this passage is being followed by Saint Matthew, only makes mention of the colt. Saint Luke also only refers to one animal, but we know that all through his gospel Saint Matthew is at pains to describe Old Testament prophecies as being fulfilled 'au pied de la lettre'.

Saint Mark tells the story in much the same words. He does however say that it was when they came to Bethphage and Bethany at the Mount of Olives a pause was made so that the donkey could be brought. In this he is followed by Saint Luke. Saint Mark also asserts that it was only one blind man that was healed on the Jericho road and gives his name as Bartimaeus, the son of Timaeus.

Saint John tells the story somewhat differently. First of all, he gives us the date, saying that it was six days before the Passover that Jesus came to Bethany, where Lazarus was whom Jesus had raised from the dead: 'So they made Him a supper there: and Martha served, but Lazarus was one of them that sat at meat with Him' (John 12:1). It was at this supper that Mary anointed the feet of Jesus with the precious ointment. After reporting this incident Saint John goes on to say:

> The common people therefore of the Jews learned that He was there: and they came not for Jesus' sake only, but that they might see Lazarus also, whom He had raised from the dead.

From this it would seem that Jesus, having come up from Jericho, went directly to Bethany, where all the Evangelists say he had stayed with Lazarus and his sisters, until the Thursday before His crucifixion. Saint John therefore gives us a timing. He certainly asserts that the Passover that year was on the Saturday. In New Testament times, when reckoning days, the first day was the day from which the calculation began. This is why the scriptures says that Jesus rose from the dead on the third day, whereas in contemporary reckoning it would be the second. It will also be remembered that in Jewish calculations, the day began at the sundown of what to us would be the previous day. For Saint John then, six days before the feast would be the Monday of Holy Week. His narrative states that the journey from Jericho was undertaken on the Sunday and that Jesus arrived in Bethany towards the evening. He and the disciples would certainly have been in need of an evening meal, as Saint John recounts, adding that quite a number came from the city both to see Him and also Lazarus. Presumably they would return to the city at nightfall, which would explain the next verse in Saint John's gospel: 'On the morrow' – that would be Monday – 'a great multitude that had come to the feast, when they heard that Jesus was coming to Jerusalem' – they would have heard it from the returning spectators from Bethany – 'took branches of palm trees and went forth to meet Him.' There is no doubt then that for Saint John the triumphal entry into Jerusalem was on the Monday of Holy Week, and not on what has come to be known as Palm Sunday.

The Synoptists do not specify the day, but they indicate that Jesus, having come up the Jericho road, paused at Bethany and Bethphage to await the delivery of the donkey, then continued into the city. On arrival He made His attack on the temple market. If that had happened on the Sunday, Jesus and His disciples would not have been able to have walked together more than the distance from the city to the summit of the Mount of Olives on the previous day, because that would have been the Sabbath. To imagine that Jesus had come all the way from Jericho, waited at Bethphage and Bethany for the ass, ridden into the city, cleansed the temple, looked round and then gone out to Bethany to spend the night there, *all in one day*, is really to stretch the imagination beyond reasonable limits. Of course, we do know that there was an inn on the Jericho road, because it is mentioned in the parable of the Good

Samaritan, but, unless there were many such places offering overnight accommodation (most unlikely), it would appear that more than a Sabbath Day's Journey would have had to have been walked. From both accounts therefore it would seem reasonable to say that Jesus made His triumphal entry into Jerusalem on the Monday, and that Saint John is more accurate, with it taking place the day after the dinner party at Bethany. If that dinner had taken place in the evening, as would be most likely, then Jesus would have arrived in Bethany, as Saint John says, six days before the Passover.

Incidentally, we do not now know where Bethphage was; it seems to have disappeared without trace. There is, however, no reason to doubt that the biblical Bethany is the same place as that which still bears its name. It could be that Bethphage was really no more than a crossroads where the path from the Jericho road turned off to the left as one travelled up from Jericho to go to Bethany, there meeting the path which came from the city which crosses the brook Kedron and the Mount of Olives. If that were the case, then 'the village that is over against you' would have been Bethany. Jesus would therefore have been able to make the necessary arrangements regarding the donkey in a place which He both knew and in which was known.

We must now consider the dinner party at which a woman anointed Jesus with a very expensive ointment. Saint Mark, and here he is followed by Saint Matthew, says that it occurred while Jesus was at Bethany. In each case the narration follows the account of an emergency meeting of the Council at which it was decided that Jesus would have to be put to death. Both Evangelists say that this meeting occurred two days before the feast. This, however, is another pericope account and it does not necessarily follow that the Council meeting preceded the dinner. The accounts of the supper are introduced with the words 'while He was at Bethany, in the house of Simon the leper', but there is no specific naming of the day. A modern reader, unfamiliar with the use of these pericopes, would assume that, because the account of the dinner was subsequent to that of the Council meeting, it would occur later in time. But that is by no means a necessary deduction. The dinner party could have happened on any evening between the Sunday and Wednesday. If Sunday were the day, then the account in the fourth gospel would receive ratification, for Saint John, it will be remembered, places it on the Sunday evening. Indeed this would make a more understandable sequence. Hearing that Jesus was expected, and curious about Lazarus, folk went from the city to see what was going on at Bethany. If this meal was being eaten in a neighbour's house, there would be more publicity about it than if Jesus had been provided with a meal in the house of Mary and Martha when He arrived there for a visit of a few days. Simon, now presumably cured of his leprosy, seems to have been a well-known person. Mary and Martha would have been invited to the house but not to the table with the men as Lazarus was, but rather to that with the women in another part of the house (it could be that Martha was helping in the kitchen!). These sightseers returned to Jerusalem and set about spreading the news that Jesus was going to make a state entry into the city the following day. This would inevitably have alarmed the government and made it vital that an emergency meeting be called. Saint John also gives an account of a Council meeting, but by implication this was a gathering of the Sanhedrin to deal with the situation which had arisen as a result of the raising of Lazarus from the dead. The sequence in the fourth gospel is as follows. Jesus raised Lazarus from the dead, after which the author goes on to say: 'Many therefore of the Jews, which came to Mary, and beheld that which He did, believed on Him. But some of them went away to the Pharisees, and told them the things which Jesus had done' (John 11:45–46). It was this that caused the Sanhedrin to be assembled. 'What do we do?' they said, 'for this man doeth many signs.' (It must be remembered that Saint John uses the word 'sign' for the miracles which Jesus performed.) 'If we let Him thus alone, all men will believe on Him: and the Romans will come and take away both our place and our nation' (John 11:47). It was at this point that Caiaphas made his prophetic statement that 'It is expedient for you that one man should die for the people'. Meanwhile we are told that 'Jesus therefore walked no more openly among the Jews, but departed thence into a country near to the wilderness, into a city called Ephraim, and there He tarried with His disciples.' We do not know for how long, because the Evangelist proceeds immediately to say: 'Now the Passover of the Jews was at hand, and many went up to Jerusalem.'

There is no reason why there should not have been two such meetings of the Council. The raising of Lazarus was one event which would create a disturbing situation. We must remember that it was vitally necessary for the Sanhedrin to keep the peace and prevent any sort of disturbance if they were to maintain what limited amount of self-government they had. The situation would most certainly have been exacerbated by the arrival of Jesus in Jerusalem, making what could only be interpreted as a Messianic claim, and by His angry disruption of the temple market. It would now be clear that the time had come to implement the resolution passed at an earlier meeting, whereby it would at some time be necessary to arrest Jesus and charge Him with a capital offence. That time had now come. Even so there was a warning: 'Not on the feast day, lest there be an uproar of the people.' This would explain the unusual haste to the legal procedures which eventually brought Jesus to the cross.

We must now return to our consideration of the dinner

party at Bethany. To recapitulate, it would seem that it was held before the triumphal entry into Jerusalem, in all probability on the Sunday evening, and that it was at the house of a well-known gentleman, probably one who had held public office. Saint Luke, it will be remembered, makes no mention of this supper, but does give us an account of a similar occasion in Galilee, at the house of a Pharisee who was also called Simon. We remember, of course, that because the author of the third gospel had no direct experience of the events which he is describing, there is obviously some confusion in his reportage of this event. This matter has already been discussed; it would seem that there were indeed two such occasions. The first would have been the one of which Saint Luke had received an account, although it is possible that either he himself or his informant mixed the names of the host. If there had been an earlier meal at which Mary had anointed Jesus, it would provide an explanation for the rather strange behaviour of Mary at the meal in Bethany, and make her action, whom Saint John clearly identifies as Mary the sister of Martha and Lazarus, entirely explicable. It would also offer an understanding of the statement that Mary Magdalene was the one from whom seven devils had been cast out. It is also understandable that Saint Luke, who was relying on the testimony of others, those 'which from the beginning were eyewitnesses and ministers of the word', having been given an account of this incident, would have been hesitant to give another which in so many particulars appeared to be a duplication. This provides an explanation that when he was reading and largely transcribing the Markan story, he decided to omit any reference to the supper at Bethany from his Passion narrative.

It would be reasonable then to say that Jesus would have kept the Sabbath of the week before that which the Christian Church terms Holy Week at Jericho and that on the first day of the week, which was to be the last of His earthly sojourn, Jesus and His disciples came up the hazardous road from Jericho towards Jerusalem, turning off it to go along the road to Bethany. It would be towards the end of the day when the party arrived there and immediately prepared to attend the dinner party which Simon the leper had arranged. The next day Jesus made His entry into Jerusalem, having made careful preparations so that by it a Messianic claim could be made.

It is not necessary to try to assign to specific days of the week the activities of our Lord during this period. All four of the Evangelists agree in saying that he preached openly in the temple and that the authorities put to Him questions which were designed to trap Him into making some statement which could be interpreted as treasonable or otherwise dangerous, and on the strength of which an arrest could be made. We can, however, with some degree of certainty, assign the cleansing of the temple to this time. Such an attack on the temple market and the dishonest practices of the traders would be unthinkable at the outset of the public ministry. This must be so, even though Jesus was not doing anything against the law or the religious feelings of the people. His protest was against the selling of inferior animals for the sacrifices, even though no doubt the religious specifications of their immaculate condition was being maintained, at inflationary prices, and against the selling of temple money at a price well above the correct exchange rate.

It was vitally important that no coins of the imperial mint should be taken within the temple area because they bore the image of the Emperor, and the second commandment strictly forbade the making of images of anything in heaven above, or in the earth beneath, or in the water under the earth. A short time earlier, Pilate had got himself into serious trouble because, seeing a minor disturbance in the temple courts, he sent in a cohort of Roman soldiers who took with them their standard, on which was a depiction of the emblematic Roman eagle. What had been a minor disturbance had immediately become a major riot. Each pilgrim, then, before entering the inner courts of the temple, was obliged to change all the Roman money he had on him for Jewish coins which bore no such image.

It was on this matter that the Synoptists demonstrate how skilfully Jesus fenced the questions which were put seeking to entrap Him. Saint Mark (12:13–17), followed by Saint Matthew (22:15–22) and Saint Luke (20:20–26), tells of the Pharisees' question as to whether it were lawful to pay tribute unto Caesar or not. It was a clever question. If the answer had been 'yes' then Jesus would have shown Himself to be an unpatriotic Jew; if it had been in the negative, He could be arrested for treason. Jesus, apparently innocently, asked if they had a piece of the tribute money, which would of course have had to have been paid in the Roman coinage. Unthinkingly, a denarius was produced. Jesus, looking at it, said 'and whose is this image?' They had to reply that it was a picture of Caesar. He had shown them that they had broken the law by bringing such a coin into the temple. The subsequent answer: 'Render unto Caesar the things that are Caesar's, and unto God the things that are God's' is then a profound statement capable of interpretation at various levels. On the surface it could mean that when in the temple one should obey the rules of the temple, and when outside obey the law prevailing, but it *also* says much more about the whole relationship of politics to religion, about the duty to the state and to God, in dealing with the human situation in which man finds himself a citizen of this world and a citizen of the Kingdom of God, and has to work out the relationship between them.

No doubt some of the other loaded questions, which Jesus parries with consummate debating skill, do indeed belong to various episodes that happened in this week. There was the question of on whose authority Jesus was exercising a public and preaching ministry and the trick question about the resurrection from the dead, all having upon them the stamp of a desperate attempt on the part of the authorities to find a reason for effecting an arrest. No doubt there would have been other questions and criticisms of a similar nature not recorded by the Evangelists, but from these few recorded ones, we can sympathise completely with the statement that 'no man after that durst ask Him any more questions' (Mark 12:34).

It is quite clear that as the week advanced things moved rapidly to a climax. At some point the breakthrough for the priests occurred when Judas went to them with a proposition that, in exchange for a financial reward, he would provide them with an opportunity to arrest Jesus with the minimum amount of publicity. There have been many attempts over the years to find a psychological reason for Judas' betrayal. The writers of many Passion Plays have endeavoured to do this, and some of them have resorted to deep theological propositions. Quite a few of them have tried to whitewash Judas in the matter. Dorothy Sayers, in her magnificent play cycle, *Man Born to be King*, gives to Judas an understanding that Jesus would be the expected Saviour and that by his betrayal he was actually bringing his own warped intelligence to create a situation which would enable the promised Messiah to fulfil His destiny. The biblical writers, however, did not feel the need to plumb the depths of such profound and convoluted psychological explanations, but merely content themselves in giving in bald statements the facts. They are very circumspect in the matter and refrain from offering any explanation for such behaviour. Sufficient for them was the enormity of the deed, and it was recorded without comment. The only suggestion about Judas' character comes from Saint John

(12:6) when he says that it was Judas who, confronted with the incident of the anointing of Jesus by Mary, proffered the criticism that the ointment might have been sold for a great deal of money (three hundred denarii) and given to the poor. The Evangelist then passes the comment that 'this he said, not because he cared for the poor, but because he was a thief, and had the bag, and bare what was put therein'. The intensity of the author's feeling of disgust is measured by the fact that this is the only comment on the character of any of the Apostles which is passed by any of the Evangelists.

We are now in a position to move into a consideration of the events of the period from Maundy Thursday to Easter Day and to examine the accounts that we have in the New Testament. All four gospels treat this period as of paramount importance. Indeed it could be said that in each of the Passion narratives is the kernel of the book and all that is recorded of the earlier life and ministry of Jesus is merely a preliminary. So important do all four consider the details of what was to them the most momentous three days in history that we must give them credit for making statements which are not only theologically significant, but also historically accurate. Some allowances must, of course, be made for certain minor defects in the recallings of memory, others for the use of historical narrative to convey theological truth, but we can reasonably assume that the Evangelists were honest men and would not deliberately invent an occurrence which would have such repercussions or knowingly pervert the essential relation of the story in the interests of evangelistic zeal or religious propaganda. They were Jews, brought up strictly in the Jewish religion and, therefore, unlike the Greeks who derived their religious beliefs from logical and mental deductions from observable physical data, their faith was based upon the experience of historical events. It was in the Exodus experience that the seeds of the subsequent and progressive revelation of God, of which the whole of the Old Testament is the chronicle, are contained. It was in the realisation that because the god of a particular mountain in Arabia, a land in which the Hebrews had never lived, had chosen them, a persecuted minority living in a foreign land, to be specially adopted by him, the reality of this being proved by the wonderful deliverance out of the land of Egypt and across the Red Sea, that it came to be realised that such a god could not be bound by local territorial limitations. It was only from these experiences of historical facts that, uniquely amongst all primitive peoples, the Jews had drawn out the knowledge of God as a loving Creator, and that holiness involved righteousness, and that love was at the heart of creation. It also led to the realisation that salvation could only be procured by the outpouring of a perfect life in a sacrificial surrender, as was demonstrated expressively by the anonymous prophet of the Exile, known to modern scholarship as Deutero-Isaiah. Men brought up in a religion such as this would not dare to present what they believed to be equally wondrous acts of God, on which they were convinced their own salvation as well as that of the whole world depended, which fulfilled all that the scriptures had foretold and which occurred in Jerusalem at the time of a particular Passover festival, except in terms of total honesty and maximum accuracy.

The night of the Wednesday and Thursday would have been spent by the Lord and His disciples at Bethany. We know from the accounts of the crucifixion that Jesus' mother, the mother of Zebedee's children and Mary the wife of Cleopas were also in Jerusalem for the feast, and it would seem natural for them to be staying in John's house. In point of fact it would be the home of Salome. There is no mention of Zebedee in any of the Passion narratives. This could mean that he had died, or that he would not be going up to Jerusalem on this occasion, or possibly that he was there but made no appearance at the foot of the cross. It would also seem that the brethren were in Jerusalem, but we have no clue as to where they would be staying. Of the other characters involved in the story, Mary Magdalene would, of course, be with her brother and sister at Bethany, and since we know that Herod's court was in residence in Jerusalem at that time, Joanna's presence would be explained, because she would be with her husband, Chuza, Herod's steward, and no doubt resident with him in Herod's palace.

Saint Mark says quite simply:

> And the first day of unleavened bread when they killed the Passover, his disciples said unto him, 'Where wilt thou that we go and prepare that thou mayest eat the Passover?' And he sendeth forth two of his disciples, and saieth unto them, 'Go ye into the city and there shall meet you a man bearing a pitcher of water: follow him. And wheresoever he shall go in, say to the goodman of the house, "Where is the guestchamber, where I shall eat the Passover with my disciples?" And he will shew you a large upper room furnished and prepared: there make ready for us.'

Saint Matthew, on the other hand, makes a few alterations to the wording of this incident. He tells that the disciples came to Jesus with the question and says that He sent them. He does not, as Saint Mark does, say that He sent two of them, yet there is no need to see in these differing words any contradiction. Twelve would be rather a large body to send to make the necessary preparations, especially as we are told that most of the furnishing of the room had already been accomplished when they got there. Neither does Saint Matthew mention the man carrying a pitcher of water, but merely tells them to 'say to such a man, "The Master saith, my time is at hand; I will keep the Passover at thy house with my disciples."' There is no contradiction here either. Saint Mark's account is somewhat fuller, that is all. Saint Luke, however, names the two disciples who were despatched to make the necessary arrangements as Peter and John. For the rest he gives the details of the man with the pitcher of water who will be seen by them and whom they must follow. He also instructs the disciples to give the pre-arranged message to the goodman of the house. The fourth gospel gives no mention of the previous arrangements for the meal, but begins its account with the words, 'Now before the feast of the Passover… And supper being ended.' In this way the narrative of the washing of the disciples' feet is introduced.

It is only the Synoptists then who give any information about the preparations. From their accounts it is quite clear that the disciples who were despatched into the city to see that all was ready could not have known the house where they were destined to go, and that very careful arrangements had been made for them to find the way. In this case it would be most unlikely that one of those disciples was John. We know that he had a house in the city and it would be unthinkable that he did not know of the house where the supper was to be eaten. It will be remembered that Jesus was John's first cousin and whoever was the owner of the house of the supper would be known to Jesus, and therefore presumably John also. At least Jesus knew the house well enough to make the arrangements, to lay a plan for the two men whom He would send to be able to find it, and He gave to them the correct formula of words by which the 'goodman' of the house would know that they were genuine. If John then were not one of these two, why does Saint Luke say that he was? It is significant that Peter and John are frequently mentioned together in the gospels.

It was Peter who asked John to find out from Jesus who was to be the traitor. It was Peter and John who went together into the court of the High Priest's house; it was Peter and John who ran together to the tomb on Easter morning. Whoever wrote the third gospel also wrote the Acts of the Apostles, and in that book, in the section dealing with the very early days of the Church's existence, Peter and John are also frequently in each other's company and are mentioned as being together. Peter and John went up together into the temple at the hour of prayer when they healed the crippled beggar: 'Now when they saw the boldness of Peter and John, and perceived that they were unlearned and ignorant men, they marvelled; and they took knowledge of them that they had been with Jesus' (Acts 4:13). It was Peter and John who were threatened by the government authorities when they were commanded not to speak at all nor teach in the name of Jesus; it was Peter and John who replied that that they could not but speak the things which they had heard and seen. (Acts 4:20). When as a result of Philip's teaching in Samaria, and 'when the Apostles which were at Jerusalem heard that Samaria had received the word of God, they sent unto them Peter and John' (Acts 8:14). There is no need to dispute the accuracy of Saint Luke's reporting of these events. Not himself being an eyewitness of the events of Maundy Thursday, it would perhaps be natural for him, when mentioning two of the disciples doing something together, to assume that they would be Peter and John. It is also interesting to note that in writing to the Galatians Saint Paul says, referring to what has come to be known as the first Synod of Jerusalem: 'When James, Cephas [that is Peter] and John, who seemed to be pillars, perceived the grace that was given unto me, they gave to me and Barnabas the right hands of fellowship' (Gal 2:9). It is of note that at this point the name of James (the Lord's brother) has been added. Presumably, as there were more calls on Peter and John to make journeys in the care of the Church, James, possibly because of his blood relationship to Jesus, had become the one who stayed in Jerusalem to preside over the Christian community there. Still, Peter and John are named as being 'pillars'.

The next question we need to ask concerns the person described as the 'goodman of the house'. The Greek word literally means 'master of the house' – οικοδεσποτης – and can mean the head of the family as well as the master of the household. It seems reasonable to assume that this house was the same as the one referred to in Acts (12:12) as the house of Mary, the mother of John whose surname was Mark, where many were gathered together praying. This is the house to which Peter went on his release from the prison where he was awaiting execution after the feast of Passover. He knew that that was where the Christian community would be meeting. We know that there was a large upper room in which the Last Supper was taken, and what could be more likely than that the same room had become the embryonic church, if we may so describe it, for normal gatherings and especially for eucharistic celebrations? Furthermore, if the young man in the Garden of Gethsemane was indeed Saint Mark, then his presence in the garden could be accounted for by the fact that he was the son of the house where the disciples had been and from which they had moved to Gethsemane. We may assume then that the house where the disciples were instructed to make the necessary preparations was that of a lady called Mary. It would be necessary for something more to be said to distinguish her from Mary the Mother, or Mary the wife of Cleopas, or Mary Magdalene. The fact that Saint Luke does this by relating her to her son would also imply that her husband was dead. She must have been a lady of considerable influence and status in Jerusalem. She must have had at least one manservant who could be despatched to the gate of the city bearing a pitcher of water; we know the upper room was a large one; we also have a reference to the Master of the House; and when in Acts we are told that at Saint Peter's arrival a 'damsel' went to the door in answer to his knocking. It could be that this girl, whose name was Rhoda, would also be a servant in the house. The goodman of the house therefore would most likely be the superior employee of Mary, who would be in charge of the household and would occupy the position of what we should know as the butler. Because the two who were sent on ahead did not know where the house was, a scheme had to be invented for someone to act as their guide. This, of course, would not be necessary when the rest of the party came, because Jesus would certainly know the way, and most likely James and John as well, who would be the neighbours, and possibly even friends, of the family.

The party, consisting of Jesus and the Twelve, then arrived and sat down for the meal. We can use the verb to sit, but in point of fact to recline would be more appropriate. All four Evangelists give an account of the supper, but the Synoptists seem to differ radically from the fourth gospel in the telling of what actually happened. Saint Mark confines his account to a narration of the forthcoming betrayal, by the announcement by Jesus that one of the company would act as a traitor, causing Him to be handed over to the authorities. Each of them asked in turn whether he were the one. Jesus does not name him, but says that it is one of the Twelve who is there present. There is no mention of Judas' departure from the table, although this could be assumed, but the narrative continues with the account of the institution of the Eucharist, concluding with the words, 'Verily I say unto you, I will drink no more of the fruit of the vine, until that day that I drink it new in the kingdom of God.' Saint Matthew gives a rather fuller account of the announcement of the betrayal. As in Mark,

Jesus makes the statement, which then causes general sorrow and provokes questions from them all: 'Lord! is it I?' Jesus replies that it is one who is at the table, and then, as though he had missed out on the previous conversation, Judas asks the question, and Jesus replies 'Thou hast said'. There is no suggestion that this last question and answer was *sotto voce*. The story then moves directly to the account of the institution, which uses almost exactly the same words as does Saint Mark.

Saint Luke on the other hand introduces the story by reporting a statement from Jesus that He had very much looked forward to this particular occasion, and he puts the remark about not partaking again 'until it be fulfilled in the kingdom of God', only referring it to eating rather than drinking. He then describes the first distribution of the cup and now uses the words of Saint Mark that He would not drink of the fruit of the vine until the kingdom of God should come. He proceeds to the institution of the Eucharist, although here there seems to be a strange duplication with the introduction of a second cup. Although some of the early versions of the New Testament do in point of fact omit the first chalice, there is a general consensus among the earliest and best attested Greek manuscripts that it accurately reflects the autograph of the gospel. We then get the announcement of the betrayal and, although the questioning is reported as being amongst themselves, there is no declaration that Judas is the traitor. Unlike the other two Synoptists, the third gospel then proceeds to give an account of a discourse from Jesus concerning greatness, which is prompted by discussion among the disciples as to who should exercise authority, leading to the announcement from the Lord that 'I appoint unto you a kingdom, as my Father hath appointed unto me; that ye may eat and drink at my table in my kingdom, and sit on thrones judging the twelve tribes of Israel.' This is followed by the prediction of Peter's denial and further advice on the way in which they should conduct their ministry. The final words are the ambiguous statement about the use of swords, when Jesus says:

> he that hath no sword, let him sell his garment and buy one. For I say unto you, that this that is written must be accomplished in me. And he was reckoned among the transgressors: for the things concerning me have an end. And they said, 'Lord, here are two swords.' And he said unto them, 'It is enough.'

He then goes out to the Mount of Olives and, on arriving at the Garden of Gethsemane, Jesus, who had been followed by the disciples, exhorts them to pray.

Saint John gives what at first sight seems to be a very different account. He has told us of the triumphal entry into Jerusalem and of the alarm that caused the Pharisees to say, 'Perceive ye how ye prevail nothing? Behold, the world is gone after him.' We next hear of the Greeks who wished to see Jesus, and their request to Philip for a meeting to be arranged. Philip takes them to Andrew and he tells Jesus of the desired introduction. We are not told whether the meeting actually took place because the Evangelist goes straight on to recount one of Jesus' discourses which begins: 'And Jesus answered them,' but it is not made clear whether this answer was given just to Philip and Andrew, or to the Greeks as well, or even whether a new pericope has started. The first words of the answer are: 'The hour is come that the Son of Man should be glorified.' Then comes one of the 'verily, verily' sayings: 'Except a corn of wheat fall into the ground and die, it abideth alone: but if it die, it bringeth forth much fruit.' A few verses later Saint John tells us that when Jesus said:

'Father, glorify thy name,' a voice came from heaven saying, 'I have both glorified it and will glorify it again.' The people therefore that stood by, and heard it, said that it thundered; others said, 'An angel spake to him.' Jesus answered and said, 'This voice came not because of me, but for your sakes. Now is the judgement of this world: now shall the prince of this world be cast out.'

Because there were people standing by it would seem that if we are still dealing with the incident of the Greeks, they too were included in the audience.

In the fourth gospel there is no account of preparations being made for the meal, there is merely the statement that:

before the feast of the Passover, when Jesus knew that his hour was come that he should depart out of this world unto the Father, having loved his own which were in the world, loved them unto the end. And supper being ended, the devil having now put into the heart of Judas Iscariot, Simon's son, to betray him: Jesus, knowing that the Father had given all things into his hands, and that he was come from God and went to God, riseth from supper and laid aside his garments, and took a towel and girded himself. After that he poureth water into a basin, and began to wash the disciples' feet. (John 13:1–5)

Saint John is the only one to record this incident and he uses it as an introduction to the last discourse which proceeds throughout the next five chapters, ending with the great High Priestly Prayer in chapter seventeen. There is no account of the institution of the Eucharist.

In addition to these four accounts of what happened on Maundy Thursday evening, we have a fifth from Saint Paul, writing in his first letter to the Corinthians, where, in chapter eleven, he is dealing with the ordering of the Eucharist in what are now the familiar Words of Institution. But first he writes:

> For I have received of the Lord that which I have delivered unto you, That the Lord Jesus the same night in which he was betrayed took bread, and, when he had given thanks, he brake it and said, 'Take, eat, this is my body, which is [broken] for you; do this, in remembrance of me.' Likewise also the cup, after supper, saying, 'This cup is the new covenant in my blood: do this as oft as ye shall drink it in remembrance of me. As often as ye eat this bread and drink this cup, ye do announce the Lord's death until when he shall come.' (1 Cor 11:23)

It is important to note that the words which introduce this passage could possibly indicate that Saint Paul was actually writing a quotation and that the formula was already beginning to establish itself as a liturgical statement.

It is also interesting to note that it is only Saint Luke and Saint Paul who give the instruction to do this. In each case the word used is not the usual Greek word that we should expect – πραττω – which would be used for 'do this action', but ποιεω, which usually means 'to make' or 'to create'. In classical Greek, however, there are times when the word is used in connection with sacrifices. Cases of this usage are to be found in the writings of the three historians, Herodotus, Thucydides and Xenophon, as well as in Plato. It is perhaps significant that Saint Luke was a Gentile and Saint Paul, at the university of Tarsus, would have been in touch with classical scholarship. In the biblical passages they give to these accounts of the institution of the Eucharist a distinctly sacrificial connotation.

Perhaps the most significant part of all four accounts is the instruction to the disciples to drink the blood. At the Passover the blood of the sacrificial victim had on no account to be drunk. Indeed all the blood had to be drained from the animal, which necessitated it being killed, so that it could be smeared on the offerer's head and poured over the altar. This was in full accordance with the law as stated in the Old Testament. This is made quite clear in Genesis 9:3–4: 'Every moving thing that liveth shall be meat for you: even as the green herb have I given you all things. But flesh with the life thereof, which is the blood thereof shall ye not eat.' Leviticus states it categorically (3:17): 'It shall be a perpetual statute for your generations throughout all your dwellings, that ye eat neither fat nor blood'; and again in 27:26: 'Moreover ye shall eat no manner of blood of fowl or of beast in any of your dwellings.' The explanation of this legal necessity is given in Leviticus 17:13:

And whatsoever man there be of the children of Israel, or of the strangers that sojourn among you, which hunteth and catcheth any beast or fowl that may be eaten; he shall even pour out the blood thereof, and cover it with dust. For it is the life of all flesh; the blood of it is for the life thereof: therefore I said unto the children of Israel, 'Ye shall eat the blood of no manner of flesh: for the life of all flesh is the blood thereof: whosoever eateth it shall be cut off.'

This is given as the reason for the ability of blood to make atonement for the soul: 'For the life of the flesh is in the blood: I have given it to you upon the altar to make an atonement for your souls: for it is the blood which maketh atonement for the soul.' The point is emphasised again and again: 'Whatsoever man there be of the house of Israel, or if the strangers which sojourn among you, that eateth any manner of blood: I will even set my face against that soul that eateth blood and will cut him off from among his people.' (Lev 17:10–11)

So explicit is this teaching about the vital quality of blood and the prohibition of human consumption that even today the Jews are supposed to eat no food which is not 'Kosher'. One of the stipulations of Kosher food is that there is no blood in it, and if it be flesh meat all the blood must have been drained away before cooking. Even in the home of every modern religious Jew there will be a draining board or grating, used to extract the last drop of blood from the meat. The flesh is first soaked in water, then sprinkled with salt, and allowed to stand for a considerable time. Before cooking it is then rinsed and placed on the board to drain.

It is hard for us to realise with what shock the disciples must have heard Jesus, after he had said that the wine in the cup was His blood and told them to drink it. This was the most revolutionary theological point that was made in the context of the institution narratives. Jesus was offering the totality of His life to become part of the lives of the disciples, and by this means they each could be taken completely and utterly into His life. One could say that in Saint Mark's gospel this particular verse is the key and solution of all that has previously been written. In the fourth gospel, however, there is no special need for this undoubted event from the Last Supper to be recorded. For Saint John the point had already been explicitly made. After all, although we can be quite certain that Jesus did go through the actions of the eucharistic consecration at the Last Supper, that itself would be a demonstration of what He was commanding the disciples to do. He made the promise that whenever they were to use bread and wine in the way that he then showed them, those elements would be for Him the means by which His life would be communicated to them. It is by our physical bodies that we express ourselves in this world, and it is because we have physical properties that we can make ourselves heard and seen, and so be able to be known to be present and to influence other people. Therefore those elements which express our life and communicate it are the body and the blood, the physical self. Jesus promised that bread and wine, used in the way that He had shown them, would be the means by which His life would be given to them, and they could therefore become His body and His blood. The self-giving was complete, signified by the instruction to drink blood, that which had up to that point always been most strictly forbidden. It must be stated that what Jesus did at the Last Supper could not have been an Eucharist. It is only after the death of the victim and the offering of the victim's life, in this instance on the cross, that the life could have been made available for such communication. The need for the Synoptists in giving their accounts of the institution of the Eucharist is to make the essential point that Jesus' life, offered sacrificially on the cross, then shown to be resurrected and thus not only released from the limitations imposed on the human condition by the dimensions of space and time, is available at all times, throughout all space, to the end of the world as the Bible says, and available fully to each and every living creature. Salvation depends upon communication in this life.

For Saint John, however, this point has already been made very clearly. After he has recounted the sign of the feeding of the five thousand, he leads into a dissertation on the bread of life. It is significant that Saint John, in telling of the miraculous feeding, uses language very redolent of that of the Synoptists in the narration of the institution of the Eucharist. He takes the bread and 'when he had given thanks he distributed to the disciples'. It is presented in what we could call Eucharistic terminology. The story is followed immediately by that of the walking on the water, an act by which Jesus showed Himself to be the Lord and Master of the created order. One is reminded of Queen Elizabeth I's doggerel, which happens to be very sound theology:

> He was the Word that made it.
> His was the word that brake it.
> And what that word doth make it
> That I believe and take it.

Saint John then continues with a narrative of what happened the day after, when the people came to ask Jesus how He had managed to get to Capernaum. He said, 'Ye seek me, not because ye saw the miracles, but because ye did eat of the loaves, and were filled.' He goes on to advise them not to work for the 'bread which perishes, but for that which endureth unto everlasting life'. Then, in reference to the provision of manna in the wilderness, Jesus says, 'Verily, verily I say unto you, Moses gave you not that bread from heaven; but my Father giveth you the true bread from heaven. For the bread of God is He which cometh down from heaven, and giveth life unto the world.' When the people ask him to give them that bread he tells them bluntly, 'I am the bread of life. He that cometh to me shall never hunger, and he that believeth in me shall never thirst.' The discourse continues on the unity of Jesus with the Father, and how the Father is working through the Son, yet it is shot through with the concept of bread, and Jesus' being available as bread, which leads to life everlasting. Eventually we get a direct declaration (John 6:53–58):

> Then Jesus said unto them, 'Verily, verily I say unto you, Except ye eat the flesh of the Son of Man and drink his blood, ye have no life in you. Whoso eateth

my flesh and drinketh my blood, hath eternal life; and I will raise him up at the last day. For my flesh is meat indeed, and my blood is drink indeed. He that eateth my flesh and drinketh my blood, dwelleth in me, and I in him. As the living Father hath sent me, and I live by the Father, so he that eateth me even he shall live by me. This is the bread that came down from heaven: not as your fathers did eat manna, and are dead: he that eateth of this bread shall live for ever.'

Nothing could be clearer than that; because of it there is clearly no need for the same teaching to be given again in the account of the Last Supper.

The Synoptists on the other hand are at pains to establish the fact that Jesus is the true sacrificial victim who gives Himself for the salvation of the world and for every living thing within it. It was in the Passover festival that the perfect victim was offered, his life, which is in the blood, was united with the worshipper's by being smeared on his forehead and offered to God by being poured over the altar. The flesh of the lamb was actually eaten at the Passover meal, so here we have a strong argument for the theological justification of making the Last Supper the Passover meal.

By telling the story of Jesus washing the disciples' feet, Saint John, at the beginning of the narration of the last discourse, stresses the fact that Jesus had come to serve mankind and was on the earth as a servant. In this dramatic performance Jesus was showing Himself to be in the true prophetic tradition, for many of the prophets effected some of their teaching by such dramatic actions. Jesus in His own person enacted the part of a slave in a typical household of the period, even to the point of dressing up (or down) to look like one. Saint Luke, on the other hand, does not put the point in such a dramatic way (although this is not to say that Jesus did not give such a telling performance), but reduced it to one verse, also contained within his last discourse (Luke 22:27): 'For whether is greater, he that sitteth at meat, or he that serveth? Is not he that sitteth at meat? But I am among you as he that serveth.'

Now, surely, we are in a position to sum up what the gospels tell us about what happened in that upper room on the first Maundy Thursday. Two disciples had gone on ahead to make the necessary preparations and, as they did not know the way, Jesus had made suitable arrangements for their guidance. The party that eventually assembled consisted of Jesus and the twelve disciples only. At some point early in the evening Judas left to go to perform the act of betrayal and to lead the arresting party to the place where he knew Jesus would be going later. At that supper Jesus went through a symbolic action, which was in the true prophetic tradition, and washed the disciples' feet. At some point in the meal He took a piece of bread, blessed it and broke it and gave it to his disciples, telling them each to eat of it, because it would be the means of communicating Himself, when He would eat it new in His kingdom, that is after His crucifixion and resurrection. He demonstrated in a similar way the use of the cup, and although it had become His blood, they were instructed each to drink it. These acts were to be done in the future, and whenever bread and wine were used in that particular way, with the conscious remembrance of Jesus who had taught them to do it, so His promise that He would be really present to give Himself to them and to take them into Himself would be realised.

From this careful reading of the accounts in the New Testament it would appear that all the narrators are describing the same event. Indeed, there appears to be a greater consistency than would be the case if five different people today described a social event of some sort that they had all visited. It is true that some will pick on one aspect of the occurrence and others will not. We have, however, been able to see that for each particular happening, there is a theological reason for each writer to have made that particular selection. The fact that the first two gospels do not include an account of a discourse at the supper, is not to say that there was not one, but that it was unnecessary to their purposes to narrate one. It could, of course, be that some of the words reported had been uttered by Jesus on some other occasion. An example of this may be the verse in Saint Luke (22:29) which reads: 'And I appoint unto you a kingdom as my Father hath appointed unto me.' This appears to be a variant of Saint John's 'As the Father hath sent me, even so send I you' (John 20:21), which comes from Jesus' lips on Easter night, but presumably to the same people and in the same place.

Next, all four gospels are united in saying that, after the supper, they adjourned across the brook Kedron, although Saint John is the only one who mentions the name specifically, and that they went into the Garden of Gethsemane. This would, as stated, have been more of an olive grove than a formal garden in the horticultural sense of the word. It is also interesting to note that it is about the only 'holy place' in Jerusalem about which there can be certainty that the place so designated today is the authentic, original site. It may even be that some of the trees there, which are certainly very old, could have been standing in our Lord's day. In those days olives were a valuable product and had great domestic and commercial value. Olive trees not only produced fruit which was edible, but oil which was necessary for culinary uses, providing fuel for artificial illumination, and also for personal application, which was vital in a hot climate with a broiling sun. Gethsemane then would almost certainly have been enclosed by a wooden fence, and no doubt there would have been a door which could be locked. That would mean that Jesus would have possession of a key, for the place would not be left insecure, especially at festival time. This is another argument for the proprietor having been someone who was on very close terms with Jesus, and the most likely candidate would seem to be Mary the mother of John whose surname was Mark. This could well explain the presence of the young man in the garden mentioned in Saint Mark's gospel, which, whilst not giving his name, had led scholars to see in this incident an indication that the young man was none other than Saint Mark himself.

Saint Mark describes the arrival at the garden by saying that they all went in, and that Jesus asked them to sit while he went to pray. Then He took Peter, James and John and presumably went further into the grove away from the other eight and asked them to watch. A question which we would like to ask is whether He asked them to watch so that they might be able to give a warning of anyone's approach or whether He wanted them to hear His prayer. No answer of course can be given. He began to be 'sore amazed and very heavy'. Saint Mark gives us the words of the prayer, so they must have been heard by someone who retained them in his memory and who could recount them later. It is interesting that Jesus addresses his Father with the familiar 'Abba' of which perhaps 'Daddy' would be a good translation. Having prayed that the cup might pass from Him but, nevertheless, that God's will would be done, Jesus returned to the three intimates and found them asleep, this happening three times. On the last occasion Jesus said that they might sleep on, so it was He who heard the approach of the arresting party and gave the warning, 'Rise up, let us go; lo! he that betrayeth me is at hand.' Apart from repeating the words of the prayer, Saint Matthew's account is, almost verbatim, that of Saint Mark's. Saint Luke, on the other hand, does not mention the separation of Peter, James and John from the others, and the instruction to watch and pray is given to the whole band. He also tells us that Jesus' agony was such that his sweat was like great drops of blood falling to the ground.

The fourth gospel gives the account somewhat differently. First of all, the brook Kedron is mentioned by name, and in this way surely Saint John wants to put his readers in mind of the fact that in a short while that little stream will be a torrent of blood from the sacrificial lambs. There is no reference to the prayer, but it will be remembered that Saint John has just given a full account of the Lord's High Priestly Prayer in the upper room. We move directly into the account of the arrival of the company sent to arrest of Jesus, and an explanation is given about how it came about: 'And Judas also, which betrayed him, knew the place; for Jesus ofttimes resorted thither with his disciples.' The personnel of the guard is described as 'a band of men and officers from the chief priests and the Pharisees', who came with lanterns and torches and weapons. Jesus goes to meet them and asks for whom they are looking. When they reply that it is Jesus of Nazareth, and if he is the one, He replies 'I am'.

This declaration above requires some explanation. Saint John has used it as a theme throughout the whole of his gospel. To understand its significance we must turn back to the Old Testament. In Exodus chapter three at verse thirteen we read:

> And Moses said unto God, 'Behold, when I come unto the children of Israel, and shall say unto them, The God of your fathers hath sent me unto you, and they shall say to me, "What is his name?" what shall I say unto them?' And God said unto Moses, 'I AM THAT I AM.' And he said, 'Thus shalt thou say unto the children of Israel, I AM hath sent me unto you.'

Thus the name of God was revealed. The Hebrew letters transliterated into Arabic ones are J.H.V.H. – we do not know how it was pronounced, because it never was spoken out loud. The Israelites, like most ancient people, had a certain reticence about the use of a person's name. The name that belongs properly to an individual is not the surname but the Christian or forename, that which is his particular possession. To use that name in address is in some way to exercise authority over the person whose name it is. To call one by name is to indicate that in a certain way that person is under the influence of and subservient to the caller. In Genesis chapter thirty-two at verse twenty-four we read:

> And Jacob was left alone; and there wrestled a man with him until the breaking of the day. And when he saw that he prevailed not against him, he touched the hollow of his thigh; and the hollow of Jacob's thigh was out of joint, as he wrestled with him. And he said, 'Let me go, for the day breaketh.' And he said, 'I will not let thee go unless thou bless me.' And he said unto him, 'What is thy name?' And he said, 'Jacob.'

The angel had asked Jacob to let him go and Jacob refused unless the angel blessed him. Jacob then recognised that he was subject to the angel, and the angel, in order to use that submission so as to put Jacob under his influence that he might receive the blessing, needed to know his name. It is also interesting to read Saint Mark's account of the Gadarene demoniac. Here is a man who is quite demented. He has discarded his clothes which to a Jew rendered the man ceremonially unclean, as also did his association with corpses (we are told that he had his dwelling among the tombs). Seeing Jesus approach, he feared the possibility of an encounter, so, to put Jesus at an immediate disadvantage, addressed Him by name: 'What have I to do with thee, Jesus, thou son of the most high God? I adjure thee by God that thou torment me not.' Jesus replies: 'What is your name?' If the demoniac gave his name, then he would have been placed under Jesus' influence. He does not therefore oblige, but instead gives his nickname: 'My name is Legion, for we are many!' For a junior to use the name of a senior or elder implies disrespect.

Because of the above, the Jews would never speak the name of God; it would be spiritually outrageous to place God under the influence of man, an infringement of the third commandment. That is why we do not know how the tetragrammaton was pronounced, simply because it *never was* pronounced. In reading the scriptures aloud, when a Jew met the word, he did not say it but substituted 'Edonai', which means 'my lord'. Originally Hebrew had no vowels, but as it was becoming a dead language in the tenth century of the Christian era, the Massoretic scholars invented a system of points and signs to write into existing manuscripts above or below the line the signification of vowels. This would not necessitate the destruction, but rather the amendment, of all existing manuscripts. When the scribes adding these points came to the tetragrammaton 'J.H.V.H.' they automatically inserted the points of Edonai. Thus in transliteration we gain the word Jehovah, which is a hybrid composed of the consonants of the name of God and the vowels of 'my lord'. Although we do not know how this name was pronounced, we do know what it means. It is a strengthened form of the first person present indicative of the verb 'to be'. That is why, in the King James version of the Bible, it is spelt in capital letters, the strengthening indicated by the 'I am that I am'. In Greek this is εγω ειμι – I am.

Throughout the gospel of Saint John these two words run like a theme. Jesus, in speaking of Himself applies them to many similes. Indeed there are seven, four of which are repeated:

'I am the bread of life.' (6:35, 51)
'I am the light of the world.' (8:12, 9:5)
'I am the door.' (10:9)
'I am the good shepherd.' (10:11, 14)
'I am the resurrection and the life.' (11:25)
'I am the way, the truth and the life.' (14:6)
'I am the true vine.' (15:1, 5)

Again, when the Samaritan woman says to Jesus that when the Messiah called Christ came he would 'tell us all things' (4:26), Jesus replied: 'I am.' Again He announces himself to the disciples when walking on the water (6:20), saying, 'I am.' In disputing with the Jews in chapter eight at verse fifty-eight, Jesus had said, 'before Abraham was, "I am".' In the same chapter, at verse twenty-eight there is: 'When ye have lifted up the Son of Man then shall ye know that I am.' Lastly in the final discourse (13:19) there is the clear declaration: 'Now I tell you before it comes to pass, that, when it is come to pass, ye may believe that I am.' Of course, Saint John was writing for Christians at a time when the inhibition about the use of the divine name no longer applied, and therefore he is at liberty to quote it many times in his gospel. When, however, our Lord would have actually spoken these things, his contemporaries would still be under that restriction. It is significant that on the occasion when Jesus says clearly to the Jews, 'Before Abraham was, I am,' the next verse tells us that the Jews 'then took up stones to cast at him'. What they heard would probably have been the first time that they had ever heard the word spoken. In any case it was a clear case of blasphemy, and in the Jewish law the penalty for the crime of blasphemy was death by stoning.

Incidentally, in the Markan account of the trial before Caiaphas, when the High Priest asks Jesus directly whether he is the Christ, the reply given is 'I am.' No wonder the High Priest tore his clothes, a symbolic act somewhat similar to a judge of donning a black cap before passing sentence of death, and said, 'Ye have heard the blasphemy what think ye?' Knowing what effect the hearing of the word would have on the members of the Sanhedrin, we need have no surprise that 'they all condemned him to be worthy of death'. In such circumstances, who of us would not have done the same?

Returning to the Johannine Passion, the Evangelist states that, in answer to the information that the band were looking for Jesus of Nazareth, He said 'I am.' This provides the explanation as to why 'they went backwards and fell to the ground'. It was only after the second announcement that they dared arrest a man who claimed to be God.

The part played by Judas in the arrest is significant. In all three Synoptists Judas kissed Jesus as he entered the garden, which was a pre-arranged signal that the guard would know which was the man they were to take into custody. Saint Matthew adds the words 'Friend, wherefore art thou come?' Saint Luke says, 'Betrayest thou the Son of man with a kiss?' In Saint John's account, however, it would be inappropriate for Judas previously to have indicated which man was Jesus, because there could be no cause for Jesus to say 'Whom seek ye?' and make the stupendous declaration. The Synoptists do not need to report this 'I am' in the garden, because it is going to appear in their account of the trial. Saint John, however, does not give an account of the trial before Caiaphas, but only of the preliminary interrogation by Annas. What the Synoptists are saying is that Judas led the company to Jesus, that they might arrest Him. John is also saying the same thing when he says that after the first 'I am' saying of Jesus, Judas also 'stood with them'. Does this mean that Saint John is saying that Judas did not kiss Jesus? By no means. What actually happened is that Judas led the way into the garden and, seeing Jesus approach, went up to Him and kissed Him. Because that was probably not the way in which Judas usually did greet Jesus (of course, it must be remembered that on any telling the events presently unfolding must have been heavily charged with emotion) the other disciples thought that it must have been a signal. It could be said that the most natural reading of these two accounts was not to say that they are different, but that they are complementary.

There is another apparent discrepancy concerning the composition of the arresting company. Saint Mark says that it was 'a great multitude with swords and staves from the chief priests and the scribes and the elders'. This threefold composition is Saint Mark's usual way of referring to the Sanhedrin or the Jewish Council. This would mean, not that they were regular soldiers, but rather a detachment of the Levitical Guard, which was at the disposal of the Council for the maintenance of order within the temple precincts. Saint Matthew omits the scribes, but that is of no moment at all. Saint Luke just says that it was 'a multitude', meaning a large company. This time it is the fourth gospel which introduces another element. Saint John says that 'Judas, having received a band of men and officers from the chief priests and Pharisees, cometh thither with lanterns and torches and weapons'. When it comes to the actual arrest, he says: 'Then the band, and captain and officers of the Jews took Jesus and bound him.' The word used for 'captain' is 'Chiliarch', which literally means an officer in charge of a thousand men, a Roman term often used for a military tribune. Does Saint John here mean that the band was so large that they had to have a whole regiment of soldiers or does he intend us to understand that as well as the officers of the Jewish force, precautions had been taken to see to it that there was a representative of the Roman Army, the occupying power, present to prevent any complaints to or from the Roman authorities? The latter explanation would seem to be the most likely; here then is another example of the attention so often paid by the author of the fourth gospel to details, the details which would be likely to impress themselves upon the mind of an onlooker and eyewitness. In any case, there is no discrepancy; it is merely differences of aspect as revealed to different witnesses.

All four Evangelists tell of one of the guardsmen having his ear cut off, but Saint Luke is the only one to say that Jesus restored it. Saint John gives names and says that it was Peter who struck the blow, and that it was Malchus who lost his ear. This must be an indication that Saint Luke had other sources of information about these events than the other Evangelists. Saint John also adds the further information that one of the people in the High Priest's palace, who questioned Peter about his association with Jesus and drew forth from him his second denial of knowing Jesus, was a kinsman of Malchus. This is another indication of the familiarity of Saint John not just with the High Priest, but also with his household. Once again it is necessary to say that because two of the Evangelists do not record an event, even in the dramatic circumstances of these closing days, it does not mean that either they did not know about it or that there is any indication that in their opinion it had not happened. It is merely a matter of selection, as any news bulletin or reportage is inevitably a matter of selection.

Before we leave the occurrences in the Garden of Gethsemane we must spend a few moments in the consideration of the young man who makes an 'on-off' appearance in a most unsuitable costume. The second gospel is the only one which carries the story. We have already noted this as an example of the Evangelists' way of using the narration of an historic event as a means of conveying a deep truth at many levels. Let us then assume for present purposes that this is an historic event. Jesus has been praying. He is out of earshot of most of the disciples, and those three who are near have fallen asleep. Yet we are told the actual words the Saviour used: someone must have heard them. It is hard indeed to imagine that Jesus would tell the disciples what had been the words of this prayer after the resurrection, and there had been no opportunity for Him to do so, even if that can be imagined, beforehand. There must have been someone else in the garden. Even if Saint Mark had not told us that there was, it would have to have been assumed. We now know that it was a young man with a sheet wrapped about his naked body. Jews were very particular about maintaining modesty when it came to revelation of their physical attributes, so this to say the least was an extraordinary costume. Certainly this young man would not have staged such a performance in order to give the author of the gospel an opportunity to proclaim a truth of deep significance. The suggestion that the youth was indeed Saint Mark himself would seem to have credibility. If this is so, we must ask the further question of how it had come about that he was there. It does not really matter whether we know the reason for it or not, but there are two possible explanations. One of these could be that the young man was indeed Saint Mark and that he would have known Jesus as a visitor to a neighbour's house and as a cousin of one of his friends, and that he may have gathered some news of impending trouble. Having gone to bed, he either could not sleep or he was awakened from sleep. We are told that the disciples sang a hymn before they went out to the Mount of Olives, and surely that would be enough to make sleep for anyone in the house difficult to say the least. This, of course, would be happening long before the introduction of night garments to wear when in bed. Being therefore anxious when he heard that the disciples and Jesus were leaving the house, and feeling an urge to see where they were going, he decided to follow them. No doubt he had gleaned the impression that Jesus was in some sort of danger, and was not a little apprehensive. Not having had time to dress, he would have picked up one of the bed covers and wrapped it around him to preserve his modesty. Not wishing it to be seen that he was following, or to appear to be inquisitive, he would have kept in the shadows and out of sight. This would explain his presence in the garden, where he would have heard the words of the Lord's prayer in His agony. Seeing Jesus arrested, in a spontaneous gesture to try to save Him, he may have leapt forward. When one of the guardsmen grabbed at him and caught the sheet, the boy could have wriggled out of it and run away with nothing on. Another, and possibly more likely, explanation of Saint Mark's presence could be that the garden belonged to his mother and that he had been sent there to act as a guard to protect the garden from robbers, when the city was crowded with all sorts of people for the festival. It could also be that there was some kind of a shed in the garden for the housing of tools and that there was somewhere in it where the lad could lie down. In any case, if it had not been for that young man, the words of Jesus' prayer to His Father would never have been known, and our understanding of its significance could never have been understood. The incident in itself would not strike the other Evangelists as of particular importance, but to Saint Mark himself it would be an indelible recollection, and we have already seen how significantly he uses the account. In any case, as Saint Mark tells the story, the young man's dart into the open occurred after he has told us that the disciples had all fled.

To sum up therefore, and put the events in the garden in

chronological order, Jesus and His disciples arrived; Jesus took Peter, James and John further into the garden, leaving the others nearer the gate and having asked them to pray; the three disciples whom Jesus had taken with Him went to sleep and had to be wakened by Jesus when He heard the approach of the company of Levitical Guard coming to arrest Him; Judas was with them and, asserting his relationship to Jesus, greeted Him with a kiss; Jesus advanced to the officers and asked for whom they were looking – when he used the divine name in answer to their reply that they sought Jesus of Nazareth, they were appalled; Peter made an attempt to prevent what was happening and in the affray cut off Malchus's ear, which Jesus promptly restored. It is fairly certain that this act was well attested because not only do we have an account of it from the fourth gospel but, although it does not appear in either of the first two Synoptists, it is found in Saint Luke, who must in this instance have been using another source of information. When Jesus was secured, the disciples all forsook Him and fled. There darts out a youth, whom no one else seemed to know was there, wearing only a sheet, out of which, when taken hold of by one of the guardsmen who made a grab at him, he wriggled and ran away. Once again there is no difficulty in reconstructing most of what happened in the garden: the four witnesses together enable us to have a clearer picture than would have been possible from any single one of them.

Jesus is now alone, under arrest, with his hands bound, and led away. He would, of course, be taken back across the brook Kedron and up the steep incline back into the city. The company would probably pass underneath the temple mound and enter the city by one of the southern gates which gave ready access to the High Priest's palace, for we are told that this is where they went. Saint Mark and Saint Matthew both tell us that 'they all forsook Him and fled'.

(Mark 14:50; Matthew 26:56) It can be assumed that at this stage that also included Judas. Quite obviously they would not have followed the band towards the city, but instead scrambled over the Mount of Olives, which was the way back to Bethany in any case, where they knew that they would find shelter. Clearly they must all have been afraid that they too would soon be arrested because of their association with the prisoner. In spite of the well attested statement that they all forsook Him and fled, all four Evangelists also say that Peter followed into the city, although the three Synoptists all say that it was at a distance, and the fourth gospel says that he was accompanied by the other disciple whom Jesus loved. It is not difficult to reconcile these accounts. The little company of twelve men (that is assuming that Judas was still with them – although it is perhaps more likely that he would go off in another direction) would have struggled up the hill away from the garden, bringing them to the track leading over the summit to Bethany. We already know quite a lot about Peter's character. Had he not sworn, only an hour or so previously, that he would never desert Jesus, even if it meant going to die with Him? Yet here he was, at the first sign of trouble, running away. 'John,' we can almost hear him say, 'I can't do this. We must go back. I promised. Even if we are to be arrested, I must go.' And so John, who was to go with him, and Peter turned back and retraced their steps, passed the garden and across the brook and up the hill. This would explain why the three Synoptists all say that he followed 'at a distance'.

It is at this point that Saint John takes up the story. The two of them arrive at the gate leading into the courtyard of the High Priest's palace, which is, of course, closed after the reception of the arresting party. Fortunately, John is known to the portress, who seeing him coming immediately opens the gate to let him in. After a mutual salutation she sees

Peter, whom she does not know, and is wary of letting him in, so closes the gate. John, finding that Peter is not with him, goes back, tells the girl that this man is a friend of his and vouches for him, so that, on John's recommendation, Peter also enters the courtyard. It would seem natural for the girl to ask Peter as he passed through the gate, 'Are you also one of the disciples of the man they have just brought in?' 'No,' was the reply, and so comes the first denial. There is general agreement that Peter said that he did not know Jesus or that he was not a disciple of Jesus three times. Saint Mark makes one of the maids of the High Priest say to him, '"And thou also wast with Jesus of Nazareth," to which Peter replied that he did not know what she was talking about, and then he went out into the porch.' In that gospel Jesus had said 'before the cock crow twice, thou shalt deny me thrice'. At this point, with great dramatic effect, Saint Mark says that the cock crew. Then 'a maid saw him again' and said to them standing about that he was one of them. It is not clear whether it was the same maid or another one. Lastly, Peter was approached by a number of people, who told him that he must be one of Jesus' party, because he was a Galilean; his north country accent had given him away. This time Peter got angry and with great vehemence said that he did not know who Jesus was. The drama is here intensified with the second crowing of the cock. Peter then remembered and collapsed, completely shattered.

Saint Matthew follows Saint Mark almost verbatim in his telling of the story, except that he makes it quite clear that the first two denials were made to different maid-servants. From a literary point of view the first gospel is couched in less dramatic writing than the second. At the supper Saint Matthew had caused Jesus to say to Peter, before the cock crowed, 'thou shalt deny.' There was no suggestion of a double crowing as in Saint Mark. Consequently the narration has lost the intensification of the suspense and the drama. We have already seen something of Saint Mark's skill in writing by his inspired ending of his gospel with a sentence begun but not completed; this is another example of a great literary ability.

The third gospel gives some additional details which are omitted by the other two Synoptists. It must always be borne in mind that the author of the first gospel had no active part to play in the events which he is here describing. The information he had, which enabled him to put in little extras, must either be his own invention or the result of conversations subsequently with some who had been closely involved. It is true that Saint Mark says that Peter was warming himself when he made his first denial, but Saint Luke adds the graphic detail that they had kindled a fire. No doubt because of the unusual activity late at night caused by the arrest, and the consequent arrangements which had to be made for the judicial procedures, it would seem that there would be coming and going for some considerable time. A fire was lit and the brazier placed in midst of the hall. The word used can certainly be used for a roofed chamber, but it more usually refers to a courtyard, and here it would probably apply to an open cloistered court, similar to the atrium of a typical Roman house. Amongst those bystanders who seized the opportunity provided by the warmth to draw close to and sit beside it was Peter. Again we have the three questions and the three denials. It is also stated that the first two enquiries came from women, and the last from a man. Also again we have the declaration that identification was aided by Peter's regional accent.

But Saint Luke contains a unique piece of dramatic irony in the telling: 'And Peter said, "Man! I know not what thou art saying." And immediately, while he yet spake, the cock crew. And the Lord turned and looked upon Peter.

And Peter remembered the word of the Lord, how he had said unto him, "Before the cock crow, thou shalt deny me thrice." And Peter went out, and wept bitterly' (Luke 22:60–62). The third question, we are told, came about an hour after the earlier denials had been made. It is quite clear that Peter was not actually present at the trial, and therefore would not have been able to see Jesus, who could turn and look upon him. To discover an explanation we are obliged to consider these verses against the Johannine account. Alone in the fourth gospel is it stated that, when Jesus had been brought into the palace, He was not conducted directly into the judgement hall. There would surely not have been time for the members of the Sanhedrin to be assembled. In this version, after Jesus had been escorted into the palace, 'The captain of the officers and Jews led Jesus away to Annas first; for he was father-in-law to Caiaphas, which was the High Priest that same year' (John 18:13). Time was not being wasted. Before the actual trial took place, it would have been desirable to hold a preliminary interrogation so that the case for the prosecution could be prepared; Caiaphas was busy assembling the Council and gathering the witnesses, so that this inquiry could be handed over to be conducted by his father-in-law. It was not a pleasant session. First Jesus answered Annas that he spoke openly to the world: 'I ever taught in the synagogue and in the temple, where the Jews always resort; and in secret have I said nothing. Why askest thou me? Ask them which heard me, what I have said unto them.' From Annas's point of view this was not at all a helpful answer. As often happens in such interrogations there was a resort to violence, to what perhaps nowadays would be described as third degree methods. One of the guards slapped Jesus hard on the face and told Him not to be impudent. Of course, we do not have a complete and full report of this interview, but it must have lasted for some considerable time. Although there was a necessity for great speed if all were to be accomplished before the onset of the feast, it would certainly be at least an hour before the trial preparations could be made and the Council, or as many of them as could be available, assembled. 'Now Annas had sent him bound unto Caiaphas the High Priest.' This would almost certainly require Jesus to be conducted through the hall, and therefore it could have been that Jesus was being led past Peter at the moment that Peter made his third denial. True, a most dramatic piece of writing, but one which nevertheless could well have been an accurate statement of what occurred.

Saint John leaves us at the point where Jesus is taken into the official trial before Caiaphas, but says nothing whatsoever about it. His next statement is, 'Then led they Jesus from Caiaphas into the hall of judgement: and it was early; and they themselves went not into the judgement hall lest they should be defiled: but that they might eat the Passover.' According to his own account Saint John was already somewhere inside the palace. Assuredly he would not have been far away from Peter, who had been allowed in on his responsibility. From the Synoptists we know that Peter had realised on this third denial what he had done. With pregnant restraint we are told that 'He wept bitterly'. He was a broken man, now incapable of anything but utter remorse, bitterness and anger with himself. He would not have known what he was doing or where he was going. In such circumstances, what would John have done? His friend was in deep distress and needed help and protection. Can one imagine John doing anything other than going to him and trying to get him to come away? And where would he have taken him? Not far away was his own house, which was the most obvious haven; it was near and it was handy. Where else could he have taken him? Besides, there were women there who would look after him. First there would be Salome, John's own mother, and almost certainly Jesus' mother would also be staying for the feast with her sister. Furthermore, it would appear most likely that Cleopas and his wife were also in the house, because they too were close relations. While Jesus was being tried before the Sanhedrin, John was busily engaged doing other things, looking after his friend and companion.

So the curtain falls on the great events of Maundy Thursday. Saint John tells us that when the trial was over and Jesus taken to be presented to Pilate for sentencing, 'it was early.' From what we have been told it is possible to build up a fairly accurate account of what had happened. There had been three scenes: the upper room, the Garden of Gethsemane and the High Priest's house. It is clear that to gain a complete picture, we need to have all four separate accounts and put them together. Every pericope is required, and although the underlying themes of each of the Evangelists may vary in emphasis and intent, causing them to make a selection of the material at their disposal, either from written documents or even from their own memories, we who read our Bibles need all the accounts that we have been given; if just one of them had been omitted, there would result an unsolved question about the historicity of the occurrences. This again is one of the considerations which cause us to say that the Bible is inspired writing, and that the Church was also inspired in making her selection of those books which are to be considered canonical.

Before our curtain rises again on the enactment of the events of the day when the world was saved from its fragmentation, humanity from its condemnation and men and women from their sin, it would be advisable to check where all the principal characters were. Jesus was in the hands of the authorities and was being led from Caiaphas to Pilate. John and Peter had gone to John's house where Mary the Mother, Salome, Mary Cleopas and her husband would also most likely be. Judas had gone to his own place, we know not where, before he made a last appearance in the temple, desperately to hurl the silver pieces back at them that had paid him. Lazarus, who was still a wanted man, together with his sisters would be, as we should say, keeping a low profile at their home in Bethany, awaiting the other nine disciples who would have made their way, no doubt expecting to be, like Lazarus, wanted men. There seems to be some uncertainty about Thomas. We do not hear of him again until after Easter. He was certainly not about on Easter Day, but he was given the news some time afterwards, and before Low Sunday. We know that he was a twin, and it could be speculated that if the brother, or perhaps a sister, were somewhere in the city or nearby, he may have gone there. But this is pure speculation for which there is no written evidence whatsoever. There were also the brethren of our Lord. It would seem that they had gone up for the feast, because after His resurrection Jesus told the women to give the news to his brethren and to tell them to go back to Galilee so that He could see them there. They do not make any appearance throughout the whole of the weekend. Of course they too would not be feeling either safe or easy. They were the accused's family and also closely related to a known felon. This would also probably explain that although Mary Cleopas is spoken of as being present at the cross, her husband receives no such recognition. He too would have wondered whether he were a suspect and therefore kept out of the way.

The world now waits for the moment in time in which occurred the most important event after the Creation: the day we call Good Friday.

Chapter V
Act Two: Good Friday

The day opens with the arrival of the escort party coming from the High Priest's palace at the Castle of Antonia, where presumably the Governor would have been in residence. Although Caiaphas had got from the Sanhedrin the verdict he wanted, it had not been done by altogether legal means. In Jewish law no one could be convicted except on the evidence of at least two independent witnesses, with the accused not permitted to be a witness in his own case. Caiaphas had not been able to produce two witnesses who could tell exactly the same tale. He had then, as it were, put Jesus, the accused, into the witness box, and asked Him directly whether He were the Messiah. According to Saint Mark's version, Jesus answered by using the divine name, adding, 'and ye shall see the Son of Man sitting on the right hand of power and coming in the clouds of heaven.' Saint Matthew balks at such a usage and writes merely 'thou has said', but does add the words about the right hand of power and the clouds of heaven. Saint Luke, to whom as a Gentile the full implications of the speaking of the name of God would not be understood as it would be by a Jew, keeps the words in substance, but makes certain adjustments, Whereas both of the first two Evangelists state that the Council met for the trial in the night time, Saint Luke says that the trial began 'as soon as it was day' (22:66). To the question 'Art thou the Christ? Tell us,' Jesus at first prevaricates, 'If I tell you, you will not believe; and if I also ask you, ye will not answer nor let me go.' He does add, however, as in the other Synoptists, that thereafter would the Son of Man sit on the right hand of the power of God. 'Then said they all, "Art thou the Son of God?"' Jesus makes the answer: 'Ye say that I am.' If this were to mean that Jesus was telling them that it was they who said that He was the son of God, it would be extremely difficult to understand what was meant. If, on the other hand, He was telling them that they spoke God's name, literally that would be untrue because they did not. This confusion probably reflects Saint Luke's Gentile upbringing. In either case the εγω ειμι is quoted, and Saint Luke must have realised from his use of Saint Mark that it had deep significance, as he ends the account with the words, 'And they said, "What need we any further witness? We ourselves have heard of his own mouth."' The charge was one of blasphemy, the trial had been conducted, not quite strictly according to law, but the evidence had been produced and the case proved. The only possible verdict was that of death. Why was the sentence then not carried out?

Saint John says (18:31) that the Jews did not have the authority themselves to implement the death penalty. This, however, as it stands, cannot strictly be true. Saint Luke, writing in the Book of Acts, gives a full account of the trial of Stephen. Certain Jewish congregations in Jerusalem, some of them composed of people from the Diaspora, found Stephen's teaching offensive, but were not equal to making a persuasive rejection of his doctrine. They then adopted other means:

They suborned men which said, 'We have heard him speak blasphemous words against Moses, and against God.' And they stirred up the people and the elders and the scribes, and came upon him, and caught him, and brought him to the Council, and set up false witnesses which said, 'This man ceaseth not to speak blasphemous words against this holy place, and the law; for we have heard him say that this Jesus of Nazareth shall destroy this place, and shall change the customs which Moses delivered us.' And all that sat in the Council, looking steadfastly upon him, saw his face as it had been the face of an angel. (Acts 6:11–15)

Saint Luke gives a long transcript of Stephen's speech of defence, which apparently caused such great annoyance and irritation that they took him out and executed him according to their law which posed as the penalty for blasphemy, death by stoning. Saint John himself also makes Pilate say to the crowd demanding the crucifixion of Jesus: 'Take ye him and crucify him; for I find no fault in him.'

Whatever were the legalities of the situation, the Jewish authorities were determined not to be responsible themselves for the death of Jesus. We know that Caiaphas was a shrewd and careful politician, and he had advised the Council that there would be occasions when it was necessary that the life of one man, who by implication might be innocent, should be sacrificed for the benefit of the people as a whole (John 11:51). Here is a further example of his political manoeuvring. Pilate, however, would never be impressed with being asked to pass sentence on one who had been convicted on a Jewish charge of blasphemy. The charge therefore had to be changed, so Caiaphas took Jesus to Pilate as a traitor to the occupying power of Rome. Saint Luke gives the deposition of Caiaphas in full: 'We found this fellow perverting the nation, and forbidding to give tribute to Caesar, saying the he himself is Christ, a king.' In giving evidence the charges were made that 'He stirreth up the people teaching throughout all Jewry, beginning from

Galilee to this place.' The mention of Galilee gives Pilate the possible 'get-out'; he obviously does not want the responsibility of doing something which might well have caused a disturbance of the peace. He had already been in trouble with the imperial authorities for not being careful enough around Jewish religious sensitivities. Saint Luke is the only one who tells of the visit to Herod, who himself was in residence in the capital at that time. Slippery as ever, he was interested to see Jesus, pleased with having an opportunity to assert his jurisdiction against the Roman Procurator; but beyond that, he wanted nothing more to do with the sensitive case. Presumably it was because of the abortive nature of this encounter that the other Evangelists did not consider it worth reporting.

It must be remembered that not one of Jesus' disciples or anyone connected with Him would have been actually present at the preliminary interrogation by Annas or at either of the trials. The Jews would not enter the court-room so as to keep themselves ceremonially clean for the feast, so there are reports of several appearances of Pilate outside to speak to the prosecutors. Indeed the dialogues which occurred in public bear a marked similarity in all four accounts, whereas the reportage of what was said and done within the Roman court must largely be deduction rather than accurate transcription. The Johannine account of the trial before Pilate is the fullest and contains some superb dramatic writing, well illustrated by Pilate's two questions: 'Am I a Jew?' and 'What is truth?' From the author's intimate knowledge of Jesus and his close association with Him, we no doubt gain a fairly truthful picture of what actually transpired.

Pilate therefore succumbed and gave the necessary orders for the crucifixion. Jesus was to be put to death by the Romans. From a judicial point of view the whole case bristles with irregularities. Caiaphas pronounced a guilty verdict after an illegal procedure, and then changed the charge. Pilate decided to retry the case, and having found the prisoner innocent, nonetheless passed on him the supreme penalty. No doubt from both their angles there were mitigating circumstances. Caiaphas needed to avoid responsibility if at all possible; Pilate had at all costs to keep the peace and prevent any riot, if his own career were to be safeguarded. He dared not risk another reproof from the Emperor. But, in the end, Jesus had been delivered into the hands of wicked men who led Him out to be crucified.

Let us now return to what was happening to the others. Presumably Peter was still 'hors de combat', completely devastated by what he had done, and he would not have been in a fit condition to take any part in the public proceedings. He certainly would not dare to meet Jesus, in those terrible circumstances under which a meeting would alone be possible. Jesus' mother, on the other hand, felt that she needed to be there to see her Son and give Him what comfort she could throughout the unspeakable agonies that were to be His. John went to give his aunt what support he could, and no doubt he himself felt the need to go to the scene of the execution. And it would also seem that the other two ladies in the house decided to go with them, Mary Cleopas and Salome. Cleopas certainly seems to have been there, because we find him walking back to Emmaus on Easter afternoon, but no doubt he would have considered that it would be safer to stay away. It would also have been safer for the women not to be seen as a group, which could have caused trouble.

Now we must go over the hill to Bethany and the house there. As Good Friday dawned there would be there Lazarus and his sisters, and eight or nine of the disciples. The disciples were in a sense in hiding. Jesus had been arrested and news had come that he had been condemned by the Procurator as a rebel. They were His disciples and therefore they were under the gravest suspicion, and it would have been dangerous at that stage for any of them to go out of doors. When you are a close associate of a rebel leader, you are also involved in the potential rising. Lazarus too was still wanted by the Jewish authorities because he had been brought back to life and was a potential source of danger to the stability of the nation. Poor Martha was, presumably, as usual much encumbered with household duties. Mary, however, was of different mettle. In the first place she would not be so well known as her other relations. Still being known as Mary of Magdala she had amongst the citizens of Jerusalem a certain anonymity. It will be recalled that she had come home after a life of some notoriety elsewhere, for it is clear the seven devils had gone out of her. She therefore was the one who had greater freedom of movement. Also, from what we know of her personality, she was of a more flamboyant nature and would have fewer qualms at making journeys herself or going into dangerous places. She therefore would be the one to go over the Mount of Olives and into the city to see what was happening. That would explain her presence on the hill of Golgotha.

We do not need to dwell upon the shame, brutality and sheer horror of the mechanics of crucifixion. Indeed they are almost past description. Traditionally Jesus spoke seven times while he was on the cross. The first of these was when He was actually being nailed, and He asked His Father to forgive the soldiers, because they did not know what they were doing. This is reported only by Saint Luke. Saint Luke is the only one also who quotes the dialogue between the thieves who were crucified with Jesus, one on either side. One joined in the general railing and barracking, the mocking and the sarcasm, while the other reproved him, saying that they two deserved their punishment, but the other man had done nothing wrong.

The placard said that He was a King of the Jews. Well, the thief would have reasoned, as that was not possible, He must have been a little deranged or suffering from delusions of grandeur, neither of which were crimes. Then as a gesture of indulgent sympathy – or could it have a tinge of sarcasm in it? – he addressed Jesus as though He really were a king: 'Lord, remember me when thou comest into thy kingdom.' Addressed as a King, as a King He replies: 'Today thou shalt be with Me in Paradise.' Paradise is a Persian concept; because of the strict rules of etiquette and protocol in the courts of Persian kings, no subject was permitted to look upon the face of Majesty. All subjects in approaching their royal master had to do the obeisance, lying prostrate on the floor, and so that the royal visage might not be seen, the king held before his face something like a fan. It was not possible for a Persian king to have any social intercourse or intimate relationship. Such an impossible way of life was rendered partially endurable by there being constructed in the midst of the palace complex a privy garden, to which from time to time the king could resort, and there meet his friends and talk with them man to man. This haven was known as the Paradison. When Jesus spoke from the cross to the dying thief, He promised that come that very day, when He would be in His realm, the robber would not only be remembered in the kingdom, but admitted into the private apartments. The only other declaration from the cross which Saint Luke reports is that 'when Jesus had cried with a loud voice, he said, "Father into thy hands I commend my spirit," and having said this, he gave up the ghost.' It is interesting to note that at the moment of His final surrender, Jesus uttered the words which His mother would have taught Him, as every Jewish mother taught her son, to say each night as he composed Himself for sleep.

Saint Mark tells that before the nailing to the cross, Jesus was offered a drink of heavy wine to blunt the pain, but says that He refused it. He tells of the casting of the lots upon the clothing which had become the perquisite of the soldiers commissioned to carry out the execution, and of the crucifixion of the other two. He tells of the mocking, the railing and the wagging of the heads, but there is no record that Jesus said anything at all. We pass into the sixth hour, when the priests would have had to depart to attend to their ceremonial duties in the temple, and when it would seem that there was an eclipse of the sun. There was darkness over the whole land from the sixth hour until the ninth hour. Then, with great dramatic intensity there is a cry from the cross, 'Eloi, Eloi, lamma Sabachthani.' – 'My God, my God why hast thou forsaken me?' Christian devotees throughout the ages have always believed that this cry has much deeper significance than that Jesus was merely saying to Himself the twenty-second psalm. It would seem that this was the nadir of the experience of self-giving. Then, says Saint Mark, when Jesus had cried again with a loud voice, He gave up the ghost. Saint Matthew follows Saint Mark verbatim in this passage, and both say that the cry of desolation was interpreted as a request for drink, and that one of them that stood by took a sponge, filled it with sour wine and put it on a reed, offering it to Jesus' lips.

Both Saint Matthew and Saint Mark say that at the moment of the Lord's death the veil of the temple was rent in twain. There is a sufficiency of evidence from the accounts to say that there was a stormy atmosphere, which resulted in at least earth tremors, if not a full scale earthquake. Such a seismic disturbance could indeed have caused the veil in the sanctuary to be torn. That veil had stood for the separation between God and man which sin had caused. Sceptics are tempted to ask whether this is simply a piece of graphic writing and literary symbolism or whether the veil was actually torn. Does it matter? Nevertheless, if one accepts the fact that the victim, whose life at that moment expired, was none other than the eternal God, God the Son, the Second Person of the most Holy and Undivided Trinity, by whom all things were made, it would perhaps be surprising if the veil had not been rent asunder.

The fourth gospel tells of a further speech from the cross in the early part of the time spent upon it. It will, however, be remembered that Saint John states definitely that it was at the sixth hour that Jesus was crucified, although we have already seen reason to believe that the time of the third hour given by the Synoptists is more likely to be the accurate one. Jesus saw His mother and His beloved cousin standing there. Not wanting His mother to see the dreadful final agonies of crucified men, Jesus commended her to John that he might take care of her, and with loving attention asked Mary to take care of John: 'And from that hour that disciple took her into his own home' (John 19:27). This has generally been interpreted by later generations to mean that Mary went to live with John and stayed with him for the rest of her life. There is even a tradition that she was still living with him when he went to be the Apostle at Ephesus, and today visitors will be shown the house where she died. Visitors to Jerusalem are also shown the house where she died in the upper city on the hill of Zion. But that is not what the gospel says. 'From that hour' means surely *at that precise moment* John took Mary to his own house, which, after all, was just around the corner. The other ladies who had accompanied her would naturally also go with them. But Mary Magdalene, who would no doubt know of the house of John, lived at Bethany. She was a younger woman, she had an enterprising nature and 'she loved much', so remained to see it through to the bitter end. That was surely the reason for the tradition that Mary

Magdalene was at the cross throughout the whole period. We do know that she was present at the deposition, when the bodies were taken down later in the afternoon.

John does not mention the cry of desolation, 'My God, my God, why hast thou forsaken me?' This is probably because he was not present when it was uttered; he had taken the ladies back to his house. It would seem, however, that when he had seen that they were settled, he did return to the scene of the crucifixion, for he reports that Jesus said 'I thirst'. Saint Mark and Saint Matthew say that there was a response to the awful 'My God, my God' cry, as though Jesus had said 'I thirst', and Saint John here gives the explanation. All three Synoptists say that just before Jesus expired, He uttered a loud cry, but do not tell us what it was that He said. Saint John, who would have returned to the scene, is able to give us the actual word. It is a great shout of triumph, the full trumpet-like sound of which can only be heard when it is spoken in the Greek – τετελεσται. It is not an easy word to translate into English. 'It is finished' is the translation offered by the Authorised Version. Others have 'It is perfected'. 'It is brought to a conclusion' would also be a possibility. The one which best catches the spirit of the word is perhaps the less literary and more colloquial 'I've done it!' When Jesus was born in Bethlehem of Judaea, He was God made man, fully and completely God, and also fully and completely man. If this had not been so, He could not have been the Saviour of the world. For then He would have been a man and, even though He could possibly be taken up into the Godhead or come to be regarded as full of the Holy Spirit even to the point of being the most godlike of all creatures, He would still be a man. Because God's creature was made for love, then freedom was inalienably made his in order that he might respond to the free love of God; for love can never be compelled, forced, bought, commanded or even cajoled.

To be love it must be freely given. It is the one freedom that can never be removed, despoiled or deprived. In the days of slavery, a man could go to the market and buy a human being. He could make that piece of property do whatever he required of him, he could force obedience in every particular. The one thing he could not make him do was to like him. Many slaves did like their masters, some even were totally devoted to them, but this was a quality which had to be freely given. If, however, that freedom was abused and one of God's creatures, in however small a capacity, decided to live his own life in his own way and go off on his own, then the whole structure of God's creation would have a piece missing. It would be fragmented, the structure broken. Every other particle of which that structure would have been made, would also share in that fragmentation, and the universe would have lost its unity. Matters could only be rectified if a perfect life, a life untainted by that fragmentation could be made available, that all might enter into it. Such a life could only be provided by the God who made it all. But the life into which human beings could be called to enter must also itself be human. This is why if Jesus were not both God and man he could not be the Saviour. Because He was perfect man, He was tempted in all things as we are. He could have succumbed to a temptation to sin. The temptation must have been at its greatest and most powerful when He said 'My God, my God, why hast thou forsaken me?' But he did not yield. His love for the Father remained, and so He could and would save the world. A perfect life was surrendered. This is no tragedy but a great and overwhelming victory: 'τετελεσται', 'I've done it.' And with this He bows His head and gives up the ghost. John is the only one who gives us the actual word, and for Saint John the Passion and crucifixion of the Lord is His glorification. The first two Synoptists give a supplementary and equally dramatic line when they report that the centurion, a soldier, Roman and a Gentile, makes his great confession: 'Truly, this man was a God!'

Almost as soon as it was seen that Jesus was well and truly dead, things began to move quickly. It is at this point that all four Evangelists introduce Joseph of Arimathaea. Saint Mark says that 'he was an honourable counsellor, who also waited for the kingdom of God'. Saint Matthew tells that 'he was a rich man of Arimathaea, named Joseph, who also himself was Jesus' disciple'. Saint Luke introduces him with the words, 'And behold, there was a man named Joseph, a counsellor, and he was a good man and a just. The same had not consented to the counsel and deed of them; he was of Arimathaea, a city of the Jews: who also himself waited for the kingdom of God.' Saint John says that he was a disciple of Jesus, but secretly, for fear of the Jews.

This man, and again all the Evangelists report it, went himself to Pilate to ask for the body of Jesus. Saint Matthew says that Pilate was astonished that Jesus was already dead. Usually men would hang on the cross for much longer, even for days on some occasions, because the mechanics of crucifixion, although causing untold and extreme agony, did not in themselves kill. Usually death came either by hypostatic pneumonia or gangrene from the untended wounds. It was also the custom to leave the bodies hanging on the crosses until picked clean by carrion or generally disintegrated. They believed that this would provide an exemplary lesson to other intending law breakers. However, according to the first Evangelist, Pilate first asked for assurance that death had occurred, before he gave the permission for an individual to be granted possession of the body. This was indeed contrary to Roman custom. It could well be that he was glad to be relieved of this matter and to have the corpse well and truly taken out of sight.

For the Jews it was most desirable that the bodies should be removed before the oncome of the Sabbath. On this particular occasion it was all the more important because of the feast, 'for that Sabbath was a high day' (John 19:31). Although we can gather from the model of the city in the hotel garden, which is archaeologically authentic according to contemporary discoveries, that it would quite easily have been possible for citizens and visitors to be able to leave and enter the walls without actually being confronted with the sight of the execution, nevertheless according to the Mosaic law to behold a naked body, and even more a corpse, was to be rendered ceremonially unclean. Because of the time taken in the rites of cleansing, if, even by chance, this sight were beheld, the viewer would have been precluded from taking part in some of the festal ceremonies. It was therefore most important, not only that Jesus' body should be removed, but also the bodies of the other two. They, however, were still alive, and certainly no permission would be given for them to be taken down until they had expired.

It is Saint John who again provides the explanation (19:31–34):

> The Jews therefore, because... the bodies should not remain upon the cross on the Sabbath day, (for that Sabbath day was a high day) besaught Pilate that their legs might be broken, and that they might be taken away. Then came the soldiers and brake the legs of the first, and of the other which was crucified with him. But when they came to Jesus, and saw that he was dead already, they brake not his legs, but one of the soldiers with a spear pierced his side, and forthwith came there out blood and water.

Used as we are to seeing artistic reproductions of the crucifixion of our Lord for devotional purposes, we are apt to forget that in actuality the later representations bear little resemblance to the real facts. In the first place the footstool attached to the upright of the cross and the loin cloth are the result of artistic convention rather than of historical reality. The victim was crucified naked and one foot was placed over the other, with one nail piercing both. This put the condemned man into an intolerable position, for with the arms stretched out, it would be necessary for the diaphragm to be expanded before the man could breathe. Each breath he took would need to have exertion put upon the leg muscles, which itself would cause acute agony. If, however, the legs were put into a condition in which that pressure was no longer able to be applied, then the diaphragm could not be expanded, and the victim would die almost instantaneously of asphyxiation.

Before the carbon dating experiment was permitted to be undertaken on the fabric known as the Holy Shroud of Turin, Ian Wilson, an Oxford history graduate, had been convinced that it was the authentic piece of material in which the Lord's body was wrapped when it was laid in the sepulchre. He had been convinced that the photographic negative image which it revealed was certainly that of a man who had been crucified, and he made the leap forward to assert that in his opinion it was none other than Jesus Himself (although he did admit that there was not a one hundred per cent proof). In discussing the piercing of the Lord's side as recorded in the New Testament, he quoted in support of his thesis certain medical authorities. One need not quote all the passage; it is to be found in what became a best-selling book entitled *The Turin Shroud*. After presenting medical evidence for the outpouring of blood creating the image imprinted on the cloth and opining that it was authentic, Wilson continues:

What about the water? No less than three different and eminent medical men have formulated theories on this. Barbet, required by French law to experiment with corpses not less than twenty-four hours old – and badly hampered by this – thought the water to have been pericardial fluid, normally present in the body only in teaspoonful quantity, but increased by the maltreatment and scourging the man of the shroud had clearly undergone. The German radiologist, Moedder, thought that it was fluid from the pleural sac, again increased in quantity because of the rough handling. But the most well formulated theory – and the most recent – appears to be that of the American, Dr Antony Sava. He has noted that in his surgical experiences of cases of severe violence against the rib cage, without an open wound, there frequently results an accumulation of bloody fluid in the pleural cavity, this being a response of the bruised lung surface to the injury. The amount of fluid can be considerable. In an experiment Sava took samples that he noted did not coagulate, but settled to the heavy dark red consistency, with clear light fluid above.

We now have the results of the experiments and the shroud has been shown to be a forgery. As was said at the time, however, there are still many questions to be asked about it. One of these must surely be how did the forger, whoever he was, come to know so much about the technique of crucifixion that he could produce an image which gave apparent accuracy to such a degree that eminent men of science had been persuaded that if the shroud were shown to be of the first century, then there could be no doubt that the body it had covered had been that of a crucified man? Assuming therefore that the image, while not being authentic, is an accurate enough depiction of what would have happened in the case of a crucifixion, the evidence given by the medical men whom Wilson quotes cannot be disregarded. It would seem, then, that it is distinctly possible that when the soldier thrust his spear into Jesus' side, there would come out both blood and water.

Or so it would appear. Saint John, the great theologian that he was, in writing about it, states it in such a way that there is a hint about a deeper understanding of the significance of the Lord's blood. If we could assume that whoever wrote the fourth gospel also wrote the first epistle which bears the name of John, we can see how the experience he had had on Good Friday remained in his mind and nurtured a profound and elemental truth of the Christian calling. In chapter five, at verse five, he writes:

> Who is he that overcometh the world, but he that believeth that Jesus is the Son of God? This is he that came by water and blood, even Jesus Christ; not by water only, but by water and blood. And it is the Spirit that beareth witness, because the Spirit is truth. For there are three that bear record in heaven, the Father, the Word and the Holy Ghost: and these three are one. And there are three that bear witness in earth, the spirit, the water and the blood, and these three agree in one.

Here we have a wonderful example of the way in which all the various parts of the New Testament hang together and supplement each other. It is also an example of the way in which the experiences of those who stood about the cross and took part in those cataclysmic events could see in them theological significance and deep spiritual meaning. Contrary to what many biblical scholars have been saying for a number of years, namely that in the New Testament we have the writings of theologians belonging to a later period of the Church's life, who are reporting (and possibly inventing) occasions whilst purporting to be historical so as to illustrate the truths they were wishing to convey, it would appear to be more likely that it was the historic event, faithfully recorded, which caused the theology to develop. This would be in the true prophetic tradition. It was from reflection upon the events of the Exodus, the deliverance from Egypt, the crossing of the Red Sea and the manifestation at Mount Sinai, that the prophets of the Old Testament were able to draw out all the great and profound religious truths which are revealed in the scriptures.

We return to Joseph of Arimathaea, having gained permission from Pilate to take possession of Jesus' body. Presumably he would return to the scene of the crucifixion and, showing his authorisation, would order the body to be taken down. It would also seem that he had taken the precaution of arming himself with a sheet in which to wrap the body temporarily, because there would not be time to complete the full ritual of the grave clothes before the onset of the Sabbath. We have already seen how skilfully Saint Mark has told this aspect of the story, using the same word for the sheet as the one he used for the piece of cloth he had wrapped around his naked body when he was in the Garden of Gethsemane.

In the Church of the Holy Sepulchre at Jerusalem, which would seem to cover the authentic sites of the crucifixion and entombment, the place has, over the centuries, been so hacked about by pious labour, and encrusted with devotional marble, gilt and tinsel, and blackened by the smoke of incense and charred by burning wicks, that for the present-day pilgrim, what was there is now altogether covered. It is not easy even in imagination to recreate the scene as it would have been on that first Good Friday. The crosses would be close to the city wall.

That indeed would be certain because we know that that was the usual kind of place where executions could be effected. Very near to the place was a garden. That too is assured because of the emphasised declaration in the fourth gospel. That the tomb belonged to Joseph of Arimathaea is quite certain, for all the Evangelists bear witness to that. Joseph was rich, and rich men liked to have their mortal remains deposited in elegant tombs. Even today, in Italy for example, there are in cemeteries tombs belonging to the well-to-do, which resemble miniature temples in their own private enclosures. This tomb was hewn out of the rock, and Joseph had got it ready for himself when his time should come, but with generosity he surrendered it for Jesus' use. (In parenthesis it is fascinating to wonder whether indeed it was used subsequently by Joseph, but on close consideration that would have been most unlikely. By the time that Joseph would be needing it for the deposition of his own body, it would have become, both for him and all those who were known as Christians, a holy place. This special sanctity would cause it to be a shrine, a place of pilgrimage, to which presumably Christians could resort, even after the destruction of Jerusalem in AD 70, because it would still be outside the city wall. No doubt this was the reason, or one of the reasons, why Hadrian, on the refounding of the city as a Roman colony in AD 135, included the site within the new wall and caused a pagan temple to be erected upon it. In this way, unwittingly, he would ensure that the place could be remembered, so that when the Empire had a ruler who professed to be a Christian, knowing of this custom of building pagan temples on the sites of local sanctuaries, he could guess where the tomb had been, demolish the temple and build a church. In point of fact this guess was made by Constantine's mother, Saint Helena, who claimed to have received the revelation in a dream. The contours of the land would not have been altered and, sure enough, there were found the remains of a tomb and a mound nearby. Constantine would then have enclosed the whole under the one great dome and building, and the Church of the Holy Sepulchre as we know it today would have arisen.)

We remember that, when Joseph went to Pilate, Mary Magdalene was in all probability still at the cross. Joseph would certainly in any case have made some sort of contact with the family. From the fact that John was able to provide the explanation as to why a soldier treated the recitation of the first verse of the twenty-second psalm as a request for a drink, by reporting that Jesus in point of fact did make a statement that He was thirsty, it can be deduced that he had returned to the scene and had arrived there in time for the last moments. In this case he would have been available as a messenger to give the news of the death to the women and to report that arrangements were being made for the burial. Because, according to Jewish custom, burial rites were usually performed by women, some of them at least would therefore have felt obliged straight away to go to this little garden where the Councillor had his tomb and be on hand to do what was needed. At this point in the narration Nicodemus makes another appearance. Saint John is the only Evangelist to mention Nicodemus at all. He was a Master in Israel, for it was as such that Jesus addressed him on the occasion of his nocturnal visit. In introducing the narration of Nicodemus' conversation with Jesus, Saint John tells us that he was a 'ruler of the Jews', which must mean that he was a member of the Sanhedrin, as indeed was Joseph of Arimathaea. These two men must also have been in close collusion with each other at the time of the crucifixion, because when Joseph arrives at the sepulchre with the body and the shroud, Nicodemus also appears (John 19:39) with a hundred pound weight of spices. Now in the preparations of a body for burial according to Jewish custom, a very great deal of spice was used. This amount, however, does seem to have been a little excessive. Transposed into contemporary measurements it would come at the lowest reckoning to about three and a half stones. It would thus have been rather a heavy load for one man, and one presumably not in the first bloom of youth at that. Perhaps John came back again to assist him! Some scholars have pointed out that the fourth Evangelist has a certain characteristic of making unduly generous provision for immediate needs, and quote the large gallonage of water which was turned into wine to rescue the celebration at Cana when the commissioned supply had been exhausted. In his reporting of the marriage it would certainly be a point that Saint John was wishing to make about the overflowing generosity of God in providing for the needs of men. But again this gracious over-provision being made could well be to the Evangelist a sign of God's superabundant love. We are also told that Joseph of Arimathaea was very rich, and rich men often like to appear somewhat flamboyant in their generosity. There is also the feeling about it being better to have too much than too little, and a lot was needed.

By this time it had become quite clear that there would not be sufficient daylight left for all the ceremonies to be done and the preparations made before the onset of the Sabbath, which was strictly at sundown. The body was therefore wrapped in the winding sheet and the load of spices left beside it in the sepulchre, and the stone was rolled against the opening. There are many such tombs which have been discovered around Jerusalem dating from this period and there seem to have been two ways of sealing them and making them secure, both involving the use of a large stone. One was to have a piece of masonry large enough to place inside the opening, rather like a stopper, and the other was to have a groove along which a stone, hewn into a circular shape, could be rolled into place, and presumably sealed in some way. This is clearly stated to have been the method used in this particular tomb because both Saint Matthew and Saint Mark say that the stone was rolled into place (Matthew 27:60; Mark 15:46). Because the body had to be left in this way, and it would not have been possible for the burial rites to have been completed until after the Sabbath, the stone would be placed in position for security. We know that it was a large one because we are told that on Easter morning, as the women went to the tomb, they were worried as to whether anyone would be available to roll it back for them, because it was too large and heavy for the women to move by themselves (Mark 16:3). It would not, however, be finally sealed, because access would be required to complete the business on the Sunday morning as early as possible. Speedy interment is still the rule in hot climates.

At this point we must pause to see who was actually present when the body was deposited in the sepulchre. For certain, Joseph and Nicodemus would have been present, and there is a strong possibility that John was also. There is no particular evidence for this, except that he is the only one to have reported the arrival on the scene of Nicodemus. He does not, however, mention any of the women who were there. It would be unthinkable that there were no women present, because as soon as the news would have been received in John's house that Jesus was dead, and that the body was being taken for burial, some at least of the ladies would undoubtedly have felt that it was their duty and obligation to go at once and do what would by law and custom be demanded of them. Saint Mark tells us that Mary Magdalene and Mary the mother of Joses were there; the second lady is of course, Mary Cleopas. Saint Matthew says that it was Mary Magdalene and the other Mary who were at the tomb, so thus far there is complete agreement. In view of Saint Luke's subsequent declaration that on Easter morning Joanna was one of the women who was early at the tomb, it would be extremely likely that she also was there. His report of the entombment however says:

> Those women who had come with Him from Galilee followed after, and beheld the sepulchre and how the body was laid. And they returned and prepared spices, and rested the Sabbath day according to the commandment.

The two ladies of whom we can be certain are the two Marys, Magdalene and Cleopas. There may have been others, but once again we are conscious that Saint Luke's evidence is always secondary. He does not say how many women there were, and certainly Mary Magdalene had come from Galilee, for Magdala is in Galilee, if not the other Mary as well.

The approach of the Sabbath made everyone depart. The body was at rest, the tomb was closed, and all could be safely left until the Sabbath was over. Where would they have gone? Presumably Joseph and Nicodemus would have gone to their own homes, which would not have been far away, in all probability in the Upper City. Mary Magdalene would have returned to Bethany. If she arrived at the summit of the Mount of Olives before sundown, she could have completed the journey home, because it was a distance which was permitted by the commandment as a Sabbath Day's Journey. We would perhaps expect Mary Cleopas to have returned to John's house, where undoubtedly John, if he were indeed present at the burial, would have gone. On the other hand, one of her sons was a disciple, and would most likely have been at Bethany with the others. Besides, Mary Magdalene herself, after the trying circumstances of the day, would probably have been in need of support and companionship, and it was not usual for ladies to walk considerable distances alone. It would be extremely likely that his mother would want to have seen how her son James was, and therefore because she was able to send a message by John as to where she had gone, she would have gone to Bethany with the other Mary. In this way she would have been able to give some comfort to the younger woman, who must have been in a dreadful state of grief and mental torment. She would have had to have remained at Bethany until the Sabbath was over. This would explain how it came about that these two ladies, in Saint Matthew's version, as it began to dawn towards the first day of the week, came to see the sepulchre. To arrive at the sepulchre as early as possible in the morning, they could have set off from Bethany, while it was yet dark, so as to be at the top of the Mount of Olives when the sun came over the horizon, when they could be released from the Sabbath discipline.

So the curtain falls on Good Friday. The Sabbath has started, the feast has begun. All over Jerusalem families would have been gathered together in their homes for the Passover meal, and the wonderful experience of the Exodus, when God chose the Hebrews to be His people and at the holy mount they accepted Him to be their God, would have been recalled. He had shown Himself to be their deliverer and their saviour having brought them out of the land of Egypt, their house of bondage, with a mighty hand and outstretched arm.

Chapter VI
Entr'acte: Easter Eve

Although the Sabbath was a day of rest, some activity and movement could be seen, as that Sabbath was a high day, being the day of the feast of Passover. In 1989 the present author and his wife were in Jerusalem at the time of the Jewish New Year's Festival, when the ram's horn or shofar was blown to announce the coming of the New Year. That year the feast also fell on the Sabbath, so that Sabbath was a high day also. It was a most interesting experience. The Friday itself was a very busy day, for in modern Israel the New Year is not unlike our observance of Christmas. Presents are given and families gather together. In the morning Jerusalem – though not the Old City – was very like an English city on the morning of Christmas Eve. There were crowds of last minute shoppers, the streets and markets were crowded, and as it moved towards midday, long bus queues formed at every stop, with many people carrying parcels wrapped in fancy paper, which were obviously to be offered as gifts to relations or friends, and there was generally an air of busy excitement. Trade was flourishing, people were busy, and a great event was obviously being expected and preparations being made. The traffic in the streets eased a little in the afternoon, but at six o'clock precisely (nowadays sunrise and sunset are regulated by the clock) it was as though someone had waved a wand. Suddenly, and to us Gentile strangers it seemed almost miraculously, it was all over. The shops were closed, the streets were empty, the cafés and bars were shut; no taxis plied trade, no buses ran. An occasional motorcar would drive quietly up a street, and there would be the odd pedestrian, but the city was silent and dead. On the following day the quiet continued. The synagogues were having their Sabbath services and people were going to them, but mostly on foot. Indeed in some places what were normally busy streets were closed to vehicular traffic. The Sunday also was a holiday and although people, mainly younger ones, were beginning to emerge into public places, it was still quiet, somewhat similar to our towns on Boxing Day. But then at six o'clock, again in a moment, in the twinkling of an eye, everything returned. The streets were crowded again, the cafés were open, the buses running, the shops ran up their shutters and vigorous trade was proceeding. We felt that we had had a taste of what the Sabbath would have been like all those years ago.

Back two thousand years, there was again some movement. Saint Matthew tells us of it:

> Now the next day, that followed the day of the preparation, the chief priests and Pharisees came together unto Pilate, saying, 'Sir, we remember that that deceiver said, while he was yet alive, "After three days I will rise again." Command therefore that the sepulchre be made sure until the third day, lest his disciples come by night, and steal him away, and say unto the people, "He is risen from the dead," so the last error shall be worse than the first.' Pilate said unto them, 'Ye have a watch: go your way, make it as sure as you can.' So they went and made the sepulchre sure, sealing the stone and setting a watch. (27:62–66)

The first question that needs to be asked after reading this account concerns the Lord's predictions of His Passion and resurrection. How did the chief priests and Pharisees know that Jesus had predicted His resurrection on the third day? Saint Mark, in his description of the trial of Jesus before Caiaphas, says (14:55–59):

> And the chief priests and all the Council sought for witness against Jesus to put him to death; and found none. For many bear false witness against him, but their witness agreed not together. And there arose certain saying, 'We heard him say, "I will destroy this temple that is made with hands, and in three days I will build another made without hands."' But neither so did their witness agree together.

Saint Matthew, following Saint Mark, makes certain minor changes in the language. He says:

> Now the chief priests and elders and all the Council sought false witnesses against Jesus to put him to death; but found none: yea, though many false witnesses came, yet found they none. At the last came two false witnesses, and said, 'This fellow said I am able to destroy the temple of God, and to build it in three days.'

In reporting the trial Saint Luke omits these implications about the destruction and rebuilding of the temple. Hearing language such as this, we must ask ourselves whether it would convey to the members of the Council a prediction of a bodily resurrection? If they already knew that Jesus had made such predictions it could possibly have acted as corroborative evidence, but stated by itself, as here reported, it would not be likely to have conveyed that particular meaning. The meaning conveyed would be that

Jesus was reported to have said that, if the temple were destroyed, He would rebuild it in three days. It must also be remembered that the Evangelists assure us that those witnesses who gave the evidence were false and implied that they had been suborned. Nevertheless, Saint John does indeed report an occasion when something very like what this evidence produced did actually happen. In chapter two at verse eighteen he says:

> Then answered the Jews and said unto him, 'What sign showest thou unto us, seeing that thou doest these things?' Jesus answered and said unto them, 'Destroy this temple, and in three days I will raise it up.' Then said the Jews, 'Forty and six years was this temple in building, and wilt thou rear it up in three days?' But he spake of the temple of his body. When therefore he was risen from the dead, his disciples remembered that he had said this unto them; and they believed the scripture, and the word that Jesus had said.

In this passage it is quite clear that the people to whom the words were spoken understood them to refer to Herod's temple in Jerusalem, the actual building, and Saint John is at pains to tell us that the disciples only understood their real significance after He was risen from the dead.

Jesus certainly did predict His Passion and His resurrection. The Synoptists report three occasions when He did so. After recounting the confession of Saint Peter on the road to Caesaraea Philippi, in the north of the country, that Jesus was the Christ, Jesus began to teach them 'that the Son of Man must suffer many things and be rejected of the elders, and of the chief priests and scribes, and be killed, and after three days rise again' (Mark 8:31). Although Saint Mark, and he is alone in this, writes that Jesus said this 'openly' – and the word really means 'with frankness' or 'freely' – there is no suggestion that it was said to anyone else other than the disciples. Indeed a few verses earlier, after Peter had made his confession, Jesus commanded that they should not tell anyone about his Messianic function.

The second prediction (Mark 9:31) comes when Jesus and the disciples were passing through Galilee, and again Saint, Mark notes that Jesus commanded secrecy: 'For he taught his disciples and said unto them, "The Son of Man is delivered into the hands of men, and they shall kill him; and after that he is killed he shall rise the third day."' The Evangelist's comment is, 'But they understood not that saying, and were afraid to ask him.' Luke (9:44), in reporting the same incident, is even more explicit:

> And they were all amazed at the mighty Power of God. But while they wondered every one, at all things which Jesus did, he said unto his disciples, 'Let these sayings sink down into your ears: for the Son of Man shall be delivered into the hands of men.' But they understood not this saying, and it was hid from them, that they perceived it not: and they feared to ask him of that saying.

Saint Matthew does not record their lack of understanding, but says that 'they were very sorry' (17:22–23).

There are also records of a third prediction. This occurs on the way up to Jerusalem for the last Passover. Saint Mark says:

> And they were in the way going up to Jerusalem: and Jesus went before them: and they were amazed: and as they followed, they were afraid. And he took again the Twelve, and began to tell them what things should happen unto him, saying, 'Behold, we go up

> to Jerusalem; and the Son of Man shall be delivered
> unto the chief priests, and unto the scribes; and they
> shall condemn him to death, and shall deliver him to
> the Gentiles; and they shall mock him, and scourge
> him, and spit upon him, and shall kill him; and the
> third day he shall rise again. (10:34)

Saint Matthew, quoting Saint Mark almost verbatim says:

> And Jesus going up to Jerusalem took the disciples
> apart in the way, and said unto them, 'Behold, we go
> up to Jerusalem; and the Son of Man shall be be-
> trayed unto the chief priests and to the scribes, and
> they shall condemn him to death, and shall deliver
> him to the Gentiles to mock, and to scourge, and to
> crucify him: and the third day he shall rise again.'

Saint Luke (18:33) again copies precisely from Saint Mark
but omits a few words. He does however make the same
addition: 'And they understood none of these things; and
this saying was hid from them, neither knew they the
things that were spoken.'

When the women arrived at the tomb on Easter
morning, according to Saint Mark, the angel said unto
them:

> Be not affrighted: Ye seek Jesus of Nazareth, which
> was crucified: he is risen; he is not here; behold the
> place where they laid him. But go your way, tell his
> disciples and Peter that he goeth before you into
> Galilee. There shall ye see him as he said unto you.

The appendage 'as he said unto you' is a clear reference to
the fact that Jesus had indeed given some sort of prognos-
tication to the disciples before his betrayal. Saint Matthew

makes the angel tell the women 'to go quickly, and tell his disciples that he is risen from the dead; and behold, he goeth before you into Galilee: lo, I have told you.' This last sentence could merely emphasise the message that the angel had to give or it could be a reference to that which Jesus had said previously. In Saint Luke's gospel (24:4–7) the angelic messenger takes the form of two men who stand by them in shining garments:

> And as they were afraid and bowed down their faces to the earth, they said unto them, 'Why seek ye the living among the dead? He is not here, but is risen: remember how he spake unto you when he was as yet in Galilee, saying, the Son of Man must be delivered into the hands of sinful men, and be crucified, and the third day rise again.' And they remembered his words.

This seems to throw a somewhat different light on the matter. In the three predictions recorded by the Synoptists, and they all do it, it is quite clear that the words were spoken only to the Twelve and that they could not understand what they meant. But in this account the angel, or angels, remind the women that Jesus told them that he would be betrayed and killed, and that he would rise again. It has often been noted that in the third gospel there are clear traces that at least a good number of the eyewitnesses, who Saint Luke tells us in the preface that he has consulted, were women. This indeed can have a ready explanation. If the 'we' passages in the Acts do indeed indicate that, after Saint Paul had crossed from Asia into Europe, Luke the beloved physician was his companion in his travels and that he stayed with him until finally they reached Rome, then there was the long period when Paul was held as a prisoner at Caesaraea waiting for the result of his application to have his case tried at the Imperial Court in Rome. During that time it would have been possible for Saint Luke to have made visits to the people who had known Jesus in the flesh and consult with them in his attempt to gather information for the account which he was intending to write. He states that others had done this sort of thing before him, but that he was anxious to have authentic material and to set it down in order:

> Forasmuch as many have taken in hand to set in order a declaration of those things which are most surely believed among us, even as they delivered them unto us, which from the beginning were eye-witnesses and ministers of the word; it seemed good to me also, having had perfect understanding of all things from the very first, to write unto thee... in order that thou mightest know the certainty of those things wherein thou has been instructed. (Luke 1:1–4)

At the time that he would be making these visits, many of the men would no longer be available, having themselves departed on missionary journeys or gone to other places where Christian congregations had been established. But there would in all probability have been quite a number of women who had known Jesus and would have been prepared to talk about Him.

Of all these ladies, the most important would inevitably be the Blessed Virgin Mary herself, if she were still living. Certainly, the birth narrative of Saint Luke seems to have been written in a somewhat different style from the rest of his writings. Could this be because of the personal nature of the information he was given? The whole document comprising the first two chapters of the gospel has a lyrical quality all its own and is very much Mary oriented. If it were not for this document we would know nothing of the Annunciation, the visitation to Elizabeth, the circumstances of the birth of Jesus in a stable, the visit of the shepherds, or of the excursion to Jerusalem for the ceremonies of purification, or even of the first visit of Jesus to Jerusalem when He was about twelve years old. After the account of the birth and the shepherds, the Evangelist writes: 'But Mary kept all these things, and pondered them in her heart.' Again after telling of the occasion when Jesus was left behind in Jerusalem and was discovered in the temple, he writes: 'And he went down with them, and came to Nazareth, and was subject unto them: but his mother kept all these sayings in her heart.' Could this not be a way in which Saint Luke is telling his readers that he has indeed acquired this information from the Lady herself; and would not this provide an explanation for the difference in the style? To anyone who reads with an unprejudiced eye, it would seem that this is quite obvious.

Others who would have been available to Saint Luke's enquiries must have figured quite a number. There were Martha and Mary; we know that Philip the deacon had four daughters who prophesied; there are Joanna and Susannah, and it may well be of some significance that it is only in the third gospel that these two ladies are mentioned by name; there were also Salome and Mary Cleopas, and again it may well be significant that Saint Luke is the only Evangelist to tell of Cleopas on the Emmaus road.

To revert to the Passion narratives, Saint Luke appears to have no doubt that Jesus, or possibly the disciples, had spoken to the women, or at least to some of them, about the forthcoming betrayal, crucifixion and resurrection. There is no doubt that in all the other accounts, the foretelling is only made to the Twelve, and they were furthermore given the impression that it was not for general publication; it is certain that they did not understand what was being told them. These facts remain, even though we could be persuaded that in the words of these predictions there is an injection of knowledge gained subsequently. So thus we can say with certainty that Jesus did predict His death and also his resurrection from the dead. He made more than one such prediction to the disciples, and He may also have, at some point, done the same to the women. From the way in which the recordings are made, it would seem to be most unlikely that either group would talk loosely about it and gossip about it to other people. How then did the information get to the priests?

We have already seen that what was said at the trial before Caiaphas would not be able to provide this knowledge. The only public declaration of which we have any record is the one reported by Saint John, but then he is careful to point out that there was no suggestion that it meant anything other to the people than that it was the temple building which was to be destroyed and rebuilt by Jesus in three days. Whence then came this information? We must not forget Judas Iscariot. He was one of the Twelve and he would have heard the predictions by being himself present when they were made. He went to the priests to betray Jesus. The priests would certainly want to have known something of his motives, if only to try to gain some information about what it was that made a faithful friend and loving disciple turn traitor. In whatever conversation Judas had with them, and indeed he must have had some session with them to apprise them of the danger which in his opinion Jesus constituted, and of the need for His destruction, it would be most unlikely that he would omit to pass on this important piece of information. He may have thought that, knowing this, the priests would consider Jesus to be an even greater menace to the safety of the community than had been previously imagined. Many have undertaken to find motives for the action that Judas took, but this is in contrast to the scriptural writers who are all most restrained and very non-committal when it comes to their treatment of Judas. It is as though they could not bring themselves to write about him. In the New Testament itself there are even contradictory accounts of the way in which he met his death. Saint Matthew tells us that, filled with remorse, he tried to give back the money to the priests, and they refused to have it. Judas then threw the silver pieces at them and 'went out and hanged himself'. The priests did not know what to do with the money because, being blood money, it could not be used for temple purposes. So they bought a field with it, to provide a cemetery for non-citizens, and it was known as Aceldama, the Hebrew for 'Field of Blood'. Saint Luke, in Acts on the other hand, says that it was Judas himself who used the money to buy the field (Acts 1:18):

> Now this man purchased a field with the reward of iniquity; and falling headlong, he burst asunder in the midst and all his bowels gushed out. And it was known unto all the dwellers at Jerusalem; insomuch as that field is called in their proper tongue, Aceldama, that is to say, the Field of blood.

The reluctance of the disciples to speak about Judas may well have caused the Gentile Luke, who came on the scenes a comparatively long time after these happenings, not to have been told the precise details of the field and its purchase, and the nature of Judas' demise. Without the restraint that the others had imposed upon themselves, Saint Luke as it were let fly with an account of a very nasty end. He seems to have had something of a taste for demise by intestinal disorders, for his account of the death of Herod carries the same stamp (Acts 12:23). It would seem that more credence should be given to Saint Matthew's bald statement.

We can now understand how the priests could have gained the information that Jesus had foretold his resurrection, though it may well have been that at the first they did not attach much importance to it. Nevertheless, it could well be that, in order to check every possibility, they sent a messenger to inspect the tomb and to see that the burial had been completed in every due manner. On the other hand, someone may have noticed certain features and reported the matter to the authorities. If anyone did visit the tomb after the departure of what we should call the mourning party, they would see that although the stone had been rolled into the closed position, the grave had not been sealed. We know that this was because the funeral rites had not been completed, and access would be required as early as possible on Sunday morning. This information, however, in the eyes of the priests would seem to indicate that a plot had been prepared. Easy access could also be afforded to someone who had planned to come and remove the body, so that when the women arrived they would find the grave empty and would jump to the conclusion that Jesus had been raised from the dead. The rumour that had been passed to them was that Jesus had said that he would rise again on the third day, from the time when the report was received, that would make it the following day. It would seem necessary then that certain precautionary measures would need to be taken. It was the Sabbath day and also a major festival. It would not therefore be easy to arrange for a detachment of the Levitical Guard to be placed on duty at the sepulchre. In any case, Jesus had been crucified by the Roman authority, and therefore the custodianship of the body was a Roman concern. It would also be much better for there to be Roman surveillance, so that if Jesus' disciples had made an attempt to remove the body, they too could have been taken into custody and tried by Roman law. This was surely Pilate's business, and Pilate certainly needed to be informed of the rumour which had been brought to their ears about a resurrection, and the evidence of a possible plot to remove the body. Therefore a visit to Pilate would be in order.

No doubt Pilate would not have been too pleased to be disturbed again by this troublesome matter that seemed never to be settled or to go away. The priests had come to tell him of some silly rumour that Jesus had said that He would rise again on the third day, and that the third day was tomorrow. It had been reported that the tomb had been left unsealed, so that it looked just possible that there may be something in it and that a plot had been hatched. The rumour could have been spread deliberately, as a preliminary part of a scheme to remove the body and give credence to the subsequent report that there had been a resurrection. We remember that Pilate, certainly according to John's account, had been very much impressed by Jesus at the trial, and all the gospels tell us that he had condemned Jesus against his own better judgement, because it was contrary to any law to put an innocent man to death. Jesus had also said some disturbing things about His kingdom not being of this world. He was therefore more than ready to accept the priests' request: 'Ye have a watch: go our way, make it as sure as you can' (Matthew 27:65). In this way the priests would have done all that they could. The tomb had been safely sealed and there was a quaternion of soldiers on guard, who would remain until after the third day had passed.

So Jerusalem could move into nightfall and prepare for sleep at the end of a long day. Pilate could feel that the whole troublesome matter, which had been such a nuisance throughout the festival, was at last over and done with; the priests could rest content that all that was humanly possible had been done to prevent any repercussions from Jesus or

His disciples. Without their leader they were not the sort of men likely to do anything to disturb the ordering of society. Mary Magdalene and Mary Cleopas had walked over the Mount of Olives to Bethany, there to join Martha, Lazarus, and eight or nine of the disciples who would still be afraid and conscious of the fact that to go out might well be to risk arrest. John would have gone back to his house in the city, and given a report to Peter, his mother and his aunt and Cleopas on what had been done at the tomb, and where the other women were. Nicodemus and Joseph of Arimathaea would be safely in their homes, and Joanna, if she had been present, would have returned to her husband in Herod's palace. The festival had passed over without there being any major disturbance, no riots or rebellions had disturbed the peace. History had not been made. Now eventide was here again and darkness was covering the earth. The world rolled on, as it had ever done, towards another day, another week.

Chapter VII
Act Three, Scene One: Easter Morning

Of the four Evangelists, Saint Matthew is the only one who tells of the guard which Pilate allowed to be placed in the garden in which the tomb was situated. The night had passed without incident, no robbers came, no disciples to steal away the body; it had been very quiet. Then, just around daybreak there was another earthquake. This one seemed to be more violent than the other tremors. Indeed it was so strong that it caused the stone, which was closing the mouth of the sepulchre, to roll back and open the door. There was a great flash of lightning which seemed to strike the stone and sizzle upon it. The soldiers were terrified and fell to the ground as though they were dead men. This was something which was altogether weird and inexplicable. Could that flash of lightning indeed have been an angel coming down from heaven and sitting upon the stone? Daring a glance inside the tomb revealed that there was nothing there; the body had gone, and yet no human being had come to take it. Added to which there were some women coming into the garden, and in the early morning light they had the appearance of wraiths. It was altogether too much, and in their terror they did what no soldier should ever do. They deserted their posts and fled.

Is not this account exactly what Saint Matthew says? Or, rather, is it what the soldiers would have said, given their condition and the historic circumstances? Let us consider the actual words of the gospel:

> In the end of the Sabbath, as it began to dawn towards the first day of the week, came Mary Magdalene and the other Mary to the sepulchre. And behold there was a great earthquake: for the angel of the Lord descended from heaven, and came and rolled back the stone from the door, and sat upon it. His countenance was like lightning, and his raiment, white as snow: and for him, the keepers did shake and became as dead men. (Matthew 28:1–4)

The appearance of the women at that early hour must also have struck the soldiers as very strange indeed. The Sabbath discipline was over when the sun had set and here they were almost at the dawning of the day. It would have been foolish to arrive at the tomb before they could see what they were doing. We have the explanation of this in the fourth gospel, when Saint John tells us that Mary Magdalene came early while it was yet dark to the tomb. In point of fact the Greek word used for 'come' implies the actual process of making the journey. In the English translation it signifies that it was still dark when she arrived at the sepulchre, but the Greek does not necessarily give that implication. It can also mean that she was in the act of making the journey very early while it was yet dark. We recall that Mary was at Bethany for the Sabbath and it seemed to be more than reasonable to suppose that Mary Cleopas had gone with her. Naturally they would both want to be at the tomb at the earliest possible moment. In a climate such as that of Palestine, obsequies were not prolonged and it was not usual to delay the disposal of a corpse for as long as twenty-four hours, let alone two days. If they had set off while it was yet dark, they could have covered the distance from Bethany to arrive at the tomb soon after dawn.

After Saint Matthew has interrupted his account of the soldiers to tell of the announcement made by the angel to the women, he returns to it:

> Now, when they [the women] were going behold some of the watch came into the city, and showed unto the chief priests all the things that were done. And when they were assembled with the elders, and had taken counsel, they gave large money unto the soldiers, saying, 'Say ye, his disciples came by night and stole him away while we slept. And if this come to the Governor's ears, we will persuade him, and secure you.' So they took the money and did as they were taught, and this saying is commonly reported among the Jews until this day. (28:11–15)

It would indeed have had to have been a very large bribe, for a Roman soldier falling asleep on guard duty would incur immediate execution by decapitation. No more serious military offence could be committed. They were in a difficult situation anyway, because they had already committed another crime by deserting their posts, and desertion was quite as serious as falling asleep on duty. They certainly would not dare to go and report themselves to Pilate, to whom they were responsible. The priests would appear to be the only people who could possibly help them in their most dangerous position. Indeed their judgement was right, because they not only got some money out of it, but they also had the assurance that, if charges were going to be proffered, the priests would stand security for them, and give then their protection. It is interesting to note that Saint Matthew says that only some of the watch went into the city. One wonders what happened to the others. This is the nearest we ever get to a description of what actually happened at the moment of the resurrection. It is graphic, it is arresting and it is convincing. It is not necessary to know more, nor would we be able to comprehend it, if more had been told.

We must now leave the soldiers to their nefarious activities and return to consider the women who were approaching. In the first gospel we read that there were two of them. We must make a note that he does not say that there were only two of them. Certainly there were two, and they are named as Mary Magdalene and the other Mary. The other Mary could only be the wife of Cleopas, and we have already had reason to believe that both these ladies had spent the Sabbath at Bethany. Saint Mark names three: Mary Magdalene, Mary the mother of James, which indeed would be Mary Cleopas, and Salome. She was the wife of Zebedee and the mother of James and John. As far as we can reckon, she would have spent the Sabbath at John's house in Jerusalem. Following the most probable route from the valley of the Kedron, the two ladies from Bethany would have climbed up and skirted the wall. If John's house were where we think it was and where traditionally it has been sited (for now it is believed that the Church of the Dormition has been erected at that place) then it would be very little trouble for the two Marys to have entered the city by one of the gates, called at the house and collected Salome, and then to have left the city by the gate nearest to Golgotha. Saint Luke says that the women were Mary Magdalene, and Joanna and Mary the mother of James. We have already noted that Saint Luke is the only Evangelist to mention Joanna, and he does so on two occasions, here and in chapter eight, verse three. An explanation of this would be that she was one of the women with whom Saint Luke had consultation when he was gathering eyewitness accounts preparatory to his writing of the two volume work, the first volume of which is the gospel. Of course, it would be inevitable that the arrangements for this visitation would have been made before the party broke up on Good Friday afternoon; they would have arranged to have met at the sepulchre as soon as possible after sunrise on the Sunday.

The fourth gospel gives us a little more information. At first sight it would seem to contradict the astonishing unanimity of the other three:

> The first day of the week cometh Mary Magdalene early, when it was yet dark, unto the sepulchre, and seeth the stone taken away from the sepulchre. Then she runneth, and cometh to Simon Peter, and the other disciple, whom Jesus loved, and saith unto them, 'They have taken away the Lord out of the sepulchre, and we know not where they have laid him.' Peter therefore went forth, and that other disciple, and came to the sepulchre. (John 20:1–3)

Let us look carefully at what Saint John actually says. He tells us that Mary Magdalene went to the sepulchre early and that she was making the journey before daylight had come. He does not say that she was the only person to have approached the tomb at that time, neither does he say that it was still dark when she arrived. He does tell us, however, that she saw that the stone had been removed. We already know enough about this Mary's character to realise that she was a somewhat volatile person and was not above jumping to conclusions. Seeing that the stone had been moved, she immediately came to the decision that someone had been to the tomb, had managed to roll away the stone and removed the body. Apparently, she did not continue to the door of the sepulchre to look inside and check whether her surmising was correct, but straight away ran back to tell

Peter and John. The other women would naturally have continued until they arrived at the tomb. When they did so, Saint Mark tells us that in the tomb there was a young man. We have already seen the literary reason he has for using this particular nomenclature. He is linking this angelic person with the young man in the garden who was shamed and returned to a condition of innocence. He also tells us that, as they were going, the women were discussing amongst themselves how they would manage to get into the tomb, for the stone was very big and heavy. He also states that they saw that the stone had been rolled away before they actually arrived at the spot, and in this we have the corroborative evidence of Saint John's account. They, presumably now without Mary Magdalene, went on and entered the tomb. On doing so they were confronted with the one who looked like a young man wearing a very shining and splendid garment. Naturally, they were frightened. The angel told them not to be afraid: 'Ye seek Jesus of Nazareth, which was crucified. He is risen, he is not here, behold the place where they laid him!' This is the first direct evidence that we have that there was no body in the tomb. He then tells them to go away and to tell the disciples and Peter that Jesus was going before them into Galilee and that He would see them there. The distinction between the disciples and Peter might well indicate that Peter was not with the main body of the disciples, who we believe were still at Bethany, whereas Peter would still be in John's house.

Saint Matthew, after he had reported that the soldiers got the impression that the lightning that came down and settled on the stone was an angelic visitation, does not tell us where the angel was who addressed the women or even whether the women went into the tomb before they saw him. He just does not mention such details, and so in no way does he contradict what Saint Mark has said. The words that the angel uses are almost identical to those reported by Saint Mark. They are:

> Fear not, for I know that ye seek Jesus which was crucified. He is not here: for He is risen, as He said. Come, see the place where the Lord lay. And go quickly, and tell his disciples that He is risen from the dead: and, behold, He goeth before you into Galilee; there shall ye see Him. Lo, I have told you.

Saint Mark next tells us that they departed quickly from the sepulchre with fear and great joy and ran to bring the disciples word. We must ask in which direction would they have gone? Most of the disciples were at Bethany, so that it would seem to be most reasonable for them to have headed in that direction. If our reconstruction is correct, they would have known that Mary Magdalene had gone back to John's house, so presumably the people who were there would already have been alerted and there would have been no need to bother about letting Peter know: that would already have been done.

Now we must turn to Saint Luke, and once again we must remind ourselves that it was a number of years afterwards when he appeared and that the passage of time does have an exaggerating effect upon the memories of significant events. However, in the main his account is, whilst making allowances for this, remarkably in accordance with what the others had told. Of course, as well as gaining information from conversations with people who had known Jesus, there would also no doubt have been available for him written documents. He does indeed seem to have known and copied passages from Saint Mark's gospel, as well as from another document, probably a collection of the sayings of Jesus which was also known to Saint Matthew. He says it was on the first day of the week;

that it was very early in the morning; he says that 'they' 'came bringing spices', but does not at that point say who 'they' were. However, after describing the angelic message, he does tell us that they were Mary Magdalene, and Joanna, and Mary the mother of James and other women that were with them. He also says that the stone was rolled away and that they entered the tomb and failed to find the body of Jesus. Up to this point in the Lukan account there is no angelic vision. As they were standing in a perplexed state, they became conscious that they had been joined by two men who were standing by them in shining garments. Recognising them as angels, the women bowed down to the ground. The angels, for such quite surely Saint Luke intends us to believe them to be, said to the women: 'Why seek ye the living among the dead? He is not here, but is risen.' The angels ask them to recall how Jesus had told them that he must be crucified and that on the third day He would rise again. 'And,' the Evangelist concludes, 'they remembered his words, and returned from the sepulchre and told all these things to the Eleven and the rest.'

The only real differences in this account are the duplication of the angel, which is an understandable development over the passage of the years, and the assumption that Jesus must have, while alive in the flesh, talked to the women about His mission, the work of salvation He had come to earth to do, and how He would do it. That, however, is not a contradiction of what the others have said but rather a deduction from the narrative as written, which gives us another valuable piece of information about our Lord's ministry. Indeed the unanimity expressed by all four of the Evangelists concerning the first recognition of the resurrection is quite astonishing. There are few newspaper reports on any one day of some event which happened only the day before which would carry such a consistency of identity. The resurrection of Jesus Christ from the dead must be one of the best attested facts in all history. No one now disbelieves that Caesar crossed the Rubicon in 49 BC or that the Athenians were victorious at the Battle of Salamis in 480 BC, and yet neither of these events is nearly so well attested as the things that were done in a little garden outside the walls of Jerusalem on the first Easter morning. If it be obtuse to cast doubts upon the historicity of either the crossing of the Rubicon or the Battle of Salamis, what would it be to aver that the tomb was not empty when the women went inside it?

Up to this point it had been established that the body of Jesus had disappeared from the tomb; the matter had been reported to the Jewish authorities, and the soldiers who reported it had been heavily bribed to say that they fell asleep while on duty and that while they slept Jesus' disciples had come and stolen the body. Women had appeared to complete the funeral procedures and had been told by an angelic messenger that Jesus was risen, and they had been made to recall that he Himself had said that this would happen. They were told to go and give the news to the disciples, and so they would have set off to go over the hill to Bethany.

In the group of women who started on this journey would have been Mary the wife of Cleopas, who had already walked over the Mount of Olives once that day; she was no longer a young woman and, of course her husband, who would not have seen her since before the Sabbath, would be waiting for her, presumably in John's house; Salome and, according to Saint Luke, Joanna. Saint Luke says that there were others. It would therefore seem to be extremely likely that Mary Cleopas did not go all the way with them to Bethany, but had decided to go to John's house, not least to be able to corroborate what Mary Magdalene would have told them. From our reconstruction Mary had not seen or heard the angel because she returned as soon as she had seen that the stone was rolled away, convinced that someone had removed the body (although she had not checked to see that it was not in the tomb). She would only have had time to blurt out her story to Peter and John, before the other Mary would have appeared and confirmed that the tomb was indeed empty, and that an angel had told them that Jesus was risen from the dead.

Now we know that as soon as Mary did impart the information that she suspected a removal of the body, Peter and John would naturally have gotten up and gone to the tomb as quickly as possible. That is exactly what Saint John tells us that they did. He also adds the fact that John, presumably a much younger man, outran Peter and came first to the sepulchre. Surely this is another of those details which make the fourth gospel so convincing as being the work of an eyewitness himself. Peter, we are told, could not understand it, but John remembered what Jesus had said, and had no doubt that He had indeed risen. A further detail is provided in that we are told about the disposition of the grave clothes, with the napkin that was about His head not lying with the linen clothes, but wrapped together in a place by itself. The full significance of this Saint John leaves to the reader to deduce for himself. Having seen these things, and been assured that there was no body in the tomb, there is no suggestion that either of the men saw or heard an angelic visitor, but rather returned to their own home. Of course, Mary would have followed them, but perhaps at a somewhat slower speed. We do not need to be percipient psychologists to know that she would not be able to stay away. Of course, she was crying. It is interesting to note that at this point Saint Luke gives corroborative evidence that Peter went to the sepulchre, thus reinforcing the Johannine account: 'Then arose Peter, and stooping down he beheld the linen clothes laid by themselves, and departed, wondering in himself what was come to pass' (Luke

14:12). The fact that Saint Luke does not say that Peter had a companion, does not necessarily indicate that he was alone. Saint Luke's interest here is to tell us that Peter went to the tomb, but returned home again, not understanding what had happened.

Meanwhile, the other women were on their way to Bethany to take the glad tidings to the disciples as instructed by the angel. Saint Mark, just before his dramatic last line to his gospel makes the interesting note that 'they went out quickly and fled from the sepulchre; for they trembled and were amazed: neither said they anything to any man: for they were afraid...' They would, of course, not be disobedient to the heavenly vision and were on their way to carry out the command to tell His disciples and Peter that He was going before them into Galilee, and that they also were to return there, and that He would be seeing them there. Surely it must mean that they moved quickly, that they were frightened in the face of this strangest of all experiences, and they did not dally to pass on any information on the way, but made every effort to get to the disciples as soon as possible. It could well be that the quickest and most direct route to get on to the Bethany path would be to have gone through the city and, even at this early hour, people would have been starting to arrive, and the business of the day would be causing the streets to fill.

It is Saint Matthew who takes up the narrative. He also says that they hurried away from the sepulchre, frightened but still full of joy, to tell the disciples. He actually says that they were running. Then suddenly, there was Jesus coming to meet them: 'And they came and held him by the feet, and worshipped him. Then said Jesus unto them, "Be not afraid; go tell my brethren that they go into Galilee, and there shall they see me"' (Matthew 28:9). We do not know whether indeed this was the first time that the risen Jesus was actually seen by anyone or whether the encounter with Mary Magdalene had already occurred. It would be silly and useless to try to argue for one or the other. Jesus Himself has now appeared. He tells the women not to be frightened, and to go to give the news to His brothers. That, of course, must mean that the brothers were staying in Jerusalem or nearby, and that the message that was given to the women was that the brethren were to go home to Galilee, and 'there shall they see me'. The ladies now had a double commission. They were to give the disciples the good news, and also the brothers, and they were to take to them a request to go back home; when they were all in Galilee, Jesus would arrange to meet them.

It is, however, well attested both by Saint Luke and Saint John that the disciples at least did see Jesus that very day, and while they were still in Jerusalem. Saint Luke indeed says that 'the Eleven were gathered together, and them that were with them... and Jesus himself stood in the midst of them' (Luke 24:33–36). In one of the most important passages in the whole of the fourth gospel, Saint John says quite clearly that the same day at evening, where the disciples were gathered together came Jesus, and stood in the midst (John 20:19).

Nevertheless, the angel had told the women to tell the disciples to go to Galilee and promised a meeting there, and Jesus Himself had asked them to arrange for the brethren to be there also. It would appear that there was to be a meeting of all who believed in Jesus and in the fact that He had arisen, and that it was to be at a certain place in Galilee. It is with an account of this meeting that Saint Matthew concludes his gospel: 'Then the Eleven went away into Galilee, and into a mountain where Jesus had appointed them. And when they saw him, they worshipped him, but some doubted.' Then the Evangelist gives what must have been a summary of Jesus' address:

All power is given unto me in heaven and in earth.
Go ye therefore and teach all nations, baptising them
in the name of the Father and of the Son, and of the
Holy Ghost: teaching them to observe all things
whatsoever I have commanded you: and, lo, I am
with you always, even unto the end of the world.
Amen.

Because of the explicit exposition of the trinitarian formula,
many people have felt that these words must be a gloss or
an intrusion into the text by a later hand. This has been
maintained by many scholars, in spite of the fact that there
is little, if any, manuscript evidence for them not being part
of the autograph. In whatever way one reads the fourth
gospel, there can be no doubt that for its author there is a
very highly developed doctrine of the three persons of the
Godhead, particularly in the last discourse. Here again there
seems to be a case of scholarship being determined by
preconceived convictions. It has also been commonly
regarded that this gathering in Galilee, as reported in the
first gospel, is Saint Matthew's account of the ascension.
But in the text itself there is no suggestion whatsoever that
it is. Rather it is reported as a great rally of those who
would soon be known as Christians, that it took place in
Galilee, and that Jesus, after His resurrection, had made
careful arrangements for it to be held. We get a hint of what
this meeting might have been from Saint Paul, when he
was writing to the Corinthians and telling them of the
information he had received about the post-resurrection
manifestations. In amongst the list of appearances he gives,
he mentions that Jesus was seen 'of above five hundred
brethren at once; of whom the greater part remain unto this
present, but some are fallen asleep' (1 Cor 15:6). Saint Paul
is certainly not the man to make a statement like that, and
even go so far as to suggest that it is abundantly possible for

it to be verified, unless indeed it were true. It would seem to be eminently probable that this passage in Corinthians is referring to the meeting on the hillside in Galilee which the first gospel reports and which our Lord was careful to arrange.

Returning now to the garden we find that Peter and John had gone away again to their own home, but Mary was left in the garden, standing by the tomb and weeping. When eventually she looked inside, she saw two angels sitting, one at the head, and the other at the feet, where the body of Jesus had lain. It will be remembered that Saint Matthew speaks of one angel, Saint Mark of a young man and Saint Luke of two men in white apparel. It is surely sufficient for any reader that there was some kind of communication, which was clear and explicit and which was not mouthed by human beings. When one is reporting angelic visitations, one is speaking of spiritual beings, the precise manifestation of which is, in every sense of the word, immaterial. To consider that it is of great importance to discover whether there were one or two angels in the tomb, is surely to miss the whole point of the story. These angels asked Mary why she was crying and heard that it was because someone had removed the Lord's body. Mary then became conscious of another presence behind her; thinking that this would be the gardener, she asked him whether he had taken the body and offered to take possession of it herself, if he would tell her where it was. Jesus addressed her by name, and in the sound of His voice, and the appellation by which he addressed her, she knew that it was Jesus. When she endeavoured to embrace Him, He asked her not to touch Him but to go and give the glad tidings to His brothers. In each of the personal appearances of Jesus so far recorded, it was to women that He spoke and He asked them to go to his brothers. To Mary, He also made reference to a future ascension to His Father and God, who was also Mary's Father and God.

In the telling of this appearance, Saint John is using the information in such a way that he is expressing and implying very much more than a retelling of the actual occurrence of historic events. After Saint John has told of the death of Christ, the piercing of His side by the soldier and the emergence of water and blood, he goes on to speak of the granting of the body to Joseph of Arimathaea and the deposition. He introduces the next section of the gospel with the words, 'Now in the place where he was crucified there was a garden; and in the garden a new sepulchre, wherein was never man yet laid.' When Saint John repeats a word in close succession, he is, as it were, emphasising it. Nowadays we should probably underline it, and so give it a stress and emphasis to make quite sure that the implications which the word aroused would be noted and retained. Saint John's gospel is a Jewish document, and to a Jew reading this sentence, there would immediately be suggested to him the Garden of Eden, which in turn would set his mind upon the creation stories to be found in Genesis. Indeed, the whole of the fourth gospel is based on the theme of creation. Saint John even begins his prologue with the identical words with which the book of Genesis opens: 'In the beginning'. Following the creation narrative as there recorded, Saint John tells us that the Word, who was very God in all the fullness and power of God, was the creator of all things. He is the agent of God in creation and He was made man. His book is about this man, who is God, creator, and who is come to manifest His glory and recreate the world which had been deranged and fragmented by sin.

As the Evangelist moves through the narration of events that occurred in Jesus' earthly life, he records miracles which he nominates as signs. These wondrous acts then are signs of the creativity of Jesus, by which He was making new the world. They follow closely the acts of creation as recorded in Genesis. The first act of creation was of water and the first miracle Saint John reports is the turning of the water into wine. The second act in the creation of the world was the making of the firmament, the dimensional universe of space and time, and the second miracle in the gospel is the healing of the nobleman's son, by which Jesus showed Himself to be the Lord of space and time; he could heal the boy at a distance, and the cure was effected at the selfsame hour in which Jesus had said to the father, 'Thy son liveth.' Thirdly, God troubled the waters by bringing out of them land, and in the third sign of Saint John the waters of the Pool of Bethesda were troubled by the angel, but Jesus could heal the cripple by direct outpouring of His own power. Then God caused vegetation to appear on the earth so that food could be provided, grass and herb-bearing seed and trees bearing fruit, which Jesus fed the five thousand in a place where there was much grass. Closely associated with this is the account of Jesus walking on the water, by which also Saint John tells that He is superior to all the forces of nature which are bound in obedience to Him. In Genesis the fifth day of creation is the day of lights, and in the fifth miracle in the gospel, light was given to the man born blind. Lastly, Genesis tells us that God made the animals and man, and the sixth sign in the gospel was the raising of Lazarus, new life given to a man. It is also very significant that after the account of the raising of Lazarus, we find a change in the tenor of the gospel. Up to that point Jesus has been the agent in all that has been recorded. He is the One who gives the signs, He is the One who performs the miracles. From the point where Lazarus is restored to life, Jesus ceases to be the agent and becomes the patient. The Evangelist proceeds immediately to tell of the betrayal by Judas, and from this point on, things happen *to* Jesus. He rests as it were from creative activity, as in Genesis God rested on the seventh day. As God was glorified on the Sabbath day, seeing everything that He had made, so for Saint John, Jesus' glorification is His Passion, crucifixion and death, and hence the conclusion of the great cry of exultant triumph. Returning to Genesis, when the days of creation were completed, the book moves on to the story of the Garden of Eden, and so the Evangelist now does the same: 'Now in the place where he was crucified there was a garden, and in the garden a new sepulchre.' We do not need to introduce any further reasoning; it is now quite clear that we move into a section of the gospel in which the story of the placing of man in the garden, the purpose and function for which Adam was made to tend it and to dress it, becomes the underlying theme.

So Mary was in the garden, and having received no information from the angels, only a question as to why she was weeping, she saw a man. It is interesting to note that in Hebrew 'Adam' is not a proper noun, it is the common noun for a man. So the Evangelist is saying that Jesus is the Man, the second Adam. Adam was put in the garden to be the gardener: so it is obvious that Mary, according to this very subtle narrative, supposes Him to be the gardener. Of course, Saint John is not making the story up in order to convey religious truth, he is still actually reporting what did indeed happen, but he is doing it in such a way that his readers could gain much more than the mere information about facts. Knowing Mary Magdalene as we already do, it would be inevitable that in the circumstances she would throw her arms around Jesus, in sheer joy and gladness. Jesus, however, restrained her with the words 'Touch me not'. He was not rejecting her love, but he was rejecting the clinging to that which had now been superseded. Jesus in the flesh had come into the world, to operate in a material environment and therefore would have to be expressed in the terms of that environment. This order of being which is confined by space and time is a universe composed of chemical properties, and men can only act upon and influence each other because they have physical bodies. Jesus, to be the Saviour of Men, therefore would Himself have to be a man. The Word was made flesh. He came to this earth to make His life available for all men, wherever or whenever they might be, to enter into it and become part of it. Therefore the life of Jesus, fully human, having died, but now raised from the dead, must be taken back into that order of being which would make it possible for Him to be present in all His fullness at every point of space and in every moment of time. Therefore Mary *could not* cling to the chemical body, because Jesus had not yet ascended into that order of being which would make this possible.

When we come next to discuss the events which occurred later in the day, we shall see how Saint John continues this theme of the Garden of Eden, and the creation of man, and how Jesus is that new creation, that new man, which, because He is God Himself, is not marred by or tainted with sin. There is a new start, a life has been lived which is life as God intended all life to be. Now all men and women have the opportunity to become a part of the perfect life which is offered to them, the new beginning, the second Adam the ascended Christ. The chemical means by which this glorified life can be made available in this physical world is no longer by means of a human body of flesh and blood, but by bread and wine, when used in that special way which had been shown to them, and in accordance with the divine promise.

It is now established that all history has a meaning, that life has a purpose, that the fallen, broken, fragmented universe can be restored and put together again. Christ is risen. There is often deep theological truth in the old familiar nursery rhymes. 'Humpty Dumpty sat on a wall, Humpty Dumpty had a great fall. All the king's horses, and all the king's men, couldn't put Humpty together again.'

Indeed God's creature had fallen, and in that fall, which was indeed great, all God's created order was shattered and fragmented. All the forces of the human race, all the earthly powers of politics and civilisation could make no reparation. Man cannot be saved by his own efforts; only God can do that. And God did do it when He raised Jesus Christ from the dead.

Easter Day had dawned. There was an earthquake, the stone was rolled away and the tomb was seen to have no body within it. The guards ran away and were bribed to make false statements. Women came to complete the burial and they saw angels who told them that Jesus was risen. Some of those women, as they went their way in obedience to their Lord's command, saw Jesus Himself. John and Peter went to the tomb; they saw no angel, they heard no voice, but they saw that the tomb was empty and that the grave clothes had been left behind. When they had returned to their own home, Jesus Himself then came to be seen by Mary Magdalene. These are the facts, well attested, and in no way contradictory. It is easy to reconstruct a consistent story of what happened, not leaving out anything that any of the Evangelists had said, but incorporating them into a continuous narrative. For this to happen in the recordings of almost any event, even making allowances for a certain amount of collusion on the part of some of them, is little short of amazing and gives surprising testimony to the integrity of the reporters and the accuracy of their reports.

It has already been observed that a detailed enquiry as to whether the risen Christ appeared first to the women on their way to tell the disciples the fact of the resurrection, as commanded by the angel, or to Mary Magdalene when Jesus came to her in the garden, is not particularly fruitful. It surely matters little in the face of the outstanding fact of the resurrection, who was the first to have received a personal encounter with Jesus Himself. Nevertheless, since certain feminist capital has been made out of the fact that it appears to be undoubted that the candidates for this honour were women, it might well behove us to look a little more closely into the matter.

The women who had gone early to the sepulchre, according to the Matthean account, were Mary Magdalene and the other Mary. The first Evangelist does not mention other women. Saint Mark, however, on whom Saint Matthew is relying for this account, states that Salome was also with them. Saint Luke, on the other hand, writes that the women who went to the tomb on Easter morning were Mary Magdalene, Joanna, and Mary the mother of James, and the other women who were with them. As neither Saint Matthew nor Saint Mark state that the names they give are of the only women who were on their way to complete the burial procedures, and in the light of Saint Luke's assertion, it would appear that they were a small company, four of whom have been specifically named. The third gospel also states that:

> they then told these things unto the Apostles. And these words appeared in their sight as idle talk, and they disbelieved them. But Peter arose, and ran unto the tomb, and, stooping and looking in, he saw the linen clothes by themselves, and he departed to his home, wondering at that which was come to pass. (Luke 24:10–12)

In this account Saint Luke agrees with Saint John who tells of Mary's arrival back from the tomb to tell Peter and John, who arise forthwith, go to the sepulchre and return to their own home. When the two who had walked that afternoon to Emmaus recognise Jesus there, they run back to Jerusalem, where they find 'the Eleven that were gathered together, and them that were with them, saying, "The Lord is risen indeed, and hath appeared unto Simon.'"

We now have an account of three appearances: one to the women as they went to tell the Apostles, presumably on the road to Bethany; one to Mary Magdalene in the garden at the sepulchre; and one to Peter in an unspecified place. In the first case, we are not told how far along the road it was that Jesus appeared to them nor how long they had been walking when He came. It would surely take well over an hour to walk from the other side of Jerusalem and over the Mount of Olives.

In the case of Mary Magdalene, she went to the garden, saw the stone rolled away, jumped to the conclusion that there had been grave robbers and ran back to John's house to tell him and Peter. They two ran to the tomb, Saint Peter a bit more slowly than Saint John, did not stay there, but went back home. This is clearly attested both by Saint Luke and Saint John. Mary followed them when they ran to the garden and remained there when the two men had gone. It must be remembered that she was still under the impression that the body had been removed by someone, for some reason or other, from the sepulchre. Even after she had seen the angels and they had spoken to her, the impression was still there, because she asked Jesus (supposing Him to be the gardener) if He were the one who had removed the corpse. We are not told for how long she had been grieving and mourning there before she saw the angels and subsequently Jesus. Saint Peter then could well have been back in the house a considerable time before Jesus showed Himself either to the women or to Mary Magdalene. He could thus have been the first to whom the resurrected Jesus manifested Himself.

Since we have embarked upon this somewhat inconsequential investigation, it would be well to ask if the New Testament provides any other indication that it could have been Saint Peter who first saw the Lord. It is significant that when the returning couple from Emmaus arrived, it was the appearance to Peter that was given as the evidence of the resurrection; he is the only one mentioned as having been so privileged. Furthermore, Saint Paul, writing to the Corinthians, gives a list of the resurrection appearances (1 Cor 15: 5–8):

> That He appeared to Cephas [Peter, the Greek word for 'rock']; then to the Twelve; then He appeared to above five hundred brethren at once of whom the greater part remain until now, but some are fallen asleep; then He appeared to James; then to all the Apostles; and last of all, as to one born out of due time, He appeared to me also.

The repeated use of the word which is translated 'then' makes it quite clear that, as far as Saint Paul is concerned, he is putting this list of appearances into chronological order, and equally clear that the first appearance was to Saint Peter.

Let us now use our own imaginations. We must remember the condition Saint Peter was in. He must still have been overcome with remorse at his threefold denial of the Saviour, particularly after his confident assurance that he would rather die with Him than deny Him. Of all the Apostles and the women and all who had been involved with Jesus, Peter was the one most in need of seeing Him and receiving the assurance of forgiveness and restoration. There is a further consideration. Jesus had replied to Peter at Caesarea Philippi when He heard his confession. Peter said: 'Thou art the Christ, the Son of the living God,' to which Jesus replied, 'Blessed art thou, Simon Bar Jonah; for flesh and blood hath not revealed it unto thee, but my Father which is in heaven. And I also say unto thee, that thou art Peter, and upon this rock I will build my church, and the gates of Hades shall not prevail against it and I will give unto thee the keys of the kingdom of heaven' (Matthew 16:17–19). By normal human calculations then, in the light of this declaration, would anyone expect Jesus to make His first appearance after the resurrection to anyone other than Saint Peter?

As has already been said, no dogmatic truth hangs upon this investigation, although some may see in it a corroborative justification for papal claims, but neither can there be any absolute certainty about the matter. It can most certainly not be affirmed that the first people to whom Jesus showed Himself after His resurrection were women.

Additional Note
The Announcement of the Resurrection

In considering the announcements of the resurrection as recorded by the Evangelists, we note that there are three. Saint Matthew's (28:5–7):

> And the angel answered and said unto the women, Fear not ye: for I know that ye seek Jesus, which hath been crucified. He is not here; for He is risen, even as He said. Come, see the place where the Lord lay. And go quickly, and tell His disciples, He is risen from the dead; and lo, He goeth before you into Galilee; there shall ye see Him: lo, I have told you.

There is the announcement of the resurrection, the reminding of the foretelling, the instruction to tell the disciples and the promise of a meeting in Galilee. Saint Mark gives the words of the angel – whom he describes as a young man for reasons which have already been considered – as:

> Be not amazed: ye seek Jesus the Nazarene, which
> hath been crucified: He is risen: He is not here: be-
> hold the place where they laid Him! But go, tell His
> disciples and Peter, He goeth before you into Galilee;
> there shall ye see Him as He said unto you.

Here there is the explicit mention of Peter, and the
instruction again is to tell the disciples. Saint Luke says that
it was after the women had entered the tomb and found it
empty that two men in dazzling apparel said to them:

> Why seek the living among the dead? He is not here,
> but is risen: remember how He spake unto you when
> He was yet in Galilee, saying that the Son of Man
> must be delivered up into the hands of wicked men,
> and crucified, and the third day rise again.

Here there is no instruction to tell anyone, but the
Evangelist continues by saying that they told all these things
to 'the Eleven, and all the rest'. Saint John does indeed
make the angels enquire of Mary Magdalene why she was
weeping, but does not record any angelic announcement of
the resurrection. Instead he mentions the appearance of
Jesus Himself.

Apart from the general assertion that Jesus had made an
early personal appearance to Peter, there are only two
references to such manifestations in the early hours of
Easter Day. The one is here in the fourth gospel, which says
that Jesus told Mary, after she had recognised Him, to tell
His brothers, and say to them, 'I ascend into my Father and
your Father, and to my God and your God.' The other is in
Saint Matthew's account of the women meeting Jesus,
presumably on the Bethany road, when He said to them,
'Fear not: go, tell my brothers that they depart into Galilee,
and there shall they see Me.' In both cases Jesus gives the

instruction to tell his brothers. This must mean, first of all, that the brothers were somewhere in Jerusalem or its environs at the time of the crucifixion, and that Jesus wanted them to go home, and promised that He would see them there in Galilee. Does this mean that they were not with the assembly of the 'Eleven, and them that were with them' whom Cleopas and his companion found gathered together in Jerusalem on their return from Emmaus? (Luke 24:33) They were certainly not present when Jesus appeared to His disciples that same day at evening where they were gathered together, the doors being shut for fear of the Jews.

Certain it is, however, that Jesus was concerned that His brothers should be informed of the resurrection and that He was intent that there should be some kind of family reunion in Galilee. Apart from the assurance that there was a private encounter between the risen Lord and Peter, these are the only two recorded occasions when Jesus needed to give an instruction for the fact of the resurrection to be announced. At all the other appearances it was sufficient that He Himself was there. No doubt much could be read into these considerations, but the one sure fact that shines through is that Jesus had a very close family relationship with His brothers.

Chapter VIII
Act Three, Scene Two: Easter Day, Later

We now move on to the latter part of the greatest day in all recorded time. It is Saint Luke who picks up the story in the chronological sequence. After he has recorded the arrival of people at the sepulchre bearing spices for the burial, and telling us that they saw that the stone had been rolled away, he says that they went into the tomb and saw that the body of Jesus was not there. Then he records the appearance of two men in white apparel who informed them that it was useless to look for the living amongst the dead and that Jesus was not there but was risen. They are then reminded that Jesus Himself had said when He was with them in Galilee, that He would be betrayed and crucified, and that He would rise again. They remembered this foretelling and went away to give the news of the resurrection to the Eleven and to all the rest. The grave party was listed as a number of women, amongst whom were Mary Magdalene and Joanna and Mary the mother of James. This accords with what we have already discussed.

He then gives an account of 'two of them', who went that same day to a village called Emmaus, which was from Jerusalem about three score furlongs, that is a distance of about seven and'a half miles. Later in the story he tells us that the name of one of them was Cleopas, but does not name his companion. There are one or two facts to note about this. Firstly, the couple who were going to Emmaus were not specified as being either disciples or brethren. They both therefore must be from amongst the others who had been attendant upon the crucifixion during these last dread days. It will be remembered that the lady whom all three Synoptists describe as Mary, the mother of James, is mentioned by Saint John as Mary the wife of Cleopas. We also remember that John was a close relation of the Holy Family. In spite of the fact that it seems generally to have been presumed throughout history that Cleopas's companion on this journey was another man, there is no scriptural evidence for such an assumption: all that Saint Luke says is that there were two of them. The most reasonable account then would be to declare that Cleopas was taking his wife back home to Emmaus, presumably where they resided. Certainly that seems to have been their home, because of the invitation that was extended to Jesus to stay with them, when it was 'towards evening and the day was far spent'.

There is an apparent objection to this theory that the two were husband and wife. When Saint Luke tells us that the name of one of them was Cleopas, he certainly establishes the fact that one of them was male. From the fourth gospel we know that Cleopas had a wife, and presumably the James and Joses who are mentioned were their children. We also know that this lady was certainly in Jerusalem on Good Friday, and as the next day was the Sabbath, she would, of course, have had to have remained there until at least the Sunday. As Saint Luke tells the story, Jesus Himself drew near and joined them on the road, but they did not recognise Him. Jesus asked them what they were talking about, because they were looking very mournful. Cleopas said 'Art thou only a stranger in Jerusalem, and hast not known the things which are come to pass there in these days?' He then proceeded to tell the stranger all about Jesus, and how they all had had hopes that He was to have been the Redeemer of Israel, but instead He had been betrayed, tried, condemned and executed, and they could not understand it. Then, almost as an afterthought, he says:

> Certain women also of our company made us astonished, which were early at the sepulchre, and when they found not his body, they came, saying that they had seen a vision of angels, which said he was alive. And certain of them which were with us went to the sepulchre, and found it even so as the women had said, but him they saw not.

The objection therefore will be raised that, if Mary had been one of the women and was his present companion, Cleopas could not have made this statement.

Let us therefore retrace our steps a little and see what the scriptures have actually told us. The women went to the tomb, one of whom was Mary the wife of Cleopas. Mary Magdalene, having seen the stone rolled away, jumped to the conclusion that there had been grave robbers and returned forthwith to tell Peter and John, who would have been in John's house. On our reconstruction it seems reasonable that Mary Cleopas, who had already walked over the hill from Bethany, elected to be the one to tell the two disciples who were nearest – that is in John's house – while the other women would go to inform the rest of them who would still be at Bethany. In that case, she would not have seen the appearance of Jesus to the women on their way, or heard His instruction to give the news also to His brethren. If this were the case, Mary would arrive at John's house only a very short while after Mary Magdalene. We know that Peter and John dashed out themselves to go to the sepulchre, and it would surely be they who were the 'certain of them which were with us', who went to the sepulchre and found even as the women had said. We know that on this occasion, although Peter and John saw that the tomb was empty and took note of the way the grave clothes had been arranged, they did not see Jesus, but returned to 'their own home'. Cleopas would have been there and then been told that they had found things just as the women had said. 'But Him they saw not' was at that moment in time an accurate statement of the information they had thus far received.

We know that Mary Magdalene had followed Peter and John to the sepulchre, and when they returned she remained there, weeping. We do not know for how long she mourned there before Jesus appeared to her. If we could convey ourselves into John's house at about this time, Cleopas, who was clearly sceptical about the vision of angels and quite sure that Jesus had not been seen by anyone, in order that his scepticism received some justification, would have said that there was no point in remaining any further in Jerusalem, which had become a distasteful and even dangerous place for him to be. Furthermore, his wife had returned from trying to do the women's work of attending to the preparation of the body for final entombment and had brought news that their son was safe at Bethany with the others, so there was really no point in staying any longer; it was high time that they were back at home. It would therefore be quite reasonable to suppose that they would not have waited for Mary Magdalene to return, because it would be by no means certain that she would have gone back there since her home was in Bethany, and it would have been quite a long time before any of the others got back, because they would have had to have gone over the Mount of Olives twice, once on their way there and once on the way back, in addition to the time they spent at Bethany giving the disciples the news. In any case, Emmaus was over seven miles away, and Cleopas would naturally want to arrive there before nightfall. In this case, his statement to Jesus about the women, the vision of angels, the journey to the tomb of 'certain that were with us', their return, and the non-appearance of Jesus, all serve to make his statement on the road completely accurate.

Saint Luke relates the substance of our Lord's discourse to the two folk as they walked, and in so doing establishes to his readers the fact that Jesus was the coming Saviour for whose coming the whole of the Old Testament is the preparation. He also establishes the theological fact that it is only through death that life can come. It behoved the Christ to suffer. In the telling of the story, he is making an important point for the readers which not only establishes a truth, but also gathers together much of what he has said in the earlier chapters. As he continues the narrative then, we would naturally expect the sequel to contain some important revelation; it will therefore be worthy of close examination.

Jesus accepted the invitation to stay the night, which means that they would of necessity have had a meal together. While they were at the table, we are told, Jesus took bread, blessed it, broke it and gave it to them, and forthwith vanished. Neither of these two people had been in the upper room on Maundy Thursday, so this particular set of actions would not have the same significance for them at the time as it would have had had they been of the Twelve. Yet, it was in those actions that He came to be recognised. Saint Luke includes this account and reports it in this way, because he is anxious to show to his readers that from then on, the presence of Jesus would be realised in the breaking of the bread and not in His presence revealed by an earthly bodily form. Jesus took the bread, broke it, and it was in that breaking that He was known. When He was present with them on the road, and even in the house up to this moment they had not known who He was, but when He took the bread and broke it they recognised Him. By vanishing at that point it was revealed that in the breaking of the bread was the fact that the real presence was known. Because it was in this act that they came to know Him, His physical body was no longer required. Therefore He vanished out of their sight. In other words it means that His risen life, which is everywhere present throughout all time to the end of the age, would be focused and made actual and recognised in the breaking of the bread. We are not told that at that time the two people were intellectually aware of all this. All they knew was that when Jesus took the bread, they knew who He was, and that the breaking of the bread was the means by which He was made known to them. Saint Luke tells it in this way to reveal the profound theological truth of the eucharistic interpretation. They knew that Jesus had been with them, alive in the fullness of His human nature, and they would come to realise that somehow or other He would continue so to be, not available to the physical senses, but still physically present in a different form: 'He was made known to them in breaking of the bread.'

Saint Luke was a Gentile and he would no doubt be cognisant of some of the teachings of the Greek philosophers, which dominated the thinking of the Hellenistic world of that time. He would know that for the Greek philosophers Plato and Aristotle, both influential and formative thinkers, the material world was not the real world. For them there was a distinction between the physical and the spiritual, and it was the spiritual which was ultimately real. The physical was the means by which the real was expressed in, and mediated to, the world of human experience. This expression had to be in the terms of the environment in which it was to operate. Therefore, the real life of Jesus was His spiritual Being risen, ascended and glorified, but it still needed expression in human terms, since He had come to save human beings from the power of sin. As the worshippers at the Passover became part of the life of the sacrificed lamb, and ate of its flesh and were united with its blood, so now men needed to become part of the risen life of Jesus, which would be mediated to them by physical means. The physical means need not always be the same, but the reality which they express would be. It therefore comes about that Jesus is made available in the bread and the wine of the Eucharist, as well as by means of the body which walked along the Emmaus road, and also in the Church which is the community of all faithful people and is indeed known to be the Body of Christ. The one material means by which this risen life could not be expressed was by that of a corpse, and all the Evangelists stress that there was no body in the tomb. 'Why seek ye the living among the dead?'

In point of fact Saint Luke is the one Evangelist who gives us the fullest account of what happened on Easter Day in the form of a continuous narrative. After recounting the coming of the women to the sepulchre and the commission by the angel to them, in which they were bidden to re-member that the resurrection had been foretold by Jesus Himself, he says that they gave the news to the Eleven and to all the rest. He then tells of the visit to the sepulchre by Peter, thus agreeing with the Johannine account, and proceeds to the full narrative of the walk by the two along the Emmaus road. Having made the point that Jesus was known to them in the breaking of bread, he proceeds to say that Cleopas and his companion rose up that same hour and returned to Jerusalem (another seven and a half miles!) and found 'the Eleven gathered together, and them that were with them' (24:33).

By this time they had been convinced that the Lord was indeed risen. The women had seen Him on their way to

Bethany, Mary Magdalene had seen Him and now also Peter had seen Him. This last agrees with the statement of Saint Paul in his letter to the Corinthians. None of the Evangelists give any further details about this encounter, but the circumstances of Peter's denials are surely a sufficient explanation of what after all any reasonable person would expect to have occurred. Now there was further evidence confirming the report which the two from Emmaus had brought. Saint Luke tells us that Jesus was made known to them in the breaking of the bread, and there would have been people there who could understand the significance of this, because they had been present at the Last Supper.

The next pericope that Saint Luke uses is the account of the appearance of Jesus to the Eleven and those who were with them, which now also included Cleopas and, presumably, his wife Mary. There was inevitably much talk and then, suddenly, there was Jesus amongst them. The unusual and the unexpected always causes an instinctive reaction of fear, and indeed we are told that they were terrified, because they thought that they were seeing a ghost. Although they had just been telling each other that Jesus was indeed arisen from the dead, they were not yet ready to accept such a sudden appearance as normal. In consideration of all future history this is quite understandable. There are still people who believe that Jesus has arisen, but are reluctant to believe that He could appear amongst them as the man whom they had known, trying to maintain that in some way the knowledge of the risen Christ is a spiritual experience incapable of material expression. On the occasion of this appearance then, Jesus would have had to have convinced them not only of the reality of the resurrection but also of the totality of it. The human nature which Jesus had accepted at the incarnation was not discarded, outmoded or superseded, but had been raised. The Jesus of the resurrection is still both man and God, fully and totally God, and fully and totally man.

First of all He set about it by giving them His usual greeting and salutation, 'Peace be unto you.' Then He asked them why they were troubled, and reasons arose in their hearts. The Greek word which is translated in the Authorised Version as 'thoughts' is indeed 'Dialogues' (διαλογισμοι). He then showed His hands and His feet so that they could see the wounds of crucifixion; more than that He actually asked them to handle Him. He then went even further and asked if they had any food about, and when they provided some fish and honey He proceeded to eat it and gave a verbal assurance that He was no ghost, but a real living person. He then proceeded, as He had with Cleopas and his wife on the road, to show that a resurrection was not against reason, and, using the scriptures, proved to their intellectual satisfaction that to those people with understanding, a resurrection was not only reasonable but to be expected. Because of this risen human and divine life, men and women could enter into the closest possible relationship with God and have their fulfilment in Him. Sorrow for sin was necessary, but the separation from God which sin had effected was now done away with because of the resurrection. 'Then opened he their understanding, that they might understand the scriptures, and said unto them, "Thus it is written, and thus it behoved Christ to suffer, and to rise from the dead on the third day"'(24:45–46). Jesus concludes His discourse with the statement that repentance and remission of sins should be preached in His name among all nations, beginning at Jerusalem. The pericope ends with the concluding line 'And ye are witnesses of these things' (24:48). What follows is an account of the ascension, and from the literary construction it is clear that it is another pericope, forming no part of the recorded events of Easter Day.

The tale is dramatically and excitedly told, and the style makes the author cover a great deal of ground in a very few verses. He tells of the women finding the tomb empty and the angelic declaration that Jesus is risen; of the visit of Peter to the sepulchre, and his subsequent return without apparently at that time seeing the risen Christ, although he does tell of an appearance to Peter later in the day; he gives a very full account of the two going to Emmaus, and of their being joined by Jesus, although they did not recognise Him, and of their conversation as they walked; of the supper at Emmaus and the recognition of Jesus when He took, blessed and broke the bread; of their return to Jerusalem and their finding the whole band gathered together in one place, presumably at John's house; and then the sudden discovery that Jesus was there amongst them. At this appearance Jesus is at pains to establish the fact that He was amongst them as a real person, expressing himself by the physical properties of body and blood. Saint Luke throughout is anxious to make the point that the risen Jesus was the incarnate Christ, raised in His totality and completeness. One can understand this emphasis when it is remembered that Saint Luke was an educated Greek and would not have been unaware of the teachings of the philosophers and would certainly have been writing for a Gentile readership. One could also say that he was by anticipation also refuting the implications for the doctrine of the resurrection of subjective idealism, which has played such a large part in the history of Western philosophy until this present time.

It is perhaps significant that Saint Luke makes no mention at all of Galilee, either of the command to the followers to go there or of the promise that Jesus would meet them there. Once again we must remind ourselves that there was a whole collection of stories about Jesus after the resurrection from which presumably the Evangelists could draw for their own purposes. The fact that Saint Luke did not choose to pick up any references to Galilee, does not mean to say that he did not believe that there had been any post-resurrection appearances in the North or that instructions had been given both to the disciples and the brethren to return there. It merely signifies that such reportage does not accord with the main thrust of Saint Luke's argument and teaching. He had to be selective and the Galileean aspects of the history did not concern him in this particular. After all there is scriptural authority for the statement that if all were told, the world itself would not be large enough to contain all that should be written.

In our consideration of the events of the first Easter Day we must now return to the study of the fourth gospel. We have already seen that Saint John introduces the Easter story with a repetition of the word 'garden', which emphasis would undoubtedly put his readers, whom he would expect to be Jews, in mind of the Garden of Eden and the creation of man. Adam was to be the gardener, and Mary here mistook Jesus for the gardener. In this way we recognise that Jesus is the second Adam, the new Man, Man made afresh in the perfection of the original creation, because He was none other than God made man, the incarnate Lord. To understand what follows the account of Mary Magdalene in the garden of the sepulchre, we must still keep these thoughts in mind, and it might be well before we do so to remind ourselves of the actual words of the Genesis account of the creation of man. 'And the Lord God formed man of the dust of the ground, and breathed into his nostrils the breath of life, and the man became a living soul.' (Gen 2:7)

It would seem that there are two conflicting accounts of the appearance of Jesus to the Apostles on the evening of Easter Day, which therefore behoves a careful examination of the text. Saint Luke states quite clearly that when the two people returned from Emmaus, they 'found the Eleven gathered together and them that were with them' (24:33). Saint John, on the other hand, says that 'the same day at evening, being the first day of the week, where the doors were shut where the disciples were assembled for fear of the Jews, came Jesus and stood in their midst.' The word here used for 'disciples' – οι μαθηται – appears in the fourth gospel no less than thirty-one times. On one of those occasions the reference is to Joseph of Arimathaea (19:38) and in this instance there is no definite article, so the translation would be 'being a disciple'. In this case the word is being used of one of a group of people which was a larger body than the original Twelve, and therefore we find the indefinite article. In the other thirty cases the word, whether in the singular or plural, and in whatever case it is used, the definite article appears with it. It would appear that in each case reference is being made to the Twelve.

In his account of the marriage at Cana, Saint John says that the mother of Jesus was there, and that Jesus was bidden and his disciples to the marriage. Here they are singled out as a constituent part of a larger community (2:2–3) After the narration of the discourse with the woman of Samaria, we read: 'then came his disciples, and marvelled that he talked with the woman' (4:27). Again, this could here only refer to the Twelve. At the beginning of the account of the feeding of the five thousand it is said that 'A great multitude followed him because they saw the miracles that he did on them that were diseased, and Jesus went up into a mountain, and there he sat with his disciples' (6:2–3). When the news of Lazarus's illness was brought to Jesus, 'he abode two days still in the same place where he was. Then after that, saith he to his disciples, "Let us go into Judaea again." The disciples say unto him, "Master, the Jews sought to stone thee, and goest thou thither again?"' (11:6–8). Later in the same story Saint Thomas is mentioned as saying to his 'fellow-disciples', 'Let us also go that we may die with him'(11:16). In this case also the designation of the disciples could only mean the Twelve. When Judas Iscariot is mentioned as making a complaint about the waste of the ointment with which Mary had anointed Jesus, he is described as 'one of his disciples', or as we should be expected to understand, 'one of the Twelve'. At the Last Supper Jesus washed 'the disciples' feet', and here too the word could only refer to the Twelve. Although there are several references to 'the disciple whom Jesus loved', in every case the definite article is used.

From this we can deduce that apart from the description of Joseph of Arimathaea as 'a' disciple, on the other thirty occasions when the word is used Saint John is making reference to the Twelve. He therefore must want us to understand that the people who had gathered together 'the same day at evening, being the first day of the week', were the disciples. Of course, two of them would not be there because Judas by this time had disappeared, and we know from what follows in the gospel that Saint Thomas was also absent on this occasion, but we are not told why. In this case, does it mean that the third and fourth Evangelists have somehow or other got the details of the evening appearance confused, or could it be that there were two appearances?

In order to answer that question let us return for a moment to the Lukan narrative. The two from Emmaus return and find the Eleven and them that were with them. The most likely place for such a gathering would have been John's house. It would seem that by this time the disciples had come out of hiding in Bethany and risked the journey into the city. The mother of Jesus, Salome, Mary Magdalene, Joanna and probably other ladies would also have been present, and in all probability Nicodemus and Joseph of Arimathaea as well, although this is pure speculation, but a not unlikely possibility. It would be unlikely that Lazarus had dared to make an appearance, however private, into the city, because he knew that the authorities were looking out for him and were wanting not only to arrest him (John 12:10–11), but to put him to death, 'because that by reason of him many of the Jews went away, and believed on Jesus'. Jesus suddenly appeared as one of the party, and He stressed the physical nature of his appearing among them. He showed them His hands and His feet, He asked them to handle Him, and He took food before them. When He was no longer there, let us ask ourselves what would have been in the minds of the disciples. First, we should remember that they too would have been thinking of themselves as wanted men: they had been the close associates of Jesus, who had been put to death as a potential rebel against Rome, and they would certainly have been thinking that suspicion would inevitably fall on them, if not from the Sanhedrin, then from the occupying power, treason against which had been the charge on which Jesus had been executed. First, surely they would have felt that it would be safer if they were not to be found with the others, upon whom no suspicion had fallen, and it would be safer for them to be in another place which was less well known. We recall yet again that John was known to the High Priest. Secondly, they would want to have been on their own for a little while. They had been specially chosen by Jesus, and He had spoken to them about a resurrection on the third day, and now they were beginning to understand. Their work and ministry, to which Jesus had called them, it would seem had not been brought to an end by the death of their Master, but in a way was only now about to begin. They needed to talk to each other. Thirdly, the most convenient place to which they could have retired would have been that upper room, the existence of which at least some of them had known nothing before the previous Thursday. The authorities would not have known that they could likely be found there, whereas John's house would have been known to the High Priest and would, from their point of view at that time, have been vulnerable. In that large upper room they could have felt safe and they could have had privacy. Saint John makes it quite clear that they were frightened men and apprehensive of being attacked in some way by the Jewish authorities. He tells us that on arrival they locked the doors 'for fear of the Jews'. If Saint John the Apostle were indeed the author of the fourth gospel, he would have been one of the men who was in this particular party. Even if young John Mark and his mother were over with the others at John's house, the domestic staff would also have provided extra protection for these ten men.

Although it may well be that the Apostles felt that they were making a wise decision for the safety of the whole community by going off on their own, it would mean that the men whom Jesus had chosen for a special ministry, and had given a special training to by means of His discourses and His associating of them with His public ministry, had now withdrawn from the others to be by themselves apart. Here they were, enclosed ('the doors being shut') ready as it were to receive some special commission or authorisation which was not to be given to the generality of all those who were with them. If there were such a withdrawal, and Jesus appeared to them while they were thus assembled, it would mean that it was the second time that they had seen Him that day. It would also mean that in the second appearance Jesus had something to say to them or do with them, which He was not willing or able to say to, or do with the whole band. It could be said that He had caused these people to be drawn apart for a specific purpose. Something needed to be done with them which was not to be done with the others. Because of this a second appearance would be necessary. Otherwise it is difficult to understand why these men should have had the privilege of seeing the risen Lord on two occasions so close to each other in time. These then must be the men who had been selected for a particular ministry which had been occasioned by the resurrection of Jesus from the dead.

It is significant that the party which left the gathering in John's house was limited to men. We do know that there were women who accompanied Jesus in His public ministry. Saint Luke indeed gives us definite information about this (8:1–3):

> And it came to pass soon afterwards that He went about through the cities and villages, preaching and giving the good tidings of the kingdom of God, and with Him the Twelve and certain women which had been healed of evil spirits and infirmities, Mary that was called Magdalene from whom seven devils had gone out, and Joanna the wife of Chuza, Herod's steward, and Susannah, and many others which ministered to them of their substance.

We know that Mary Magdalene and Joanna were in Jerusalem at the time of which we are thinking, and no doubt there would have been others. These two, however, are each named in the Passion narrative and they would certainly have been present amongst the people present when Jesus made His appearance to 'the Eleven, and them that were with them' as recorded by Saint Luke. Saint Mark speaks of 'Many other women which came up with Him unto Jerusalem' (15:41) and Saint Matthew says that 'many women were there [at the crucifixion] which had followed Jesus from Galilee.' Some of these at least must have been amongst those who were with the Eleven.

We must now pick up again the threads of the Johannine account. We have seen how carefully the author has put into the minds of his readers at this point the story of the creation of man, the first Adam as recorded in the book of Genesis. We have also seen how he has established the fact that Jesus is the New Man, the second Adam, and that in Him God, by becoming incarnate, had produced a perfect man, man as God originally intended, a Man who because He was also God made man, was a man who was untainted by sin and had not been affected by the fragmentation effects of the fall. With these matters in mind Saint John has prepared us to receive the account of this manifestation of Jesus to the Apostles, the disciples gathered together in the upper room. 'Came Jesus,' he writes, 'and stood in the midst, and saith unto them, "Peace be unto you."' This was His normal greeting. He then showed them His hands and His side. If our reconstruction is correct, this action had already been experienced by the men to whom the mark of the nails and the spear were revealed. It would seem that this too was becoming the normal way in which Jesus revealed Himself after His resurrection. 'Then,' we are told, 'were the disciples glad when they saw the Lord.' The next words are particularly significant. 'Then said Jesus to them again, "Peace be unto you: as my Father hath sent me even so send I you."' Why was it necessary for the giving of the peace to be reiterated?

To understand this we must turn back to the last discourse. We are bound to recall that the last time Jesus had been together with His disciples would have been in this same room three days previously, and that He had not had any words with them on their own as a group since then. In the record of the conversation on that occasion, Saint John records that Jesus said: 'Peace I leave with you, my peace I give unto you: not as the world giveth, give I unto you.' Then He breaks off and continues with the words 'Let not your heart be troubled, neither let it be afraid.' Surely the first part of this sentence would have excited in the disciples' minds the question about the nature of the peace which He was going to give, whether it was to be different from peace as understood by the world. Instead of providing an explanation concerning this peace, Jesus breaks off and leaves the matter as it were in mid air. Now, at their next meeting, they have the answer. This is the peace of which He spoke; they can have that peace because they have Jesus alive with them for all time. Peace as this world understands it can be broken, it can be disturbed, it can give place to strife and war, but this peace 'not as the world giveth' can never depart or be broken, because Jesus has returned from the dead to be alive for ever. Jesus goes on to say, 'As my Father hath sent me, even so send I you.' That which the Father gave to the Son, to have life within Himself, the Son now passes on to the disciples whom He had chosen. In this way the disciples could indeed be taken up into the very life of God through the commission which the Father gave to the Son, and the Son is about to give to them. It must also surely mean that these words also convey the meaning that what Jesus is going to give to them can be transferred. He received it from the Father, He is passing it on to them. Reason would therefore demand that if this gift is a transferable one it could be passed on by the disciples to others. This also links with the words in the High Priestly Prayer: 'Neither pray I for these alone, but for them also which shall believe on me through their word' (17:20).

We now proceed to what must be the administration of an unique sacrament, that of the sufflation: 'And when he had said this, he breathed on them.' Once more we are taken back into the Book of Genesis. 'God formed man of the dust of the ground, and breathed into his nostrils the breath of life, and the man became a living soul.' As God in the old myth had collected together particles of clay or dust to make a statue and animated it by breathing into it, so Jesus has now gathered together, not this time particles of clay, but living human beings, in this case ten of them, the men whom He had specially selected and called for this particular ministry and function, and breathed into them, not going round the circle and giving each one an individual sufflation, but rather a general expiration, so that the new body becomes a living organism. '"As the Father hath sent me, even so send I you. Now that which I received from the Father I am giving unto you." As this was done He said...' Here we come up against a difficulty. All the English translations from the Authorised Version onwards, through all the welter of modern attempts, say 'Receive ye the Holy Ghost', or the Holy Spirit, and have this as the gift of the third person of the Trinity. But in the Greek, there is no definite article, and the word translated by ghost or spirit can equally well and with equal accuracy be translated as 'wind' or ' breath'. The same word in Hebrew (*ruach*) can also bear all three meanings. In most of the contemporary editions of the Greek Testament, the words are given capital letters, but that does not get us anywhere at all, for in the earliest manuscripts which have survived, the whole text is written in capital letters, so that the use of capitals here for Πνευμα Αγιον is quite irrelevant, being just an accommodation by recent compositors to fit the English mistranslations. The only possible translation here must then be 'Receive ye holy breath', and this makes sense. If the words are made to mean the Holy Spirit, what then happened on the feast of Pentecost? There cannot possibly have been a duplication. In Acts, Saint Luke, having given an account of the ascension, says that 'they returned unto Jerusalem from the mount called Olivet, which is near to Jerusalem, a Sabbath Day's Journey.' He states that they went up into an upper room, which must have been the room of the Cenacle or the Last Supper. The party who met there are described as the Eleven, each of whom is mentioned by name: 'and these all continued with one accord in prayer and supplication with the women, and Mary the mother of Jesus, and his brethren.' This was the community which proceeded to ask the Lord to indicate which of the two candidates they had selected, He wished to appoint to fill the place and apostleship of Judas Iscariot. Neither of these candidates would appear to be one of Jesus' brothers, therefore that the community must have been somewhat larger than Saint Luke lists. When he comes to describe the events of Pentecost he says that 'they were all with one accord in one place'. In the Johannine account of the Easter Evening appearance it was the ten only. Now, at Pentecost, the wind was heard and there appeared cloven tongues, 'like as of fire, and it sat upon each of them, and they spake as the Spirit gave them utterance.' This is the gift of the spirit, and it is made to each and every one individually, whereas the Apostles were constituted and animated as the Church, as a body corporate.

On Easter evening then Jesus gave to the body of the Apostles the breath of sanctification as distinct from the breath of life as recorded in Genesis, and it is possible to go on to say that the Church became a living organism, the means by which Jesus, risen and glorified, was to be expressed in and mediated to the world. To this body was given an authority which only God can give: 'Whosoever's sins ye forgive, they are forgiven, and whosoever's sins ye retain, they are retained.' Many preachers and teachers in the past have described Whitsunday as the birthday of the Church, but surely this must be a misnomer. The Church was born on Easter Day, when Jesus breathed upon His disciples and gave them the power to bind and loose. When a child is born it has the gift of life, it is fully a member of the human race, but it has no strength. It cannot support itself, it cannot stand or walk, it can only be where it is put. But as the days go by, strength is given and soon the child can sit up and then stand up; in time he can support himself and walk unaided. There is a distinction then between the gift of life and the gift of strength. Life was given to the Church on Easter evening, the strength came to the individual members on Whitsunday. The power to bind and loose was given to the Ten as to a body corporate, but it had been made quite clear that the Ten were also given the authority to pass on that gift to others, whereas the gift of the Power of God the Holy Spirit was made to each individual member of the Church, enabling him or her to exercise ministry and also themselves to partake in the risen life of Jesus.

Saint John has managed to cram an enormous amount of theology into this last chapter. He has established the fact of the resurrection and given the evidence of the tomb with no body in it; he has made a point about the nature of the risen Christ by the disposition of the grave clothes; he has told of the visit to the tomb of the two leading Apostles and made the point about belief in the resurrection; he has made the story of Mary in the garden establish the fact that the risen Christ, although He is the second Adam sent into the world, is not to be confined within the limitations of a physical body, but will ascend to the Father of all, and therefore be everywhere and always present; he has spoken about the gathering of the Apostles as God gathered the particles of dust with which to create man and shown how the new man, Christ Himself, gave His life to be expressed by His church; and he has recounted that He gave to that Church the power to bind and loose, making it the agency of God in the world. Each of these theological principles could well have filled a volume, but in a matter of twenty-three verses, all has been said.

He now adds on a tailpiece. From a literary point of view, 'whosoever's sins ye remit, they are remitted, and whosoever's sins ye retain' is not a curtain line. Something more climactic is required to give a fitting conclusion to what is, as well as everything else, a composite work of art and an example of good and stylish writing. These concluding verses however are not just a winding up of the book, Saint John never wastes words on merely trying to create a dramatic effect, in spite of the tremendous impression made by 'And it was night' when Judas left to effect the betrayal, or 'And the cock crew' after the telling of Peter's denials. Thus he still has something to say in this postlude. First, he tells us that Saint Thomas was not present in the upper room on Easter night. He does not tell us where he was, but the use of the word 'dydimus', which means a twin, may have been inserted here to give a hint, or perhaps a clue. Was this twin brother or sister also resident in Jerusalem, and had Thomas fled there instead of going over the hill to Bethany? In any case it is not important where he was, for the making of the Evangelist's point requires the knowledge that he was absent. It would seem that he surfaced again sometime during the week, and by this time he had dared to come out of hiding and go in search of the others, which would surely mean entry into the city. We have another possible hint when Saint John is speaking of Jesus' decision to go to Bethany which was in Judaea; having heard of the illness of Lazarus, and having received the knowledge that he was dead, it was Thomas who had said, 'Let us also go with Him that we may die with Him.' Saint Thomas does seem to have been very conscious of the dangers in Judaea, which stemmed from association with Jesus.

So Thomas heard the news, and we must remember that not only would he have been told of the empty tomb and the message of the angels, but also of the appearances to Mary, Peter, the women, the two at Emmaus, the whole company, and the Apostles on their own (and probably of other events as well which none of the Evangelists saw as necessary to report) – but still he needed tangible proof: 'Except I shall see in his hands the print of the nails, and put my finger into the print of the nails and thrust my hand into his side, I will not believe' (20:25). Saint John knew that Thomas was a typical example, not only of people of his own day, but of many men in every age, who will not accept verbal evidence, but need to have a personal experience, and not only mental, psychological or spiritual, but material and mediated by means of the senses as well. Indeed this attitude has been recommended and formed the base of much educational theory propounded in the twentieth century: one should not believe something because a teacher says so, but rather go and find it out for oneself. One should not accept knowledge on the authority of others, but use the authority of one's own experience. Authority arbitrarily exercised is despotism, and to expect to have statements accepted without question is indoctrination. There are still many Thomases in the world.

Then the Evangelist tells us that eight days had passed. Presumably it was eight days since the appearances on Easter Day, not eight days after the information had been given to Thomas, and his disbelief had been expressed. This brings us to a second Sunday. If the John who wrote the gospel is the same as the John who wrote the Apocalypse, it can be noted that he was the first writer to use the phrase 'the Lord's Day' (Rev 1:10). Once again Saint John is careful to say that it was the disciples who were in the one place on this occasion also. We have seen that when Saint John uses the word 'disciple' it refers to the Apostles, and if there are others in the company he is careful to say so. Once again also, the doors were locked because they were still afraid of the Jews, and presumably this fear would not have been lessened by the fact that Thomas was now with them; once again, Jesus came and stood in their midst, once more giving His usual greeting, 'Peace be unto you.' Then Thomas is directly addressed and invited to do exactly what he said he would have to do before he would accept the fact of the resurrection. Again with dramatic intent, Saint John does not tell us whether he actually accepted the invitation or not, but leads directly to what is undoubtedly a curtain line, 'and Thomas answered and said unto him, "My Lord and my God."' No other Evangelist has stressed the divinity of Jesus, 'who came forth from God,' 'who was with the Father from the beginning,' and in countless other similar phrases, more strongly than the fourth. The entirety of the gospel message is presented most dramatically and succinctly in this fine declaration of Saint Thomas. This is surely the great climax of the gospel, the declaration to which all that precedes has been leading and its great affirmation. Then comes the denouement: 'Thomas, because thou hast seen me thou hast believed; blessed are they that have not seen, and yet have believed.' Belief depends not only upon the information conveyed to the mind by the senses, but by other means, by preaching and by reading the written evidence of those who know.

The above is stressed and emphasised in the next two concluding verses. They provide the final underlining at the conclusion of the work, the explanation of the whole purpose of writing:

And many other signs truly did Jesus in the presence of his disciples, which are not written in this book: but these are written that ye might believe that Jesus is the Christ, the Son of God, and that believing ye might have life through his name.

These last words are worthy of a little closer analysis. The author tells us that he has made a selection of the things that Jesus did and said, which are also signs of his creative power and divine sonship. Here we have a direct acknowledgement that there were in existence a great deal of recorded episodes, and that they, being signs, are brief illustrations of the ways in which the truth about Jesus was revealed, rather than prolonged treatises or dissertations. Secondly, the use of the word sign indicates that the actions of Jesus were symbolic of His true nature. What we casually call miracles, such as the turning of the water into wine at Cana, or the healing of the nobleman's son, Saint John calls 'signs', because he presents them as expressions in the affairs of men of the creative power of Jesus, who, in the Prologue that John has presented as The Word, was God, with God, co-eternal with God, by whom all things were made. The Word, being made flesh and dwelling among us, is now creating anew, making a new creation to replace that which had been disrupted by sin, causing all who were born of blood, of the will of the flesh, or of the will of man, to be part of that fragmented universe and disordered cosmos. Thirdly, the purpose of writing the book is to give what evidence is needed to inspire belief in the reader that Jesus is the Son of God, or God the Son, who is the Anointed One, the Messiah, the Saviour. Such a belief will cause the believer to react to the very name of Jesus, and in so doing to find life for his redemption. In this way the book itself is a sign, because inspired writing, as this book undoubtedly is on any counting, can take the reader beyond the words he sees written on the pages and can bring him into touch with that living power, which as Saint John promised in the Prologue, would be granted to 'as many as received him, power to become the sons of God, even to them that believe on his name'.

Chapter IX
Epilogue: The Great Forty Days

In the book of Acts, Saint Luke tells us that Jesus showed Himself alive after His Passion by many infallible proofs, being seen for forty days and speaking of things pertaining to the kingdom of God. Nothing could be clearer than that. This period has come to be known as the Great Forty Days, and the implication is that there were many more appearances of the risen Christ than have been recorded in the books of the New Testament. The last of such appearances was the occasion which has come to be known as the Ascension. Saint Luke gives two accounts of this experience, one at the conclusion of the gospel and the other at the beginning of Acts, and in one of the attempted reconstructed endings of Saint Mark's gospel there is a reference to the fact that Jesus ascended and sat down at the right hand of God. In the biblical accounts there are only a few references to the appearances of Jesus to His disciples between Easter Day and Ascension Day, but it is suggested that there were many more appearances than the Evangelists have recorded. Saint Paul also provides for the Corinthians a catena of such appearances which corroborates the gospel records, but adds a reference to an appearance to Saint James.

The first of these appearances is that recorded by Saint Matthew. In his account of the events of Easter Day he says that the angel said unto the women:

> Fear not ye; for I know that ye seek Jesus, which was crucified. He is not here: for he is risen as he said. Come, see the place where the Lord lay. And go quickly, and tell his disciples that he is risen from the dead; and, behold, he goeth before you into Galilee; there shall ye see him. Lo, I have told you.

As the women went on their way to execute the angelic command, Jesus met them on the way and said, 'Be not afraid. Go tell my brethren that they go into Galilee, and there shall they see me.' On both these occasions there is the promise that Jesus would meet the disciples and the brethren in Galilee. The command to 'stay in Jerusalem until they be endued with power from on high' as recorded by Saint Luke doubtless belongs to the ascensiontide experiences rather than to the events on Easter Day.

In Saint Matthew's gospel it is quite clear that Jesus arranged for appearances to happen in Galilee, for the angel at the tomb said to the women, 'Go quickly and tell His disciples, He is risen from the dead; and lo, He goeth before you into Galilee, there shall ye see Him.' The author goes on to say that 'the eleven disciples went away into Galilee into a mountain where Jesus had appointed them'. Somehow or other Jesus had chosen a place where the meeting was to be held, named the particular hillside and communicated it to the people he wished to be present. We do not know how or where this was done, but there can be no doubt that such a projected assembly was held and may even be that occasion to which Saint Paul refers when he says that Jesus appeared on one occasion to more than five hundred brethren at once, of whom the greater part were still living (1 Corinthians 15:6). Saint Matthew continues:

> And when they saw him, they worshipped him, but some doubted. And Jesus came and spake unto them,

saying, 'All power is given unto me in heaven and on earth. Go ye therefore and teach all nations, baptising them in the name of the Father, and of the Son, and of the Holy Ghost; teaching them to observe all things whatsoever I have commanded you: and lo! I am with you always, even unto the end of the world.'

This surely must be a digest of the actual sermon or talk which Jesus had given to the company on this occasion. Because of the insertion of the baptismal formula and the use of the threefold Name, many scholars have presumed that these could not be the *ipsissima verba* of Jesus Himself, but must reflect the use of the Church in a later period of its existence.

Although the doctrine of the Trinity is not explicitly stated in formula form in any of the books of the New Testament, it is quite clearly adumbrated. The fourth gospel indeed has very sure teaching about the divinity of Jesus as well as His humanity, and also regarding the personality of the Comforter, the Paraclete or the Holy Spirit. The unity of the Godhead is also explicitly maintained. In view of the fact that baptism into the threefold Name appears in all the ancient manuscripts, and especially after the redating of the Magdalen papyri by Dr Thiede to which reference has already been made, it would seem that the use of this formula is very ancient and could indeed have been expressed by Jesus Himself on this occasion.

It must be noted that in the Matthean account of this gathering there is no mention of the ascension. There is therefore no reason to suppose that these words belong to the Ascension experience, or that that event is stated by Saint Matthew to have taken place in Galilee. Indeed there is the Lukan evidence that it was on the Mount of Olives, and there is no reason to dispute this. Neither does the statement recorded by Saint Luke at the time of the ascension, that the disciples were to be witnesses unto Him, both in Jerusalem, and in all Judaea, and in Samaria, and unto the uttermost part of the earth, in any way preclude the issuing of the command to preach the gospel in every place in all the world on the hillside in Galilee. In fact, both the command and the declaration have their proper places and significance in the contexts in which they appear in scripture. There then seems to have been some sort of a rally called for a hillside in Galilee, at which Jesus appeared, and gave a discourse in which He stressed the missionary and evangelistic nature of the ministry of all who wished to follow Him and accept Him as Saviour and Lord. If Saint Paul is correct, and this is the meeting to which he makes reference and states was attended by above five hundred brethren at once, it must have been a large body of folk who gathered there. Yet Saint Paul is not the man to make wild statements or not to check his references, so that we can say with full assurance that he himself certainly believed that there had been a gathering of a very large body of people. Because he seems to have anticipated some doubtfulness in his readers, he goes on to state that there was a majority of those who had been present on that occasion still alive, whose evidence could be checked. The pains with which the Synoptists show Jesus to have taken to ensure that there was to be a meeting in Galilee, and the fact that He summoned the brethren as well as the disciples, would seem to render corroborative evidence for a meeting in the North of some considerable size. It still seems that there is a close affinity between the canonical accounts of the happenings on these momentous days. There is also what is perhaps another significant fact about this gathering which makes it different from the appearances already considered. In the earlier manifestations Jesus appeared without invitation or expectation on the part of those to whom He appeared. In this instance not only had

Jesus made arrangements for the meeting to be convened, but the people who attended it were confident of His promise that He would meet them there. Even so, there were still some who in all probability had not been present at the Easter appearances, and the implication is that they had not previously seen the risen Jesus, and still could not take it in that He was indeed fully raised from the dead. This would undoubtedly point the way to the fact that in the continuing life of the Church, the presence of Jesus is assured by His promises, and that worshippers gather together in the expectation of experiencing that presence; equally undoubtedly, this would have been in the mind of the author of the first gospel, who would have intended the point to be taken by his readers.

The other manifestation of the risen Christ within the period of the Great Forty Days to be reported in the New Testament is that by the shore of the Sea of Galilee, narrated in the twenty-first chapter of Saint John's gospel. Although there are no ancient manuscripts which have survived without this chapter being an essential part of the book, it is quite certain that it has a different authorship from the other twenty chapters. In the first place, the last verses of chapter twenty appear to bring the book to a climax and are intended to be a conclusion. In the second place, there are differences of style in this extra chapter, and thirdly, and most importantly, at the end the author writes a commendation of the gospel, saying that the he knows that the disciple whom Jesus loved, who had written these things, was speaking the truth. 'This is the disciple which testifieth of these things, and wrote these things: and we know that his testimony is true.' From these words it is clear that whoever wrote the rest of the gospel, and the events to which the disciple whom Jesus loved is testifying, must have been someone other than the person who wrote this last verse. We must therefore conclude that it was added as an appendix and a commendation, either at the time of publication or subsequently. It must have, however, been written very soon after the first twenty chapters, because of its general acceptance as part of the book.

The chapter begins with an account of an appearance of Jesus on the shore of the Sea of Galilee. The story opens with an assembling of a number of the disciples, Simon Peter, Thomas the twin, Nathanael of Cana, the sons of Zebedee and two others. It is interesting to note that Zebedee is mentioned by name and that he has two sons who were disciples. Nowhere else in the fourth gospel is Zebedee spoken of, and neither are James and John, or the sons of Zebedee. Yet one of this party must have been the beloved disciple, because a little later on the author says that he was in the boat. He is not likely to have been one of the two disciples who are not named, so that means that he must be one of the sons of Zebedee. Later on in the chapter we learn that there was a saying that the beloved disciple would not die, but since we already know that James the brother of John was the first of the Twelve to be martyred, being killed by Herod so as to please the Jews (Acts 12:1–2), by a process of elimination we have the evidence that John was the beloved disciple.

This group of seven men are together, and Peter announces that he would go fishing. This must indicate that they had all returned to Galilee and were back at the jobs which they had left when Jesus called them to be His disciples. The others say that they will accompany him, so they go down to the shore, take out a boat and spend the whole night on the operation which is wholly unsuccessful. As dawn breaks and they are rowing towards the shore, a man standing there, whom they do not recognise, calls out to them asking them if they have anything to eat with them. The actual words are 'Children, have ye any meat?' which translated into modern English would be something like,

'Hey, lads, have you got any food there?' When they say that they do not, the stranger invites them to cast their nets on the right side of the ship. Something very similar to this had happened once before, which is recorded in the gospels, but not, significantly in the fourth. The disciples do as they are told and catch so many fish that the net becomes so heavy it was only with difficulty that they can row the boat shorewards. No doubt it was this similarity to an earlier occasion which caused John to guess that it was Jesus standing there, and he says so to Peter. Impulsive as ever, Peter cannot wait upon the slow progress of the boat to the shore and jumps overboard, leaving the others to bring the boat to the land dragging their net behind them. To their astonishment they see that Jesus had made a fire, had cooked some fish and had also provided some bread. Practical as ever (it will be remembered that when He had raised Jairus's daughter, He had to remind her parents that she would be hungry), Jesus now tells them not to leave their catch dangling in the water but to bring it to land. Did they count the fish there and then? It is not beyond the realms of possibility, but it is more likely that the author is merely guessing at a large number. Saint Jerome states that ancient naturalists believed that there were that number of species of fishes, but unfortunately he does not give his references for this remark, and so far no statement of this kind by ancient sources has been revealed. It is true that the ancient world was fascinated by the significance of numbers and was in the habit of using them cryptically. Ancient Christian commentators on this passage noticed very early that a hundred and fifty-three was a significant number because it is the total of all the numbers from one to seventeen being added together. It can also be noted that an equilateral triangle of dots, with seventeen on each side, will give a total of a hundred and fifty-three dots and could therefore well have been used as a symbol of totality or perfection. It could be that, if this were so, the author, having this in his mind just pulled the figure out of his subconscious and put it down merely to indicate that this catch was not only large but that the fishes were so great that it was the perfect fisherman's dream. It must remain, however, that the story does in no way depend upon the number of fishes caught, and it is really a waste of time to try to find some cryptic significance in this number.

Having given this account of an appearance of Jesus to the disciples, the writer affirms that it was the third time that He had done so. Presumably, the previous two occasions would have been the one in the upper room on Easter Day and the second one eight days after. If we consider that the disciples were also present in Jerusalem at the appearance to all the company after Cleopas and his companion had returned from Emmaus, then it would be the fourth, but if we are counting the appearances to the disciples alone, then it would be correct. In the story as it is told there is a distinct suggestion that there existed some sort of rapport or understanding between Peter and the beloved disciple. Here then is another picture of these two men being in collusion.

Now we move on to the next section of the chapter, which is told as having happened after the breakfast on the shore. Jesus asks Peter three times if he loves him, and three times Peter answers yes. On the superficial level it would appear that the reason for the threefold questioning is the threefold denial in the High Priest's palace. Nevertheless, there is some significance in the actual words which are used. When one is dealing with the emotion or experience which we call love, the English language, rich in so much else, is notoriously impoverished. Where we have only the one word, the Greek language has no less than four. The first of these is eros (ερος) from which the English word 'erotic' derives. It was also the name that was given by the ancient Greeks to the God of Love. We must make no mistake about it: in classical thinking Eros was by no means a naughty boy, but a highly respectable young man. Unfortunately in English the word erotic has acquired salacious or even pornographic undertones, which are totally absent in the Greek. It is used there for that strong emotion which attracts one to another, but it is based on a sense of need, whether that need be physical, mental or spiritual. It is the attempt to make up that which is lacking, and to complement and fulfil some deficiency.

The second Greek word for love is 'philia'(φιλια) which is often translated as friendship or friendliness. It is used for a warm desire for closeness and association which is not based upon need, but more upon an untrammelled self-giving. We find it used in such words as philanthropy, philosophy, Anglophile, or even philately. The English word 'like' is too weak to express adequately what is meant by philia. It is something much stronger than mere pleasure in another's company, even moving very close to an association which could be described as romantic.

The third Greek word for love is 'storge' (στοργη). This is the parental and filial love within the family. It is not easy to describe in English because we have no word for it, but it signifies that emotional attachment which undoubtedly exists between teachers and their pupils, or sovereigns and their subjects. When Queen Elizabeth I, addressing a deputation from her Parliament at the close of her life, said, 'Though God hath raised me high, yet this I count the glory of my crown, that I have reigned with your loves,' and when Sir John Harrington commenting on this statement said, 'We loved her, for she said she did love us,' both Sovereign and subject, if they had been speaking in Greek, would have used the word storge.

The fourth word used is 'agape'(αγαπη) and this is a love which is based upon the will, but which grows from that into the warmest of associations and the strongest of emotions. It is a common human experience that there are colleagues who are not in any way attractive to each other and with whom there would be no desire for personal friendship. Yet because of the circumstances which throw such people together, if life is not to become intolerable, they have to learn to 'get on' with each other. There is a determination not only not to quarrel and bicker, but also to make a very real effort to find in that colleague features which can even be considered attractive. In such cases as this, it is a common experience that as time goes on, the one feels a developing regard for the other, which even deepens into a genuine desire for the other's well-being. Beyond even that, it often leads into a warm and loving association, and this, in the end, draws into itself the other three aspects of love. Such a love is known to the poets as being stronger than death. This is the word which Saint Paul used in his well-known hymn to love in his first letter to the Corinthians. When the word came to be translated into Latin, the word 'caritas' was used, which literally means the state of being dear or precious, and it is from this Latin word that the English charity has been derived. Surely there is significance in the fact that in the marriage service, the first question asked of the couple is not 'Do you love this man/woman?' or even 'Are you in love with each other?' but 'Wilt thou…?' The marriage vow is for life, and if the love of the bride and groom is to survive, it must not only be based upon emotion, however strong, or even upon the fulfilment of a very real need, however pressing. Although both 'eros' and 'philia' are involved, it must be based upon the will, and that is the surest safeguard of its continuance.

In the questions that Jesus puts to Peter, the first two use the word 'agape', but Peter replies by using 'philia'. In the last question however Jesus Himself uses 'philia' and

Peter similarly responds. We must not make too much of this; both words do indeed carry the meaning of love, and throughout Peter is determined to show Jesus that he has great affection for Him and is warmly attached to Him. So Saint Peter had been completely rehabilitated and the denials have been obliterated. He is entrusted with the responsibility of caring for the flock.

Then comes a strange addendum in that Peter questions Jesus about the status of the beloved disciple, saying, 'and what shall this man do?' Jesus' reply is also not easy to interpret: 'If I will that he tarry till I come, what is that to thee? Follow thou me.' Clearly the saying which the author says is abroad among the brethren, that that disciple should not die, is one that needed some sort of explanation, and here it is given as being based upon a misinterpretation of a saying of Jesus. The falsification is rectified and it is pointed out that Jesus had not said that that disciple should not die. Traditionally, Saint John was the only one of the Twelve who did not suffer a martyr's death, but lived to a great age as the Bishop at Ephesus and had care of all the seven churches of the Roman Province of Asia. It would appear then, in part at least, that by the inclusion of this extraordinary conversation, the author is seeking to correct a rumour which was persisting in certain quarters, and making it quite clear that, although the 'parousia' or second coming was expected, there was no guarantee that Saint John would still be alive when indeed it did occur.

It would seem, however, that there has to be another explanation, for the author is at pains to reconcile the ministries of Peter and John. For there to be a reconciliation, there must be some sort of division. Saint John and Saint Peter, both in the gospels and in the Acts, are repeatedly shown as being in each other's company and being closely associated with each other. Nevertheless, in the early Church, Christians were not unknown for having personal loyalties to such an extent that they caused divisions. Saint Paul had to deal with such a situation among the Christians at Corinth. In writing to them he says:

> It hath been declared unto me of you, my brethren, by them which are of the house of Chloe, that there are contentions among you. Now this I say, that every one of you saith, I am of Paul; and I of Apollos; and I of Cephas; and I of Christ. Is Christ divided? Was Paul crucified for you? Or were ye baptised into the name of Paul? (1 Cor 1:11–13)

He goes on to say that he was glad that he did not in point of fact baptise any of them, except Crispus and Gaius, so that no one could say that they had been baptised into the name of Paul. He then remembers that he also baptised the household of Stephanas; then, almost by way of apology, he says that he cannot remember baptising anyone else. He is obviously very disturbed by the loyalty of Corinthian Christians to the person who baptised them rather than to Christ. Any parish priest knows full well that this is a constant temptation in the Church, that men and women should be attentive because of their appreciation of, or affection for, the parson, and we all know of clergymen who have built up a large and active congregation on the cult of their own personalities. It has often been seen that the great danger of this is that, when that particular vicar leaves, the whole set-up collapses.

It would appear that there had been something of the same sort of personality cult amongst some of the very early members of Christ's Church. Some of His followers could have been heard to maintain that they were Petrines and others that they were Johannines. It would also seem from this passage in the appendix to the fourth gospel that the writer was doing what he could to show the falseness of such claims and the great dangers that lay in this attitude by maintaining that both Peter and John were lovers of Jesus. This explains the association of the dialogue with Peter about his love for the Lord and the reference to the disciple whom Jesus loved. Both are together in the service of Jesus and their love for the Master. It could well have been that such a saying as 'Thou art Peter, and upon this rock I will build my Church', and the reference to the keys of the kingdom being given to him, seemed to give Peter a certain pre-eminence. On the other hand the mere fact that John was known as the disciple whom Jesus loved would also seem to set him above the other ten Apostles. It could well be that this sectarianism manifested itself very early and had caused a distinct division in the primitive Christian community, and it was this that led the Evangelists to make such a careful point of showing that between the two Apostles themselves there was complete accord. If this were true, the mere fact that there is no record of it that has survived, and we can at best only surmise that it existed by making reasonable deductions from the written accounts, bears witness to the success of those men who were doing what they could to remove a cause of dissension from the Church.

In one of the attempted endings to Saint Mark's gospel, there is a brief reference to the ascension. It is to be found in chapter sixteen verse nineteen: 'So then, after the Lord had spoken unto them, he was received up into heaven and sate on the right hand of God.' This is a mere bald statement of a fact. No details are given either as to place or personnel. By being received into Heaven and sitting on the right hand of God, the author would understand that these facts made it possible for Jesus to be everywhere available, as is God the Father. Apart from this one verse, the only other two accounts of the post-resurrection ascension appearance of Jesus are to be found at the end of Saint Luke's gospel and at the beginning of the Acts of the Apostles. As both these books have the same author it means that there is only one narrator of the ascension event. In the gospel Saint Luke has told us that Jesus had instructed them to remain in Jerusalem 'until they be endued with power from on high'. This is part of the narration of the appearance of Jesus in Jerusalem after the return of Cleopas and his companion from Emmaus. He tells us that the company consisted of 'the Eleven, and them that were with them'. In this case there were more present on that occasion than the disciples, and these others would certainly be at least the women or some of them, though the Evangelist is not specific. He then begins a new pericope and says:

> And he led them out as far at to Bethany [we have already seen that this would better be translated towards Bethany, that is on the path over the Mount of Olives to that village] and he lifted up his hands and blessed them. And it came to pass, while he blessed them, he was parted from them, and carried up into Heaven. And they worshipped him, and returned to Jerusalem with great joy: and were continually in the temple praising and blessing God. Amen.

Again there are no details given of the circumstances of the experience, but it is significant that, although there was a parting, there was no sorrow, but they – whoever 'they' happened to be – returned to Jerusalem in a very joyful condition. Surely this must intend to convey the idea that, although Jesus would not again appear in bodily form as He had been doing since Easter Day, there was the recognition that never more would there be a parting from Him. It will be recalled that the first gospel reported that Jesus had said in Galilee that He would be with them, even unto the end of the age.

For a fuller account of this event we have to turn to the book of Acts. The book opens with a declaration that the earlier volume, that is the third gospel, had reported all that Jesus had done and taught until the day that He was taken:

> after that he through the Holy Ghost had given commandment unto the Apostles whom he had chosen: to whom also he showed himself alive after his passion by many infallible proofs, being seen of them forty days, and speaking of the things pertaining to the kingdom of God.

Here there is a specific period of time mentioned. The command had been given that they should wait in Jerusalem until they 'shall be baptised with the Holy Ghost not many days hence'. We know that the forty days after Easter were fulfilled on the sixth Thursday thereafter and that the outpouring of the Holy Spirit occurred on the feast of Pentecost, because Saint Luke in writing about it tells us so, and that makes the brief period to which the Lord referred one of ten days. The timetable is precise and there appears to be no reason for any doubt to be expressed about it. The words seem to imply that this instruction happened before the actual day when the ascension occurred, for Saint Luke goes on to say 'When they therefore were come together', and this would appear to indicate that it is a reference to a subsequent meeting, which had been explicitly arranged. When He was asked whether this was to be the moment when the kingdom of Israel would be restored, Jesus replied that the exact moment of the final consummation is a matter which is known, of course, to God, but of which the people on earth are to remain in ignorance. But again the assurance is given that the Spirit of God would descend upon them and empower them to be witnesses unto Jesus, in Jerusalem, in Judaea, in Samaria and unto the uttermost parts of the earth.

The next verse is the only one in the whole of the New Testament which gives a description of what happened next. 'And when He had spoken these things, while they beheld, He was taken up: and a cloud received Him out of their sight.' Anyone who has stood on high ground and a cloud has enveloped where he is standing knows how quite suddenly all vision is obscured; one cannot see clearly even the accompanying party. Then, when the cloud has passed, almost as though someone had switched on the light, all is clear again. Saint Luke seems to make it apparent that something of this kind occurred on that Thursday morning. When the cloud had cleared, Jesus was not to be seen; He was no longer there in bodily appearance. The men on the mount could only assume therefore that He had ascended, that is gone upwards. We no longer believe in a three-tier universe; we no longer accept it that heaven is somewhere above the bright blue sky; we know that heaven is not a place, but that it is present in every point of space; all this we know, and yet we still think of an upward direction as a movement towards a superior state and condition of being, so deeply is this symbolism engrained in our consciousness. It is therefore inevitable that in describing what happened at the Ascension, we, as those men of old did, should continue to think of an upward movement; it is folly to endeavour to eradicate such symbolic thinking or to use the symbolic nature of the language to try to assert that the event which is so described did not in point of fact happen. Jesus must have appeared to some at least of His followers, and there was a disappearance, which somehow or other convinced them that they would not see Him in that form again. Because if they did, they would not be able to have the realisation that wherever they went He would always be with them to the end of time.

Saint Luke then goes on to assert that as well as those who were there, they had been joined by two men who stood by them in white apparel. This seems to be the formula which Saint Luke adopts when he is describing an angelic appearance and visitation. It will be remembered that on Easter Day in Saint Luke's account of what happened when the women arrived at the sepulchre, he tells us that two men stood by them in shining garments. This seems then to be Saint Luke's convention in describing that which is ultimately indescribable. Having been told by the angelic visitor(s) that Jesus will come again in the manner in which they have seen Him go, they returned to Jerusalem from the mount called Olivet, which from Jerusalem was a Sabbath Day's Journey. 'And when they were come in, they went up into an upper room,' and then there are listed the eleven disciples. This reference to an upper room must indicate that same place in which Jesus had taken such care that it should be prepared for the Last Supper, and the same place that on Easter evening Jesus came where the Apostles were assembled, the doors being shut. The mention of the eleven names would also seem to indicate that this was the totality of the party which had returned from the Mount of Olives, though this is an inference and not specifically stated.

Moving on in his history Saint Luke then says that these Apostles just named, 'continued in one accord in prayer and supplication, with the women, and Mary the mother of Jesus, and with his brethren.' From this we can gather that this upper room had become the headquarters, if one may so describe it, of the Church in Jerusalem, and we are also given a summary of the people who constituted the body corporate. We do not need to read anything into the fact that both Lazarus and Cleopas are never mentioned again.

Surely Saint Luke is not compiling an exact register, but giving us the general picture of the men and women who constituted the body of people who could be described as followers of Jesus and who believed in His resurrection. This was the company that obeyed the Lord's command to wait in Jerusalem until they received power from on high. It is significant that when Saint Luke does come to give an account of the events that happened on the feast of Pentecost, he begins by saying, 'They were all with one accord in one place.' This would indicate that it was not only the disciples who were there assembled, but that it was a meeting of the whole company, the women, and the brethren as well, and also Mary the Mother. They were all to receive the power from on high, the gift of the Spirit, but it was only to the disciples that was given the authority to bind and loose.

There is still in the New Testament one more account of the post-resurrection appearances of our Lord, which is to be found in the fifteenth chapter of the former epistle to the Corinthians, verses three to seven:

> For I delivered unto you first of all that which I also received, how that Christ died for our sins according to the scriptures: and that he was seen of Cephas [that is Peter], then of the Twelve: after that he was seen of above five hundred brethren at once; of whom the greater part remain unto this present, but some are fallen asleep. After that he was seen of James, then of all the Apostles, and last of all he was seen of me also, as of one born out of due time.

Apart from the mention of an appearance to James, the list as given by Saint Paul can find its basis in the four gospels. The appearance to Peter is recorded second hand in the gospels, but no details are given as to what transpired on that occasion. He was seen by the Twelve on Easter evening, and this is a pardonable exaggeration, because we know that on that occasion Judas had gone his own way and Thomas was not there. Nevertheless the Twelve had become a title for the original disciples who had accompanied Jesus throughout His public ministry. The rally of over five hundred, it would seem, was that recorded as taking place in Galilee by Saint Matthew, and the appearance to all the Apostles could be a reference to the Ascension experience. The four Evangelists do not record the appearance to James, but they do indicate that Jesus was most anxious that His brethren should be informed of the resurrection from the dead. This James is presumably the one who was the brother of the Lord, who later became, doubtless because of his kinship to Jesus, the presiding Apostle at the Church in Jerusalem.

The appearance to Saint Paul, 'as to one born out of due time', is surely a reference to the conversion experience on the Damascus Road. There are no less than three accounts of this event in the New Testament. Saint Luke in Acts tells the story in a straightforward narrative style:

And as he journeyed, he came near to Damascus: and suddenly there shined round about him a light from heaven: and he fell to the earth, and heard a voice saying unto him, 'Saul, Saul, why persecutest thou me?' And he said, 'Who art thou, Lord?' And the Lord said, 'I am Jesus, whom thou persecutest: it is hard for thee to kick against the pricks.' And he, trembling and astonished, said, 'Lord, what wilt thou have me to do?' And the Lord said unto him, 'Arise, and go into the city, and it shall be told thee what thou must do.' And the men which journeyed with him stood speechless, hearing a voice, but seeing no man. And Saul arose from the earth, and, when his eyes were opened, he saw no man: but they led him by the hand, and brought him into Damascus. And he was three days without sight, and neither did eat nor drink. (Acts 9:3–9)

Later in the same book Saint Luke is giving an account of the taking of Paul into custody in Jerusalem. Saint Paul asked permission to address the Jews from the comparatively safe platform of the stairs which presumably led into the Castle of Antonia and, his request being granted, he spoke to them in Hebrew, a fact which we are told caused the company to listen with even greater attention. Saint Luke proceeds to give the speech, or its substance, translated into Greek. In it he makes Saint Paul say:

And it came to pass that as I made my journey, and was come nigh unto Damascus, about noon, suddenly there shone from heaven a great light round about me. And I fell unto the ground, and heard a voice saying unto me, 'Saul, Saul, why persecutest thou me?' And I answered, 'Who art thou, Lord?' And he said unto me, 'I am Jesus of Nazareth, whom thou persecutest.' And they that were with me saw indeed the light and were afraid; but they heard not the voice of him that spake unto me. And I said, 'What shall I do, Lord?' And the Lord said unto me, 'Arise and go into Damascus, and there it shall be told thee of all things that are appointed unto thee to do.' And when I could not see, for the glory of that light, being led by the hand of them that were with me, I came into Damascus. (Acts 22:6–11)

The third account, also from Acts, is contained in the defence of himself that Saint Paul delivered before King Agrippa, Bernice, and Festus the Governor:

Whereupon as I went to Damascus with authority and commission from the chief priests, at midday, O King, I saw in the way a light from heaven, above the brightness of the sun, shining round about me and them which journeyed with me. And when we were all fallen to the earth, I heard a voice speaking unto me, and saying in the Hebrew tongue, 'Saul, Saul, why persecutest thou me? It is hard for thee to kick against the pricks.' And I said, 'Who art thou, Lord?' And he said, 'I am Jesus, whom thou persecutest, but rise, and stand upon thy feet.' (Acts 26:12–16)

There follows a commission to Saint Paul to exercise a ministry to the Gentiles. In this third telling, there is no reference to the blindness that the vision had caused, but then there was no need for Saint Paul at this stage to make mention of it. His anxiety was to prove the point that 'he was not disobedient' to the heavenly vision.

It will be noted that there is a great similarity of wording in all three accounts. Nevertheless, if one has heard a friend or relation telling of some experience which has possessed special significance on many different occasions, it is remarkable how the accounts are produced each time in almost the same words. Saint Luke, it would seem, had been Saint Paul's companion for a number of years, and he must have heard the Apostle tell this story on very many occasions. In all the accounts however, it would seem that Saint Paul did not actually see Jesus. He heard His voice speaking to him in Hebrew, he reports a conversation between them, but each time the story is told it would seem that the appearance was of such brilliance, 'above the brightness of the sun', that not only could Saint Paul not bear to look at it, but it was so devastating that it caused blindness, which lasted for three days, and could only be cured by the putting on of hands by Ananias.

Saint Paul was most anxious to assure others that he had indeed been granted a vision of the risen Christ. It was thus that he established his credentials to be an Apostle, and it is the same doctrine which makes Saint Paul also record the appearance to James, who himself had been admitted into the apostolic fraternity after the resurrection. However, the appearances which are recorded in the gospels all occurred before the Ascension, and the disciples were convinced that that day marked the last of the appearances of that kind. If, after that, the risen Christ was to manifest Himself to anyone, it could not be in the form in which He had invited the disciples to handle Him and see that it was indeed He Himself. In the accounts of the conversion of Saint Paul this is indeed the case. The appearance of the risen Jesus was here as real as it had been to Mary Magdalene and the others, but it could not be in the same manner.

In this way we have been able to retrace the events which occurred in Jerusalem and thereabouts over the period of the Passover festival in what is probably most likely to be the year AD 27. We have been able to understand why certain episodes have been chosen by one of the Evangelists and not by the others. We are also left with the assurance that there is much else that could have been told and the implication that there were many more post-resurrection appearances than those written of in the New Testament. The editor of Saint John's gospel says that a selection had had to be made, because if all were told, 'the world itself would not be able to contain all the books that should be written' (John 21:25). Saint Luke also makes it abundantly clear that Jesus showed Himself alive after His Passion by many infallible proofs. It would appear that from the very beginning there were some people who could not bring themselves to believe that the resurrection really had happened. Each writer in the New Testament who reports it makes it clear that his evidence is authentic and there are plenty more who could corroborate. It surely is not too much to say that if an historic event had had the same sort of publicity, the same kind of testimony, and the same mutual agreement between the various accounts, there would not be any doubt that the event had happened and that the circumstances had been correctly reported. There can be no better attested fact in all history than the things that came to pass in Jerusalem in those days. When Cleopas said to Jesus, 'Art thou only a stranger in Jerusalem and hast not known the things that are come to pass there in these days?' he was expressing the practical voice of common sense. When people deny the physical resurrection, or that the tomb was empty, or that the disciples who saw the risen Christ were only having subjective experiences, they are flying in the face of evidence that is overwhelmingly convincing. The modern habit of stating that what we read in the books of the New Testament is not so much accurate reportage as the opinions and reflections of Christians after a period of time had elapsed, and that it is the duty of scholars to try to get back to the origins of the stories and sayings which are put into the documents, can only be a pathetic way of trying to excuse an inability to believe the things that have been attested.

Surely no one can believe seriously that the men who wrote the books which became, and became very quickly, the canonical scriptures of the Christian Church, were liars and cheats, or even deluded fools. We must surely give them the credit of being men of integrity. Even so, when these books first appeared there were many people still living who could have contradicted them, if their testimony had been false. Recent scholarship is tending to date the writing of the gospels to an earlier period than that which it had become fashionable to affirm: that brings them to a time when there were still people alive who could remember the events described. At that times memories had to be better trained than they have been since the invention of the printing press has made references to easily available records possible. These considerations enhance the authority and reliability of the scriptural documents.

Index

X

Xenophon, 32, 136

Z

Zarephath, 18, 19